Critical Reflections on Australian Public Policy

Selected Essays

Critical Reflections on Australian Public Policy

Selected Essays

Edited by John Wanna

ANU
THE AUSTRALIAN NATIONAL UNIVERSITY

E PRESS

Published by ANU E Press
The Australian National University
Canberra ACT 0200, Australia
Email: anuepress@anu.edu.au
This title is also available online at: http://epress.anu.edu.au/critical_citation.html

---

National Library of Australia
Cataloguing-in-Publication entry

Title:	Critical reflections on Australian public policy : selected essays / editor, John Wanna.
ISBN:	9781921536700 (pbk.) 9781921536717 (pdf)
Series:	ANZSOG series.
Subjects:	Political planning--Australia Policy sciences. Federal government--Australia. Australia--Politics and government--21st century. Australia--Economic policy. Australia--Social policy.

Other Authors/Contributors:
        Wanna, John.

Dewey Number: 320.60994

Cover design by John Butcher

Funding for this monograph series has been provided by the Australia and New Zealand School of Government Research Program.

John Wanna, *Series Editor*

Professor John Wanna is the Sir John Bunting Chair of Public Administration at the Research School of Social Sciences at The Australian National University. He is the director of research for the Australian and New Zealand School of Government (ANZSOG). He is also a joint appointment with the Department of Politics and Public Policy at Griffith University and a principal researcher with two research centres: the Governance and Public Policy Research Centre and the nationally-funded Key Centre in Ethics, Law, Justice and Governance at Griffith University. Professor Wanna has produced around 20 books including two national text books on policy and public management. He has produced a number of research-based studies on budgeting and financial management including: *Budgetary Management and Control* (1990); *Managing Public Expenditure* (2000), *From Accounting to Accountability* (2001); *Controlling Public Expenditure* (2003); *Yes Premier* (2005); *Westminster Legacies: Democracy and Responsible Government in Asia and the Pacific* (2005); *Westminster Compared* (forthcoming) and most recently *The Reality of Budget Reform in the OECD* (forthcoming). He is completing, with John Butcher and Ben Freyens, a study of service delivery in the Australian government, entitled *Policy in Action* (with UNSW Press). He was a chief investigator in a major Australian Research Council funded study of the Future of Governance in Australia (1999-2001) involving Griffith and the ANU. His research interests include Australian and comparative politics, public expenditure and budgeting, and government-business relations. He also writes on Australian politics in newspapers such as *The Australian*, the *Courier-Mail* and *The Canberra Times* and has been a regular state political commentator on ABC radio and TV.

Table of Contents

Part 3. Reflections on governance and leadership

Part 4. Reflections on adaptive change

Foreword

This collection of 'critical reflections' on Australian public policy offers a valuable contribution to public discussion of important political and policy issues facing our nation and society. These essays are important not only because of the reputation and position of the various contributors, but because they are incredibly 'content rich' and brimming with new ideas.

Contributors to this volume include politicians, senior public servants, respected academics and civil society leaders. Their views matter—whether or not one agrees with the propositions put—because of *who* they are and their capacity to influence and shape events. With few exceptions, the contributors are active *players*, not dispassionate observers of the issues in which they are engaged.

Their observations and commentary on Australian public affairs reach back into the recent past and, in some cases, the essays need to be viewed through the lens of antecedent and subsequent events. For example, readers of Ian Gill's essay on creating a conservation economy in indigenous communities (Chapter 15), will compare and contrast his experience with Australia's experience of the Northern Territory intervention. Readers of Air Chief Marshall Angus Houston's essay on leadership in the Australian Defence Force (Chapter 12) will reflect on his remarks in light of recent controversies concerning the relationship between the Defence Minister and the civilian and military arms of the Defence portfolio.

Many of the essays in this collection are 'primary sources' insofar as they provide an important record of the views, hopes and frustrations of key decision makers working at the coalface of Australian political, social and economic affairs. It must be borne in mind, when reading some of these contributions, that the views expressed by the authors reflect a particular point in time: for example, John Brumby has contributed two essays to this collection, one prepared on the back of the National Reform Agenda (see Chapter 5) from a speech given while he was still the Victorian Treasurer and John Howard was still Prime Minister, and the other (Chapter 2) from a speech given after he became Premier and John Howard had given way to Kevin Rudd. Taken together, the two essays chart the political and policy trajectory of the development of his ideas as the federal reform agenda progressed.

The essays in this collection were originally presented either as part of the Australia and New Zealand School of Government (ANZSOG) Public Lecture Series in 2007 and 2008 or at the ANZSOG Annual Conference 'Making Federalism Work' held on 11 and 12 September 2008, in Melbourne. The sole exception is Peter Thompson's essay reflecting on changes in the media landscape during his lifetime, which was prepared for a special ANZSOG workshop on strategic media management held in August 2006. The essays in this volume are grouped into four broad themes.

Part 1, *Reflections on Australian federalism*, contains essays by the Federal Treasurer, Wayne Swan, Queensland Premier, Anna Bligh, Victorian Premier, John Brumby, and ANU academic Mark Matthews, each of whom outlines cogent arguments and prescriptions for a renewed and reinvigorated federalism.

In Part 2, *Reflections on Australian politics and policy*, Griffith University's Pat Weller paints a compelling—and at times amusing—portrait of cabinet government and Solicitor-General, David Bennett, Australian Competition and Consumer Commission (ACCC) Chairman, Graeme Samuel, and Productivity Commission Chairman, Gary Banks, reflect on matters as diverse as constitutional litigation, the operation of the *Trade Practices Act* and the many iterations of evidenced-based policy.

In Part 3, *Reflections on leadership and governance*, the colourful former Telstra executive Phil Burgess [1] reflects on the cultural divide between public and private sector leadership; former Senator Andrew Murray speculates on the inclusion of political governance, transparency and accountability as part of a broader reform agenda alongside burning issues such as climate change, education and infrastructure; and Air Chief Marshall Angus Houston reflects on the principles on which successful leadership of the Australian Defence Force must be based.

In Part 4, *Reflections on adaptive change*, The Australian National University's Vice-Chancellor—sometimes dubbed the most powerful vice-chancellor in Australia—presents a compelling argument for 'rethinking, renewal and reinvigoration' in Australian higher education; social entrepreneur Ian Gill, President of Ecotrust Canada, outlines the Canadian experience in building a 'conservation economy' in indigenous communities and draws comparisons with the Australian situation; and, finally, well-known journalist Peter Thompson reflects on the technological revolutions shaping Australian media and popular culture.

Whether the authors are actors in the events and issues under discussion (such as Wayne Swan, John Brumby, Ian Gill or Graeme Samuel) or keen observers of events (Patrick Weller, Peter Thompson or Mark Matthews), the critical reflections contained within these pages offer much to those with an interest in the main currents of contemporary Australian policy and politics. I commend this volume to you.

John Wanna
Sir John Bunting Chair of Public Administration
Research School of Social Science
The Australian National University
March 2009

ENDNOTES

[1] Burgess, of course, was one of a trio of American executive imports (the others being Greg Winn and Bill Stewart) dubbed the 'three amigos', who, under the direction of Chief Executive, Sol Trujillo, saw a normally subservient Telstra muscle up to the Howard Government in the policy tussle over the regulatory burden borne by the telco.

Contributors

Gary Banks

Gary Banks AO has been Chairman of the Productivity Commission since its inception and was reappointed in April 2008. In addition to overseeing the commission's activities, he has personally headed national inquiries into such topics as the National Competition Policy, the National Reform Agenda and the economic implications of an ageing Australia. He also chaired the Australian Government's Regulation Taskforce in 2006 and is presiding over the Productivity Commission's gambling inquiry. Banks chairs the intergovernmental Steering Committee for the Review of Government Services and was the initial convenor for its report on Indigenous disadvantage. In 1998, he was a member of the West Review of Higher Education. In 2007, he was made an Officer of the Order of Australia for services to the development of public policy in microeconomic reform and regulation.

David Bennett

David Bennett AC QC was the Solicitor-General of the Commonwealth of Australia, appointed for a five-year term in August 1998 and for a second five-year term in August 2003. In August 2008, Dr Bennett returned to private practice at the legal firm 5 Wentworth, founded by Sir Garfield Barwick in 1932, where he had been a member between 1982 and 1998. Dr Bennett was appointed as a Queen's Counsel in 1979 and practised in the areas of appellate law generally, constitutional law, administrative law, revenue law, trade practices and competition law, among others. Dr Bennett served as president of the NSW Bar Association from November 1995 to November 1997 and President of the Australian Bar Association from November 1995 to February 1997. Dr Bennett was appointed an Officer of the Order of Australia on 12 June 2000 for service to the law and the legal profession in the areas of administration, education and practice. Dr Bennett was appointed a Companion in the Order of Australia in the Queen's Birthday Honours List 2008 for services to the law, particularly as Commonwealth Solicitor-General, through the provision of advice on matters of national interest and the international promotion of Australian legal services and education. He was also the recipient of a Centenary Medal in 2003.

Anna Bligh

Anna Bligh MP was sworn in as Premier of Queensland on 13 September 2007, after the resignation of Peter Beattie. She is the state's first female premier and, in the 2009 Queensland state election, earned the distinction of being the first *elected* female State premier. Bligh was appointed Deputy Premier of Queensland in July 2005—the same month she celebrated 10 years as Member for South Brisbane. As Deputy Premier, she was also Treasurer and Minister for

Infrastructure, running the $33 billion Queensland State Budget and leading construction of the $9 billion South-East Queensland Water Grid. She was formerly Minister for Finance, State Development, Trade and Innovation. Before that, she was Queensland's first female Education Minister, spending almost five years overseeing significant reforms to the state's education system, during which time she also had responsibilities for the arts portfolio, overseeing construction of the Millennium Arts Precinct. After the election of the Beattie Labor Government in June 1998, her first ministerial responsibility was as Minister for Families, Youth and Community Care and Disability Services. Before her election, on 15 July 1995, Bligh worked in many community organisations and in the Queensland Public Service, in employment, training and industrial relations policy. Bligh graduated with an Arts Degree from the University of Queensland in 1980.

John Brumby

John Brumby MP was sworn in as the forty-fifth Premier of Victoria on 30 July 2007. Before becoming Premier, Brumby served as Treasurer and Minister for Regional and Rural Development. He was also appointed as Victoria's first Minister for Innovation in February 2002. Brumby was elected to the Victorian Parliament in 1993. He was Leader of the Opposition for almost six years. Between 1983 and 1990, he was the Federal Member for Bendigo during the Hawke Government and served as Chairman of the Parliamentary Committee on Employment, Education and Training. Brumby completed a Bachelor of Commerce from Melbourne University in 1974 and a Diploma of Education from the State College of Victoria, Rusden, in 1975. He was the recipient of a Centenary Medal in 2001, a National Leadership Award for Tourism and Infrastructure Contribution in 2005 and a Research Australia Leadership and Innovation Award in 2006.

Phil Burgess

Phil Burgess is a writer and commentator on economic, political and cultural trends. He is also a Visiting Professor of Policy Studies at the University of California at Los Angeles' public policy school, where he teaches in the graduate program on communications and culture, and a non-resident Senior Fellow for Technology and Culture at the Center for the New West, where he was the founding president from 1988–2000. He is the former Group Managing Director for Public Policy and Communications at Telstra. He now lives in the United States and is President of The Annapolis Institute, a private, non-partisan think tank.

Ian Chubb

Ian Chubb AC was appointed Vice-Chancellor of The Australian National University in January 2001, having previously been Vice-Chancellor of Flinders University from 1995 to 2000. He was the Senior Deputy Vice-Chancellor at Monash University from 1993 to 1995, for part of that time simultaneously holding the position of Foundation Dean of the Faculty of Business and Economics. From 1986 to 1990, Professor Chubb was Deputy Vice-Chancellor of the University of Wollongong. Between 1990 and 1993, Professor Chubb was the full-time Chair of the Higher Education Council and concurrently Deputy Chair of the National Board of Employment, Education and Training. He served as a member and, subsequently, Chair of the Higher Education Council in a part-time capacity from 1994 to 1997. He also served as Interim Chair, then Deputy Chair, of the National Committee for Quality in Higher Education from 1993 to 1994. Professor Chubb was Chair of the Group of Eight universities in 2004 and 2005 and has served in various capacities on the National Health and Medical Research Council and the Australian Research Committee. Professor Chubb began his university career as a neuroscientist. The recipient of a number of academic awards and named fellowships at the University of Ghent and Oxford University, he returned to Australia to take up a position in human physiology at Flinders University in 1977. In June 1999, Professor Chubb was made an Officer of the Order of Australia for his services to 'the development of higher education policy and its implementation at state, national and international levels, as an administrator in the tertiary education sector, and to research, particularly in the field of neuroscience'. In April 2003, he was awarded the Centenary Medal for service to Australian society through tertiary education and university administration. In June 2006, Professor Chubb was appointed a Companion of the Order of Australia for 'service to higher education including research and development policy in the pursuit of advancing the national interest socially, economically, culturally and environmentally and to the facilitation of a knowledge-based global economy'.

Ian Gill

Ian Gill is President of Ecotrust Canada, an enterprising non-profit organisation whose purpose is to build the conservation economy in coastal British Columbia. Ecotrust Canada works at the intersection of conservation and community economic development by promoting innovation and enabling communities, First Nations and enterprises to green and grow their local economies. Gill was born in Australia and now holds dual Australian and Canadian citizenship. He began his career as a journalist, covering federal politics from Canberra for *The Land*. After moving to Canada in 1981, he furthered his journalistic career, first with the *Vancouver Sun* and then with the Canadian Broadcasting Corporation—as its environmental reporter and as a host and producer of documentaries that won local, national and international awards. In 1994, Gill founded Ecotrust Canada and today serves as President of Ecotrust Canada and its subsidiary, Ecotrust Canada Capital.

Allan Grant (Angus) Houston

Allan Grant (Angus) Houston AO AFC joined the Royal Australian Air Force (RAAF) as a cadet pilot in 1970. Air Chief Marshal Houston has wide staff experience, having served on the Joint Operations staff at Headquarters Australian Defence during the Gulf crisis of 1990–91. He was the Director of Air Force Policy during 1992–93 and also served at Headquarters Australian Theatre from 1997 to 1999 as Chief of Staff, and Head of Strategic Command from 2000 to 2001. He was promoted to Air Chief Marshal and assumed his current appointment as Chief of the Defence Force on 4 July 2005 after four years as Chief of Air Force. In 2003, Air Chief Marshal Houston was advanced as an Officer in the Order of Australia, having previously been appointed a Member in 1990. In 1980, he was awarded the Air Force Cross. Air Chief Marshal Houston is the third RAAF officer to be appointed to the most senior position in the Australian Defence Force.

Mark Matthews

Mark Matthews is Director of Policy and Engagement at the new Centre for Policy Innovation in the Research School of Social Sciences, The Australian National University. Since April 2007, Matthews has also served as Executive Director of the Forum for European-Australian Science and Technology cooperation (FEAST), established by the Australian Government and the European Union to highlight, promote and facilitate research collaboration between their respective communities. The FEAST Secretariat is hosted by The Australian National University on behalf of the research community. Matthews has extensive private sector experience in public policy consulting in the United Kingdom and Australia, with a particular emphasis on science and innovation policy. In addition to his business experience, he has held academic positions in the Universities of Sussex (Research Fellow, Science Policy Research Unit), Bath (Research Fellow, School of Management) and Warwick (Senior Fellow, Warwick Manufacturing Group, Department of Engineering). Matthews' research focuses on international political aspects of national differences in science and innovation capability and on the potential for using insights from engineering management and finance to inform how uncertainty and risk are managed in public policy settings.

Terry Moran

Terry Moran AO was appointed to the position of Secretary, Department of Prime Minister and Cabinet, in February 2008. Moran has had a varied career as a public servant, working with successive Australian federal and state governments, with roles in public policy and public sector management. He was Chief Executive of the Office of the State Training Board (OSTB) in Victoria from late 1987 to May 1993. In May 1993, he was appointed as the first Chief Executive Officer of the Australian National Training Authority and was subsequently appointed Director-General of Education Queensland in August 1998. In July 2000, Moran was appointed Secretary of the Victorian Department of Premier and Cabinet. As part of this role, Moran advised the Victorian Premier on the development of major policy initiatives by the Victorian Government. He advised the Victorian Government in relation to public sector reform initiatives that led to the establishment of the Victorian State Services Authority in 2005 and also took a leading role in the development of a new National Reform Agenda, a broad reform program aimed at improving productivity and workforce participation. Moran has a strong interest in public policy capacity and was instrumental in establishing the Australia and New Zealand School of Government—a joint initiative by six governments and 10 universities—in 2003.

Andrew Murray

Andrew Murray was born in England and has lived and worked in Rhodesia, South Africa, England and Australia. Raised and schooled in Rhodesia (now Zimbabwe), he went to university in South Africa and later to Oxford as a Rhodes Scholar. Murray migrated to Australia in 1989 and was a senator for Western Australia from July 1996 to June 2008. He has direct experience of complex and difficult environments, including those affected by war, economic sanctions and major political, social, environmental and economic problems. Pre-Senate, his business career included positions as an executive and director in large public and private corporations, and owning and managing his own businesses. He has also been in the armed forces, a consultant, occasional media writer and occasional academic, and is a published author. He is best known in politics for his work on finance, economic, business, industrial relations and tax issues; on accountability and electoral reform; and for his work on institutionalised children.

Graeme Samuel

Graeme Samuel AO is the Chairman of the Australian Competition and Consumer Commission (ACCC). He took up the position in July 2003. Until then he was President of the National Competition Council, Chairman of the Melbourne and Olympics Parks Trust, a commissioner of the Australian Football League, a member of the board of the Docklands Authority and a director of Thakral Holdings Limited. He relinquished all these offices to assume his position with the ACCC. Samuel is also an Associate Member of the Australian Communications and Media Authority. He is a past president of the Australian Chamber of Commerce and Industry and a past chairman of Playbox Theatre Company. Samuel holds a Bachelor of Laws (Melbourne) and Master of Laws (Monash). In

1998, Samuel was appointed an Officer in the General Division of the Order of Australia.

Wayne Swan

Wayne Swan MP was sworn in as Treasurer of the Commonwealth of Australia after Labor's election victory on 24 November 2007. He was elected to Parliament as the Member for the Brisbane seat of Lilley from 1993 to 1996, and from 1998 to the present. Swan is the author of *Postcode: The splintering of a nation*, published by Pluto Press Australia in June 2005. Before his appointment to his current role, he was Labor's Shadow Treasurer from 2004. Before that, he was Shadow Minister for Family and Community Services from 1998 to 2004. Before entering Parliament, Swan was for 12 years a lecturer in public policy at the Queensland Institute of Technology (now QUT), then State Secretary of the Queensland Branch of the Australian Labor Party and campaign director for Wayne Goss's historic election victories in 1989 and 1992. He has also worked as a policy analyst in the Office of Youth Affairs and as an adviser to the Hon Bill Hayden MP, the Hon Mick Young MP and the Hon Kim Beazley MP. Swan has a Bachelor of Arts (Hons) degree from the University of Queensland.

Peter Thompson

Peter Thompson is a leading educator, communications consultant, broadcaster and author. For many years he has been an ABC radio and television broadcaster and currently hosts the successful *Talking Heads* program on ABC TV. His publications include *Persuading Aristotle*, *The Secrets of the Great Communicators* and the audio publications *Communication: A winning strategy* and *The Astute Negotiator*. Thompson is an ANZSOG Fellow and has taught senior public sector managers in the school's Executive Fellows Program about the complex relationship between the media and government. Thompson has also taught communication to MBA and executive programs at the Australian Graduate School of Management, and advises governments and non-governmental organisations on communication strategy. He is an alumnus of the Kennedy School of Government and the Australian Graduate School of Management.

Patrick Weller

Patrick Weller AO holds an ANZSOG Chair at Griffith University, where he is also Professor of Politics and Public Policy and Director of the Centre for Governance and Public Policy. His principal interests are the operations of executive government, in Australia and internationally, the impact of political leadership and the role of international civil servants in international organisations. Professor Weller is the author of many books, articles, book chapters, reviews, conference papers and reports.

Part 1. Reflections on federalism

1. Federalism and the engine room of prosperity[1]

The Hon Wayne Swan MP, Treasurer of Australia

Australian legal scholar Professor Greg Craven once described federalism as the topic most likely to clear an Australian barbecue. In the past 50 years, he wrote, 'Australian federalism has received more bad press than morbid obesity'. Whether you agree or disagree with Craven's views on federalism itself, it is hard to argue with his description of it as our own constitutional 'F' word.

To most Australians, federalism is probably about as popular as a politician appearing onstage at a grand final. Yet while it might not so far have become the lead topic of conversation in the nation's lounge rooms and pubs, Australians do care about making public services work better. And in a system such as ours, it's hard to get better outcomes in areas such as housing, health and Indigenous affairs unless all governments work together.

I want to say something about the ambitious reforms we're implementing through the Council of Australian Governments (COAG), to offer a sense of the new architecture we propose and why it represents a fundamental improvement over the way we've done things in the past. Reforming the architecture of Commonwealth–state relations can sound a little *airy*, so I also want to provide a practical example of how our new approach will affect the lives of Australians. I want to describe what we're doing with school reform and how it exemplifies what we can achieve from modern federalism. There's no better reason to get federalism right than the opportunity it provides to improve our schools.

My whole political life I have believed education is the engine room of prosperity and the key to overcoming social disadvantage. It's why I devoted a big chunk of 2005 to writing *Postcode: The splintering of a nation*, my book on social disadvantage in Australia. Creating prosperity and spreading opportunity are why I entered politics. Education is what brings these two objectives together. I am relishing the opportunity we've been given to modernise the federation, so we can build a platform from which to reform Australia's education system.

As the government goes about lifting national productivity and creating a more inclusive society, Commonwealth–state relations and education reform is the place where Julia Gillard's policy agendas and mine frequently meet. Education reform—especially school reform—has been proposed in this country for a decade. Half-hearted attempts have been made, but they have not been backed up with the leadership and conviction needed to deliver structural change. Our predecessors never succeeded in navigating Australia's future—and there is no better example of this than the former treasurer's failure to invest in the education of our children.

In a number of developed countries, imaginative public policies have substantially improved the quality of school education and student outcomes. Greater transparency, along with new investment and greater flexibility, has been key to these improvements. By comparison, Australia's reform effort has been lacklustre. And one of the key reasons why is they have foundered on the rock of unreformed federalism. It's only now that we are creating a more flexible, market-driven set of Commonwealth–state relations that substantial education reforms can finally be realised. Ultimately, this is a major structural difference between the Rudd Government's school reforms and those that have been floated before them—not only because we have the will to revolutionise Australia's education system, but because we are modernising the federal structures to enable necessary education reforms and investments to be made.

Modern federalism

Every economy in the world today is facing tough economic conditions. The global credit crunch and global oil price shock have buffeted confidence and share markets and are slowing global growth. But as the National Accounts for the September Quarter 2008 demonstrated, while Australia is not immune, we are well placed in comparison with a number of other developed economies. And the Rudd Government is determined to press home this advantage. This means undertaking serious microeconomic reform—to boost our productivity, lift our international competitiveness and invest in our human capital.

In many respects, the COAG reforms are the centrepiece of the government's microeconomic reform agenda. The reforms are focused on what economists call 'enhancing public sector productivity'—or what just about everyone else simply calls 'better public services'. The changes in the financial relationship between the Commonwealth and the states that we are putting in place represent a major revamp of Australian federalism. The old ways of doing things have obviously not worked.

For decades, the Commonwealth imposed input controls on Commonwealth funding to the states—tough conditions to dictate the way funding was to be used. These conditions constrained flexibility and innovation in service delivery. This made it difficult for the states to set their own priorities. It also created inefficiencies, as the Commonwealth devoted unnecessary time to administering them. Most importantly, Commonwealth intervention in areas of state responsibility blurred the lines of accountability. The conditions imposed on Commonwealth funding confused the public because it was no longer clear whether the states or the Commonwealth was accountable for poor service delivery, or indeed good service delivery. If you doubt this, I suggest you go to a suburban shopping centre and ask the shoppers which level of government is responsible for improving their child's school.

This lack of public accountability is the reason COAG meetings became a routine blame game, with both levels of government blaming the other for poor service delivery and trying to shift expenditure responsibility. Voters were left unsure who was ultimately at fault, but quite sure that they wouldn't tolerate that kind of squabbling from their children. Old-style federalism was conducive to short-term fixes and political machinations—but it stood fundamentally at odds with delivering high-quality services and the necessary reforms to underpin future economic prosperity. We are committed to leaving it permanently in our wake.

There's been a lot written and a lot said about the future of federalism if the Carpenter Government is not returned in Western Australia.[2] This misses the point. We've always said that we want to build a modern federalism that looks beyond current governments. The reforms we envisage are too important to be caught up in partisan politics. In education, for example, the future of our kids is far more important than any party political differences we have. That is why I am proud of the new financial framework that Australian treasurers have hammered out this year.

New financial framework reforms

In modernising Commonwealth–state financial relations in Australia, we have been guided by some commonsense principles. The states have a wealth of experience in how best to deliver services in their jurisdictions. The Commonwealth should leave them the scope to innovate and tailor solutions in a way that best fits the needs of their populations. This is not to say that there is no role for policy leadership by the Commonwealth. Many of the big challenges facing the economy are issues that need to be addressed through the Commonwealth working in partnership with the states.

So what do the new financial framework reforms mean in practice? The Commonwealth will continue to assist the states in their endeavours, but the states will be responsible and accountable. The new framework for federal financial relations will help to make that clear. That clarity in accountability will be achieved in several ways. First, the number of Specific Purpose Payments will be reduced from more than 90 to just a handful—in the areas of health care, early years education and schools, vocational education, disabilities and housing. To see what a fundamental break this is with the past, you have to recall that the number of Specific Purpose Payments has sat at about 100 for decades now. In this sense, our approach is radically different from what has gone before. This rationalisation will reduce wastage at a time when we can no longer sustain the excesses of the past.

Second, the Commonwealth will give the states the budget flexibility they need to allocate resources where they will produce the best results. The Commonwealth will move away from the prescription of the past and remove the input controls that inhibit state service delivery and priority setting. Instead, the focus will be on the achievement of outcomes.

Third, the Commonwealth will provide the states with more funding certainty. States will be better off financially and will no longer be plagued with the uncertainty of not knowing whether they will receive Commonwealth payments. There will be no more five-year agreements with 'take it or leave it' offers when they expire. Instead, the new National Specific Purpose Payments will be ongoing agreements, reviewed periodically to ensure the maintenance of funding adequacy.

Fourth, and central to the new framework, there will be simpler, standardised and more transparent public performance reporting. The new reporting framework will focus on the achievement of results, value for money and timely provision of publicly available and comparable performance information. Roles and responsibilities will be clarified and the performance of each jurisdiction will be independently assessed by the COAG Reform Council.

Also central to the new financial framework reforms will be additional incentive payments to drive key economic and social reforms. National Partnership Payments will reward those states that best deliver the services and outcomes to their citizens, and not reward those that don't. In so doing, they will drive a new microeconomic reform agenda in this country. Most importantly of all, they will improve the quality of services available to the Australian people—including schools.

Schools reform

Australia has not traditionally been a highly educated country. It is easy to forget that in 1983, when the Hawke Government came to power, only four in 10 Australian children finished year 12. When Labor left office in 1996, that number had risen to seven in 10. Since then, there has been relatively little change in school completion rates. Higher educational attainment has a substantial productivity pay-off. On average, each additional year of education raises earnings by 10 per cent.

Education is particularly important at a time when developed-country labour markets are in a state of flux. Manual low-skilled jobs are increasingly disappearing, while employment growth has been concentrated in jobs requiring abstract cognitive skills, complex communication and exercising judgment in the face of uncertainty. Of course, manual jobs will not disappear, but there is also a trend towards higher skill requirements within occupations.

As a recent Organisation for Economic Cooperation and Development (OECD) working paper pointed out, 'a bank teller today spends more time than in the past selling financial services, and less time performing routine tasks such as processing deposits and withdrawals. Similarly a mechanic can no longer function without the ability to read and to work with computerised testing equipment.'[3] What is driving these changes? One factor is the rapid advance of technology.

In a new book, Harvard economists Claudia Goldin and Larry Katz refer to the 'race' between education and technology.[4] At times when technology outstrips education, inequality rises. Conversely, when education increases faster than technology, inequality falls. The other factor is globalisation. In the past few decades, India has opened its economy to the world, China has shifted to market capitalism and the former Soviet empire has collapsed. Another Harvard economist, Richard Freeman, vividly refers to these events as equivalent to another 1.5 billion unskilled workers joining the global economy.[5]

On balance, the expansion of the global economy has benefited Australians. But as immigration, trade and *offshoring* have expanded, many Australian workers suddenly find themselves in a global labour market. These findings have profound implications for anyone who cares about the most disadvantaged in our society. Although technological advances and globalisation are major contributors to rising living standards in Australia, they do not lift all boats equally. Public policy needs to recognise this and ensure that the gains from technology, trade and immigration are shared across society. Central to this is raising the quantity and quality of education.

It isn't easy to predict the occupational mix of the Australian labour market in the future. But it's a fair bet that one of the best things we can give to a young Australian today is a broad-based education—the foundation for lifelong learning. This will benefit the individuals themselves, but it will also have positive spill-overs. Better-educated adults pay more tax, are less reliant on income support and are less likely to commit crimes.

A comprehensive discussion of the government's schools reforms would take much longer than I have available to me here. So let me simply focus on two aspects of our reforms, which are symbolic of what we are working towards. These are transparency in school reporting and improving schools in low socioeconomic status communities.

Transparency in school reporting

In the private sector, it has long been recognised that information is central to well-functioning markets. It turns out that the same is true in the public sector. Giving people information about the performance of public services empowers them to spur reform. It is also consistent with this government's belief in transparency. We are ultimately accountable to voters, whose taxes fund government services. Those voters have a right to know how well these services are performing.

I've talked previously about the importance of reporting health outcomes at a hospital level—an agenda that Health Minister, Nicola Roxon, has been vigorously promoting. In this essay, I want to speak about a parallel agenda: reporting test score results at a school level.

During the past month, the Prime Minister and Deputy Prime Minister have made clear that we are committed to reporting test scores at a school level. This has not been uncontroversial, with some critics referring to it as 'unreliable and misleading', a 'divisive sideshow' and suggesting that we are engaging in 'bullying tactics'.

It is important that we engage with our critics on this issue. For the most part, they care about the same things that we do: ensuring that our education system is as good as it can be and that it particularly serves the needs of the most needy students. You cannot be serious about equality of opportunity unless you are committed to improving the quality of schools in disadvantaged communities. In achieving this goal, it is critical that we measure the performance of schools, so we can learn from the best and identify problems early.

But measuring school performance is not as simple as comparing their raw scores. In part, the differences between schools are due to their socioeconomic mix. We should not blame a school because it enrols children from low-income households or shower it with plaudits because it admits only the more affluent. That is why this government is committed to 'like school' reporting.

Separating what students bring to the classroom on day one from the value added by the school is not trivial—but it is not impossible either. Indeed, the challenge is similar to the one we face in separating hospital performance from case-load mix. We need to take account of whether one hospital treats sicker patients than another in determining hospital effectiveness.

A student's family background is an important influence on his or her success at school. But it would be a mistake to think that is all that matters. There are persistent and systematic differences between schools and we owe it to Australia's children to learn as much as we can about why one school does better than another. It is also important to remember that we are requiring all schools to be accountable—government and non-government.

For the first time in the nation's history, parents will be able to compare the performance of schools across Australia, taking into account the mix of students at those schools. If one school is performing far better than its socioeconomic mix would predict, why don't we see what we can learn from it? Sometimes the answer will be something that is hard to replicate—a charismatic principal, perhaps. But other times, we might find that schools can learn lessons from one another that can raise the performance of all.

In theory, information should matter—and in practice, we have good evidence that it does. Looking at accountability across all 50 states of the United States, Stanford academics Martin Carnoy and Susanna Loeb found that the largest test score gains were experienced in those states that published school-level results. White, black and Hispanic students all did better when schools in their state became more accountable. A strong and transparent accountability framework is a non-negotiable part of the COAG schools reform agenda, which reaches further and deeper than anything Australia has seen in the past decade and more.

For too long, public policy in this area has been made with an eye to short-term politics, not long-term improvements in policy outcomes. That's not the way this government does business. We believe that parents and the community have a right to know how their schools are performing and to compare them with other schools that serve similar populations.

Schools in low socioeconomic status communities

While greater transparency is necessary for improving underachieving schools, it's not sufficient. The government has therefore set out to provide new resources to schools in low socioeconomic status communities in order to spur reform in those schools. In my book *Postcode*, I described a quality education as 'a one-way ticket out of poverty'. But at the time of writing—2005—I also noted that 'education policies seem to be designed with the purpose of making it harder for students from poorer communities to compete with their wealthier peers'. According to OECD research, students in the lowest socioeconomic quartile lag behind those in the highest socioeconomic quartile by 2.5 years. It's time to change that.

Through the COAG process, we're aiming to help improve schools in low socioeconomic status communities. This involves targeting additional resources—about $500 000 per annum for a typical sized school—to the schools that serve the most disadvantaged children in Australia. Making these schools work better will raise gross domestic product (GDP) in the long run, but it's about more than that. We want poor children in Australia to enjoy an education as good—or better—than anyone else.

Our low socioeconomic status school reforms are about more than money. In aggregate, there is very little evidence to show that spending more money alone will result in better education performance.[6] So we are committed to ensuring that this new spending spurs fundamental changes in these schools.

Over time, we hope that many of these reforms will be adopted in other schools. But we are starting at the place we believe is most important: the neediest neighbourhoods of Australia. Our reforms will provide more funding and greater discretion to principals and local school communities. They will help schools attract high-performing teachers and principals, and reward them for success.

Teaching in a disadvantaged area is one of the most important jobs in the nation. We need to ensure that more talented young Australians choose teaching in the future, and create incentives for them to work in the nation's neediest schools.

Through our low socioeconomic status reforms, schools will also have the flexibility to help students through after-school study support, new sporting programs, strong networks with the local community and links with local businesses. Private schools in leafy suburbs have long offered programs such as these to their students. But in low socioeconomic status communities, they have been the exception rather than the norm. With these extra resources, we also expect greater accountability.

We do not apologise for insisting that high standards should apply in every community. These proposed reforms have been criticised from some quarters as anti-teacher and even anti-public education. The opposite, in fact, is true. They are motivated by a passionate belief in the importance of good public schools and good teachers—a belief founded in personal experience, shared with the Prime Minister, during our years at Nambour High School.

Under these policies, school funding will follow need and be used to raise the quality, standing and remuneration of the teaching profession. And given the predominance of public schools in the ranks of disadvantage, this means the policies represent a new future for public education and for the teaching profession.

In many cases, there are excellent, dedicated principals and teachers doing a great job in these communities. Our task is to recognise those professionals and strengthen their efforts. Our policies are a lifeline for these teachers, should they choose to grasp it. I suspect the overwhelming majority of parents are hoping they will.

The reforms have also been dismissed as a copy of the previous government's policy. That too is wrong. The policies of the Howard Government set out to create something completely different: a set of 'dumb' league tables that offered no analysis of why some schools were underperforming and no strategy for addressing their underperformance. In contrast, our 'like schools' approach takes account of differences in family backgrounds across schools. And where we identify underperformance, we'll be in there doing our utmost to make sure those schools fulfil their potential.

Conclusion

I've aimed to give you a flavour of what we are doing to modernise Commonwealth–state relations—and to give you two examples of the types of reforms we will be able to deliver, building on this new federal platform. My examples have focused on school reform because it brings together two of my longstanding policy interests. Education is both economic policy and social policy. It is now the key policy area where good economics and good moral values combine to produce the best results. This is the reason why social democratic parties around the world run for office promising their three top priorities will be 'education, education and education'. In a world of technological change and globalisation, we owe it to the next generation of Australians to provide the best possible education. This matters for all children—but it matters especially for the most disadvantaged.

For Labor, better schools are the cornerstone of a decent society. Indeed, quality schools might well be the best anti-poverty program available. Education increases productivity and participation, it builds prosperity and it also offers the hope of breaking the intergenerational cycle of poverty.

Modern federalism will enable us to finally undertake bold reforms to Australia's school system—notwithstanding the fact that the responsibility for schools policy in this country straddles Commonwealth–state boundaries. Our modernisation of the federation is driven by the same practical spirit that inspired Federation itself: a desire to create systems that stand the best chance of delivering for the Australian people.

We want to encourage innovation and problem solving at the local level—providing states with greater budgetary flexibility in return for greater transparency and accountability. And we are committed to major reforms to make public services work better, which we are backing with substantial new funding. Underpinning what we are doing is what I have called 'the Australian way'. The Australian way is the idea that we are all richer when we are able to participate in the economy, that inequality is bad economics and that better education is vital to creating a better society.

For me, these are moral certainties and they inspire the reforms that we are undertaking today.

ENDNOTES

[1] This essay was originally presented as a keynote address at the ANZSOG Annual Conference on 11 September 2008.

[2] The Labor Government of Alan Carpenter was narrowly defeated in the Western Australia state election on 6 September 2008.

[3] Brook, Anne-Marie 2008, *Raising education achievement and breaking the cycle of inequality in the United Kingdom*, Economics Department Working Papers No. 663, Organisation for Economic Cooperation and Development, Paris.

[4] Goldin, Claudia and Katz, Lawrence 2008, *The Race Between Education and Technology*, Harvard University Press, Cambridge, Mass.

[5] Freeman, Richard 2005, 'What really ails Europe (and America): the doubling of the global workforce', *The Globalist*, 3 June 2005.

[6] See *2008–09 Budget Statement*, vol. 4, pp. 4.24–25.

2. Does federalism work?[1]

The Hon John Brumby MP, Premier of Victoria

Does a system of government drawn up at the end of the nineteenth century and activated at the dawn of the twentieth century still have currency in the twenty-first century?

In a word: yes. Federalism does work. It is a robust and flexible system that has stood the test of time and made us one of the world's most stable democracies. It is an efficient system that, according to analysis done for the Withers and Twomey report *Australia's Federal Future*, boosts our per capita GDP by 10.5 per cent—or $11 402 per household—through the greater efficiencies of political and fiscal decentralisation.

But, it needs to be said, there is room for improvement. Given the size and scope of challenges Australia faces—such as climate change, the rise of the BRIC economies (Brazil, Russia, India and China) and our ageing and growing population—we need to make federalism work better.

Federalism needs to change to adapt to our changing circumstances and benefit the community. For instance, Withers and Twomey found that if Australia went further with fiscal decentralisation—in line with the best federal practice of Canada, Germany and Switzerland—average annual incomes would increase by $4188.

However, in changing, we must resist the temptation to go back to the future—and re-litigate the old arguments of state versus Commonwealth. For instance, the question of who holds the financial levers is well and truly settled.

As our second Prime Minister, Alfred Deakin, accurately predicted in 1902, 'The rights of self-government of the states have been fondly supposed to be safeguarded by the Constitution. It has left them legally free, but financially chained to the chariot wheels of the Commonwealth.'

Equally, it would be a mistake to confuse the Commonwealth's fiscal power with constitutional power. As Sir Henry Winneke, the former Governor and Chief Justice of the Supreme Court of Victoria, said in 1965:

> As a consequence of our federal way of life, based as it is upon a division of powers between Commonwealth and state, there is no absolute sovereignty in Australia. Citizens who value their individual liberties may see in this an effective safeguard against the development of…a new despotism.

In other words, no Australian government operates in isolation. Every Australian government—be they state or territory or Commonwealth—has an equal share in our federation. And that egalitarian and quintessentially Australian approach to federalism is the best way to deliver the policies and investments we need to meet the challenges of our time, secure Australia's productivity, sustainability and liveability and deliver the Australian people the opportunities they deserve.

Victoria's reform record

I have spoken many times about what needs to be done to make federalism work better. For instance, in April 2005, I delivered a speech to the Melbourne Institute that laid out the framework for what became the National Reform Agenda. I said Australia needed:

- a new model of cooperative federalism
- a national effort to improve competition and regulation
- greater investment in world-class infrastructure
- a national target for boosting workforce participation
- a national approach to Australia's growing population.

The last time I addressed ANZSOG—in February last year—I spoke about how cooperative Commonwealth–state relations were crucial to meet the reform challenges. The quote from me that features on today's program is taken from that speech: 'New solutions, new reforms and a recommitment to co-operative federalism are crucial to meeting the challenges facing our country.'

More importantly, those words have been backed with action. Victoria has not just developed the National Reform Agenda, we've:

- quadrupled infrastructure spending
- led the nation in regulatory reform
- and led the nation in skills training and jobs creation.

In the past month, we've launched a major innovation statement to drive new economic growth, and a major skills statement to boost jobs training. Securing Jobs for Your Future is a $316 million reform package that will give 172 000 Victorians the opportunity to train, retrain or boost their qualifications, as well as transforming the skills base of our workforce and boosting productivity and labour-force participation.

We will shortly release a manufacturing statement to drive innovation and investment across the sector. And, at the end of 2008, we will release a landmark transport statement that sets out how we will expand Victoria's transport network.

We understand the importance of innovation and reform. That's why—despite a two-tiered economy and a global economic slowdown—Victoria is, according to *The Age*'s reading of the latest National Accounts figures, the 'surprise engine room of the Australian economy', contributing almost half of the nation's growth in domestic demand.

However, the size and scope of the challenges we face are too great for any one level of government to tackle on their own. That's why we need cooperative federalism.

Cooperative federalism

The past 10 months demonstrate what can be achieved if all the stakeholders work together. Since the election of the Rudd Government, COAG has met three times: in December 2007, then in March and July 2008.

The December 2007 COAG meeting saw the Prime Minister, premiers and chief ministers commit to:

- a blitz on elective surgery waiting times
- a national partnership to close the gap in life expectancy that exists between Indigenous and non-Indigenous Australians.

The March 2008 COAG saw the Prime Minister, premiers and chief ministers:

- agree to draw up a new model for federal financial relations—with the priority being modernising Special Purpose Payments and developing National Partnership Payments
- agree for the first time on a common framework for the reform of education—including early childhood development, schooling, skills and workforce development
- sign a historic memorandum of understanding for the reform of the Murray-Darling Basin to restore the environment and ensure sustainable agriculture in the future.

The July 2008 COAG meeting agreed to a major overhaul of overlapping and inconsistent regulations that will make life easier for business and consumers and usher in a seamless national economy. And we have—in July and September 2008—seen the release of draft and supplementary draft reports by the landmark Garnaut Climate Change Review, with the final report to be released on 30 September 2008.

The Garnaut Review was initiated by the states and territories through the Council for the Australian Federation in February 2007. The Council for the Australian Federation complements COAG by providing a forum for new policy innovations such as committing to improve vehicle safety standards to ensure new vehicles are safer and that the benefits of new technologies are realised.

Of these COAG reforms the one with the highest profile was the agreement on the Murray-Darling Basin. This was a reform first discussed in 1901, and earmarked again for reform by Paul Keating in 1996 and John Howard in 2006. It was only when the issue was approached as an exercise in cooperative federalism that real progress was made—with an agreement reached in less than six months.

There's another point about the Murray-Darling that needs to be made. There was a perception that the magic solution for the Murray-Darling was to give the Commonwealth total control over the Murray-Darling Basin. Not only was this scenario constitutionally impossible, it was environmentally nonsensical.

The fact is that federalism can't make it rain—and only rain will make the Murray-Darling Basin bloom. If the Commonwealth had been running the Murray-Darling before the drought, the basin would still be in dire straits.

The new agreement is a good outcome for the Murray-Darling and demonstrates what can be achieved when governments work together. And the year's still not over.

COAG will meet again in October and December 2008, with major discussions on the agenda for the new Carbon Pollution Reduction Scheme and a complete rewriting of federal–state financial relations, with 90 former Special Purpose Payment agreements collapsed down to five and a set of new National Partnerships to deliver incentives for agreed reform outcomes.

The COAG working groups are also developing a substantial agenda for reform, including 27 areas for rationalisation of regulation. I can honestly say that, in 25 years of public life as a federal and state parliamentarian, I have never seen the Commonwealth, states and territories work together with such focus and with such positive outcomes. Put it this way:

- with the Keating Government, COAG's first five meetings were held over a period of three-and-a-half years
- with the Howard Government, its first five COAGs were held over five years—and its last five over two years
- with the Rudd Government, by December 2008, the past five meetings will have been held over 12 months.

Since the last federal election, the COAG process has doubled in frequency—and intensity. But we need to do more.

Making federalism work better

As I said earlier, Australia is facing enormous challenges. Our global economy is changing rapidly, with the emergence of Brazil, Russia, India and China. Our environment is changing rapidly, with the drought and climate change. And our community is changing rapidly, with our rapidly growing and ageing population.

Not only that, the challenges we face are all interrelated. That's one of the lessons of climate change: the way we live and work has an impact on the world in which we live. Everything is connected.

The great challenge we face as a nation is to change the way we live and work for the better—to improve our sustainability and productivity and create a fairer and more liveable community. And the best way we can do that is for governments of all jurisdictions—no matter where they sit in the electoral cycle, no matter what their political persuasion—to take decisive action and take that decisive action in a coordinated manner.

We need to turn what's been a year of action by COAG into a decade of action and national reform. And, to do so, we need to elevate the status of and clarify the agenda of COAG. COAG has always been a forum for national progress. Its purpose—when first established in 1992 by the Keating Government—was to coordinate and focus the authority of the heads of governments, improve intergovernmental relations and drive microeconomic reform.

But COAG has no constitutional or legislative standing, and its secretariat is an appendix of the Department of Prime Minister and Cabinet. And the COAG Reform Council operates based on an intergovernmental agreement that sets out broad objectives and functions, but with no clear powers or independence. The current status and structure of COAG is outmoded. Just as we are modernising federal finances, we need to modernise what is, in effect, federation's cabinet of first ministers.

With that in mind, I am here calling for COAG to be underpinned by a new intergovernmental agreement—with the role and governance of the COAG Secretariat formalised. This agreement should require:

- regular meetings of COAG
- an effective and independent secretariat
- the right for states to place items on the agenda.

COAG is an increasingly important decision-making body that drives the reform process, makes collective decisions and resolves deadlocks. The fact that COAG has ceased the practice of always sitting in Canberra has changed the dynamic. But Australia needs COAG to become an enduring institution that rises above the ebb and flow of governments.

A new intergovernmental agreement would:

- reflect that COAG is an equal partnership between all levels of government
- set out COAG's vision and objectives
- have a strong emphasis on joint accountability and direct all Australian governments to meet high performance benchmarks
- provide flexibility for COAG to adapt and evolve

- make COAG transparent to the community—using plain language that all Australians can understand
- drive the cultural change required to support a mature federalism.

I am also calling for the drawing up of a comprehensive forward plan for action by COAG—tackling key social and environmental challenges and the tighter global economy with short, medium and long-term targets.

Australia faces serious challenges to its diverse economic foundations—particularly in the area of manufacturing skills and self-reliance. We need to find new opportunities for export markets, import replacements and to expand into the growth markets of the future.

Over the next decade, it's likely that Australian governments will spend more than $10 billion buying new trains to provide for the significant shift back to public transport as petrol prices rise. There is an opportunity for COAG to show leadership in procurement and industry development by coordinating the purchase and assembly of new rolling stock and maximising the benefits for Australia from this massive investment.

Australian manufacturing already makes everything from family sedans to naval frigates. There's no reason why we shouldn't be also involved in the manufacturing and assembly of trains.

And when it comes to equipping the next generation of Australians with the skills and education they need to make their way in the world, we need to look to the value of a place-based approach to education.

In areas of disadvantage and underperformance, this will mean breaking down the barriers between state and federal government funding arrangements, as well as between government and non-government schools.

Such an approach could deliver stronger partnerships with clear goals, so that all children in a targeted area—whether in a government or non-government school—could experience an even better education.

This approach is being driven in Victoria through the Education Blueprint our government released in September 2008, which is based on our solid belief that every Victorian child deserves every opportunity in life.

Reform of ministerial councils

Another area for significant reform is the plethora of ministerial councils. We need to look at ways to rationalise their number in order to foster interaction between areas—such as natural resources and primary industries, early childhood development and school education. And we also need to strengthen their effectiveness so that they retain a clear focus on resolving issues within deadlines.

Currently, there are 31 separate ministerial councils. Those councils are expensive to run, often have overlapping responsibilities and consume too much time for too little outcome. Different jurisdictions have different portfolio arrangements, sometimes leading to confusion and large entourages at council meetings. Some ministerial councils now have statutory functions or decision-making powers that can create ambiguities.

Over the past year, the reform task has been given to a small group of COAG working groups, chaired by federal ministers, and these have achieved a great deal. However, the accountability of COAG working groups could be improved and there is a mismatch, with the states represented at an officer level and the Commonwealth at a ministerial level.

The review of the COAG working groups due at the end of 2008 is an opportunity to simplify the system. That review should also extend to a consideration of the relationship between the working groups and our 31 ministerial councils. In my view, the review should focus on the merger of the working groups and ministerial councils and a net reduction in the number of councils—perhaps to less than a dozen covering major portfolio groups.

It should also consider the relationship of the ministerial councils to COAG—including clarifying the role of COAG in being the final arbiter of disputes, with power to cut through deadlocks that have repeatedly arisen to slow the pace of reform.

The outcome of the review should be reflected in the intergovernmental agreement. In short, we need to foster a federal culture that encourages harmonisation and innovation without imposing uniformity.

Clarifying overlapping responsibilities

There have also been recent calls for the transferral of various state responsibilities holus-bolus to the Commonwealth, with unsubstantiated claims about potential savings. Those claims don't stand up to scrutiny. As the Withers and Twomey report found, the federal system of government is more efficient and flexible than the unitary system, with more transparency and less corruption.

Unitary states in 21 OECD countries employ nearly 11 per cent more public servants than federations. Public spending as a proportion of GDP is also 13 per cent higher in those OECD countries with a unitary system of government.

That's why, internationally, the trend is towards developing a more federal style of government that is able to juggle the competing demands of globalisation and local communities.

Yet, in Australia, federalism seems to be a scapegoat. The Withers Twomey report found that many of the arguments against federalism were based on misconceptions and false assumptions, such as that it was incompatible with globalisation, too costly, had one tier of government too many and promoted buck-passing and conflict.

As the Withers Twomey report says: 'There are many popular myths in Australia concerning federalism that are not borne out by the evidence...Australian attitudes towards federalism are out of step with those in the rest of the world.'

In this hyper-critical climate, it is easy to lose perspective. There is a double standard when it comes to measuring the relative performance of state and federal governments. Why is it that whenever a state government is perceived to have failed it is, inevitably, seen as proof that the states should be abolished? That's like arguing that the Commonwealth should be abolished and Canberra turned back into a sheep paddock because the Howard Government mishandled the $1 billion Seasprite helicopter project.

Historically, many reform initiatives were first proposed and trialled by state governments. For example, new approaches to social and environmental policy were trialled by the Dunstan and Hamer Governments and public sector reform was introduced by the Cain Government and adopted Australia-wide.

The states also ensure the voices of regional communities are heard and their interests represented in Canberra.

The point I am driving at is that we need to set aside our myths and preconceptions of federalism and focus on the reality, such as sorting out overlapping responsibilities. Clarifying responsibilities is one of the most practical actions we can take to make federalism work better, but there are no easy solutions. Recent discussions have highlighted how hard reform within a federal system can be at the practical, day-to-day level.

Let me be clear: I am not an advocate of a grand exchange of responsibilities. Instead, I want to see governments work together on areas where there are strong overlaps in responsibilities so that we can present a seamless service to the public. Four areas where we could start—as part of the new funding agreements currently under negotiation—are:

- aged-care services and disability services
- universities, TAFE and apprenticeships
- early childhood development services and child care
- hospitals and Medicare-funded primary health services.

Conclusion

In conclusion, let me leave you with a thought. Right now, most federations are working towards subsidiarity—shifting the focus of government decision making to a more local level. Globally, Australia is an exception to that rule: rather than becoming more localised, we are becoming more centralised.

The new Chief Justice of the High Court of Australia, Robert French, characterised the trend somewhat fatalistically in a speech in August 2008 when he said:

> Despite the benefits of co-operative federalism the wide range of its application may have an overall tendency to define as national that which was once local. A shrinking federation will continue to shrink. The logical outcome is the singular state of a unitary federation. That is the federation you have when you do not have a federation.

It is in our national interest to resist a slide into a 'Clayton's' federation—because cooperative federalism is the system best able to juggle the competing global and local demands of the future.

The challenge ahead of us is not to make federalism work—but work better.

Over the past nine months we have seen what can be achieved through cooperative federalism, with the states and the Commonwealth working together to:

- target elective surgery waiting times
- create a seamless national economy
- secure a historic agreement on the Murray-Darling Basin
- close the gap in life expectancy between Indigenous and non-Indigenous Australians
- draw up a new model for federal financial relations
- agree to a common framework for education reform
- establish the building blocks of an emissions trading scheme.

The new actions I have suggested here propose an even broader vision for cooperative federalism, with the prospect of further real and tangible gains for the nation. At this time of economic, social and environmental challenges, we need to take the next step and ensure that the performance of our federation is up there with the very best in the world.

ENDNOTES

[1] This essay was originally presented as a keynote address at the ANZSOG Annual Conference on 11 September 2008.

3. What has federalism ever done for us?[1]

The Hon Anna Bligh MP, Premier of Queensland

In April 2008, our new Prime Minister gathered together 1000 of our country's best and brightest to imagine the Australia we could be in 2020. As I left Canberra on that cold Sunday afternoon, I was both inspired and alarmed. Inspired by the wealth of ideas and the many new voices that had been unearthed by the process and alarmed that the most recurring theme and, without doubt, the most popular idea was the abolition of the states.

Here were some of the country's brightest, most educated, most experienced and publicly engaged thinkers cheering rapturously at a throwaway line from Tim Fischer about getting rid of the states. It gave me real pause for thought.

A century ago, as the fathers of the federation shaped the constitution, the preservation and protection of the states were pivotal to their deliberations, and yet today there seems to be a headlong, popular rush to abandon them. I was struck by how comprehensively John Howard had demonised the states, but I was also acutely aware that this alone could not explain the phenomenon.

At the very least, the summiteers' reaction articulated a real sense of disappointment and frustration with many key areas of social service provision. States ignore this at their peril.

So, a century on from federation, against a backdrop of an emerging cooperative federalism and fresh from a meeting of COAG, I thought it would be useful here to reflect on federalism as a form of government and contemplate the future of our own federation. In doing so, I intend to mount a spirited defence of the federation.

I will, no doubt, be accused of self-interest in this respect; I note that the wheels of constitutional change turn at a glacial pace in this country and any radical change in the federation is unlikely to happen during my political career. So, I speak as a citizen as much as a premier and I caution against the inevitable, perhaps intoxicating, rush to simple solutions.

In essence, I believe that, in a country of 21 million people, spread across 7.6 million square kilometres, providing services to people in some of the great cities of the world and some of the most remote places on Earth, a federation of states is the most effective way to govern, to manage and to provide services.

What has federalism ever done for us?

A century ago, Australia's colonies were able to design the government they wanted. They examined governments around the world and they chose a federation. They were not alone in so choosing. The United States, Switzerland and Canada were among the nations that had already decided on a federation. Looking back over 107 years of federalism in Australia, we might well ask: what has federalism ever done for us?

Well, how about this: federalism divides and limits power, providing checks and balances that protect individuals, mitigate against an overly powerful central government and assist accountability. Federalism allows for coordinated national action on issues of national importance, such as responses to natural disasters like cyclones. It also encourages healthy competition and creativity between the states and territories, both of which lead to improvements in performance, efficiency and outcomes.

For example, consider how uncompetitive our state tax arrangements would be if there was not a healthy competition between states to lower the tax burden in every budget. Federalism recognises the distinctive nature and identity of the regions of Australia through the states and territories, thereby allowing for policies and services to be tailored to the different needs of different people and communities across vast and varied country.

Federalism offers a number of other advantages, as detailed in a report by Anne Twomey and Glenn Withers for the Council for the Australian Federation in 2007. They point out that many Australians see our structure of government as old-fashioned, cumbersome and inefficient. Yet, in other places, federalism is viewed as modern, flexible and efficient in dealing with the increasing pressures faced by communities. This report shows that, when compared with centralised, unitary governments, federated structures such as Australia have:

- more efficient governments
- higher rates of economic growth
- higher per capita GDP.

Further, their research demonstrates that increasing centralisation threatens these benefits.

The foundation of our current prosperity as a nation is built on significant economic, social and environmental reforms, negotiated and put in place through our federal structure. As the report demonstrates, of the G8 nations—the countries with the greatest economies in the world—four are federations and seven have at least three tiers of government. The success of federations—and of countries with three tiers of government—is not transitory, as Twomey and Withers state: 'In the past 50 years, federations have consistently out-performed unitary systems in economic terms…the more centralised the federation, the better the performance.'

What have the states ever done for us?

If some Australians question the value of federalism, I think many more might ask: what have the states ever done for us? For most Australians, most of the time, most of the government services they use are delivered by the states, such as the schools their children attend, the public hospitals where they seek emergency care and surgery, the roads they drive on, the buses and trains they catch, the clean water provided to their homes.

Why is it that the states deliver most services, even though the Commonwealth funds at least some of them? One reason is that our federation is built on the principle of subsidiarity—the idea that matters should be dealt with, and services provided by, competent government closest to the community.

Given the scale usually required to deliver universally available services, that generally means the state and territory governments, and in some cases it means local government. Under the subsidiarity principle, matters of national interest, such as defence, and areas that require a nationally equitable approach across state borders, such as income support, should sit with the national government.

Similarly, cross-jurisdictional matters or areas where harmonisation is required, such as corporation laws, and where economies of scale can be derived, also sit naturally with the national government. However, where services need to be delivered in person or tailored to local circumstances, other levels of government are best placed to manage service delivery.

And we should remember that these large, and sometimes challenging, service delivery systems deliver some extraordinary results across our country. In Australia today, 2.268 million children will be taught in a state school classroom and about 120 000 people will be treated as non-admitted patients in public hospitals. In Queensland today, some 478 000 children are being educated in state schools and more than 28 800 people will be treated as non-admitted patients in public hospitals.

The system isn't perfect

However, neither the federation nor the states are perfect. The problems have been well documented: creeping centralism in all areas of public policy and service delivery; complexity and confusion about the roles and responsibilities of the Commonwealth and the states; a system that can be bureaucratic, cumbersome and slow to respond to cross-jurisdictional or emerging issues; duplication of services, wastage of funds, cost-shifting and buck-passing; and financial arrangements that have produced an extreme vertical fiscal imbalance.

No wonder there is frustration and disappointment at service delivery failures. Government doesn't always deliver services well, on time, on budget or to expectation. There have been some awful failures, as Queensland experienced recently with the poor maintenance of nurses' accommodation in the Torres Strait, with the resultant threat to the safety and security of our staff in an isolated part of the state, which, in turn, has led to problems in recruiting and retaining qualified staff.

I understand, and share, people's frustration and I have to say the states, including my own, can do much better on service delivery. Accompanying this is a belief that another level of government—in most cases, the federal government—could do a better job, as we saw from the preliminary results of a survey on constitutional values by Griffith University, which were published in *The Australian* on 3 July 2008. The survey of 1200 voters showed that half of them believed the Commonwealth was the level of government that was most effective at doing its job; just under 20 per cent nominated local government; and just over 18 per cent nominated the states. And just over 79 per cent thought the Commonwealth should get involved in issues that were the responsibility of state governments.

This rush to a seemingly simple solution is underpinned, in my view, by the fact that most people have limited experience of the Commonwealth as a direct service provider. They are just blindly hoping the Commonwealth will do a better job. They are also apparently in the grip of collective amnesia about the Commonwealth's record when it does actually deliver services. So let's stop for a moment and remember:

- the kerosene baths for frail aged people in a nursing home under the purview of a Commonwealth department
- the long-running and expensive saga of defence procurement, such as the Collins-class submarines
- unjust and unlawful detentions by an immigration department that was assessed as incompetent by the Commonwealth itself.

Contemplate the alternative. Imagine the lack of coherence if all of Australia's schools, more than 9500 in all, were run out of Canberra. Consider the challenge for a mum in Broome seeking to influence a federal Education Minister from Melbourne about the toilet block at the local public school, or worse still, imagine if schools were the responsibility of some 700 local governments. I raise these examples not as a partisan political attack or as a Canberra-bashing exercise but to highlight that service delivery problems are not the exclusive preserve of any one level of government, but rather that they are endemic to the business of delivering services.

Appetite for change

I am not alone in identifying the problems with our federation and the need for reform. Debate about federalism, which cooled after the failure of the republic referendum, has been rekindled in the past few years. We've had some significant contributions from, among others, former premiers Peter Beattie and Steve Bracks, the states and territories through the Council for the Australian Federation, Kevin Rudd as Opposition Leader and as Prime Minister, the Business Council of Australia and delegates to the Australia 2020 Summit and the Queensland 2020 Summit. I think it's fair to say there is widespread agreement that we need reform.

But before we start tearing up our constitution, or abolishing our states, let's acknowledge that federations have much to offer. Let's acknowledge that there is a global move towards federalism rather than away from it. Countries such as Spain, Belgium and South Africa, which had been unitary, have adopted federal structures, thereby maintaining some central control while also permitting some regional control. The United Kingdom is creating legislatures and devolving responsibilities in Scotland, Wales and Northern Ireland. And of course there is the European Union, a federation of sovereign nations that more often than not also have very strong provincial governments. So, let's keep our federation but let's make it work better.

Some proposals

I'd like to offer some proposals to reinforce and reinvigorate our system. My proposals are built on three key beliefs:

- a belief in the principle of subsidiarity
- a belief in the need for clear roles and responsibilities—and in many major services of importance, shared responsibilities, based on changing needs, challenges and opportunities facing our citizens
- a belief that the Commonwealth and the states must be willing to both assume and surrender responsibilities.

I can best articulate these beliefs by explaining how they would apply to three key policy areas, and to Commonwealth–state financial relations. I will start with the roles and responsibilities in two key human services that are in great need of reform—that is, education and training, and health—and, finally, move on to climate change, a new public policy challenge that will have an enormous impact on each of us.

Education and training

As a former education minister and as a parent, I know that education is the key that unlocks a child's potential. Education, skills, innovation—these are the keys to our individual and collective prosperity.

Given their importance, education and training are the first policy areas in which I propose reform of state and federal relations. Some of you might be aware that in the lead-up to the Australia 2020 Summit, I proposed the introduction of a full national curriculum progressively from the beginning of the 2010 school year, supported by a new national curriculum authority incorporating the state, Catholic and independent sectors.

Here, I want to go further. In a globalised economy, with an increasingly mobile population, in the midst of a skills shortage, we need greater consistency in our education and training system. Currently, we have a mishmash of inconsistent responsibilities and accountability requirements.

In early childhood education and care, the states are largely responsible for licensing and regulating childcare centres, which the Commonwealth funds and accredits and with its own quality-assurance system attached. The end result is massive duplication, with childcare centres having to report on policies and practices to two levels of government. Notwithstanding the Commonwealth's recent commitment to universal access to preschool for all four year olds, currently the states are the primary funders and regulators of preschool services and accredit the programs that are used.

In primary and secondary education, the states provide public education, but regulate private schools. However, we fund, register teachers and approve the curriculum for both sectors. Meanwhile, the Commonwealth chips in some funding for public schools, most of the funding for private schools and has its own accountability requirements for both sectors, in addition to those of the states.

In vocational education and training, states regulate the training system, purchase training from public and private training providers and provide training through TAFE and community colleges. The Commonwealth provides about one-quarter of training funds and also subsidises employers to take on apprentices. And universities are created under state legislation, get most of their funding from the Commonwealth and face the accountability requirements of both. It's time for a radical rethinking of roles and responsibilities.

One option is for the states to take primary responsibility for service delivery in early childhood and care as well as school education and for the Commonwealth to assume primary responsibility for delivery of post-school qualifications in the vocational education and training (VET) system and universities. I am not proposing a complete takeover of early childhood and school education by the states. The Commonwealth could usefully retain lead responsibility for setting overall national goals and a national curriculum. But the delivery would be the responsibility of the states, as provider in the public system and regulator in the private system.

I think it's time for us to view early childhood and school education as one seamless system, whether it is publicly or privately provided. And surely the quality of care and education provided in all early childhood centres and schools should be the responsibility of one level of government. Similarly, responsibilities for post-secondary education and training should be reformed.

One of the key points of agreement at the Australia 2020 Summit was that we should develop a seamless national economy. Given the importance of skilled labour to our economy, surely this must mean streamlining our post-school education system. As with early childhood and school education, we need to see this system as a whole. Making the Commonwealth solely responsible for VET and universities would be a major step in delivering the skilled workforce we need as a nation. Importantly, it would also significantly improve the efficiency of our university and VET providers and reduce red tape and major duplication in financial and performance accountability requirements of the state and federal governments. It will also increase the national and international portability of the skills of our workforce.

Health

All states face significant challenges in delivering health services. Some of Queensland's challenges are unique. Each week, up to 1800 extra people arrive in our state and contribute to surging demand. The majority of residents live outside the capital, some in remote communities and some in regional centres such as Cairns, which is further away from Brisbane than Melbourne.

We have boosted spending on our health system, investing more than $10 billion over five years. But over the past 10 years under the Howard Government, federal funding for our public health system fell from 50 to about 35 per cent. Frankly, we are struggling to keep pace with growth and demand.

If Queensland's current rates of population growth, economic growth and public health spending continue unabated, by 2042 our public health spending will consume the entire state budget. This is not in the public interest. That's my motivation for proposing some major changes in the way we manage health, as a nation.

In our submission to the National Hospitals and Health Reform Commission, we suggest key reforms. In my view, states should be responsible for health services that are likely to require an integrated service delivery response. For example, many of the problems we encounter in relation to Indigenous health in remote communities cannot be addressed solely through the health system; there is sometimes a housing issue, sometimes a need for upgraded water supplies or better sewerage systems, which, of course, the state delivers.

This means the states should be responsible for Indigenous health. Queensland agrees with the commission that the states should continue to be responsible for acute-care services—those that require hospital admissions. However, we need the Commonwealth to take responsibility for things that are making the job of running hospitals that much harder. At the moment, there are people waiting in hospital emergency wards who really just need to see a GP, and a shortage of nursing home beds—controlled by the Commonwealth—means that every day an average of 468 Queenslanders who need a nursing home bed are in fact in acute-care beds in public hospitals and Queensland bears the extra cost of almost $400 000 a day.

The problem is that public hospitals are run by state governments and nursing homes are overseen by the Commonwealth. There is no imperative, no incentive for the two sectors to work together. Queensland's submission proposes that the Commonwealth should pay the states the full cost of providing such services in a hospital. I'm confident that pressure on the Commonwealth's hip-pocket nerve would lead to a rapid appreciation of the need to fix these anomalies. The National Health and Hospitals Reform Commission is a good example of the way in which we can maturely and systemically renegotiate roles and responsibilities to achieve better health care for all Australians.

Climate change

Professor Ross Garnaut's report to the government—*The Garnaut Climate Change Review*— examines, for the first time, the costs of climate change to Australia. His findings will be challenging. The report doesn't offer easy solutions. Climate change is the most critical challenge facing Australia and the world. We must get it right. And given the embryonic nature of policy making regarding climate change, we have the chance to get it right from the very beginning rather than reworking an existing system. We have the chance to ensure the different levels of government do not end up tripping over each other. We must ensure our federation is sufficiently responsive, agile and coordinated to deal with the complex issues relating to challenges from climate change.

Opportunity for change

My argument for reform is not about the states, it's about the health and sustainability of our federation. It is, by no means, a perfect system. But, to misquote Winston Churchill, just 'a little federalism is the worst form of governance, except for all the others'.

One hundred and eleven years ago, a proponent of federalism, Sir Isaac Isaacs, spoke of the colonies being at a point of great tension as they considered whether to form a federation. I think we are at another point in our history where there is great tension around how we work together. Our nation has evolved and our world has changed greatly since 1901 but our federal system and our constitution have not. We are at a point of great opportunity, with governments of the same political persuasion in power across Australia, a Prime Minister committed to a new federalism and state and territory leaders who want a real partnership. We have an appetite for change. There is also an opportunity for change—a once-in-a-generation opportunity. Let's make the most of it.

ENDNOTES

[1] This essay was originally presented as an ANZSOG Public Lecture on 4 July 2008.

4. Splicing the perspectives of the Commonwealth and states into a workable federation[1]

Terry Moran AO

In my view, we are on the verge of a revived federalism, which holds great possibilities for Australia in the twenty-first century. By this I do not mean we are about to eliminate or radically diminish the power of the states or any other critical element of the institutions of the federal system. Rather, we are on the threshold of entering into a new compact between governments, which contains the potential to confer several benefits on the Australian people:

- improved levels of service from government, based on a strategic agreement on what the focus should be
- better outcomes across a wide front
- increased productivity that will lift our living standards still further
- important new strategic initiatives.

Having been in public administration at the Commonwealth and state level, I can say that talent and creativity are to be found at both levels of government. We can harness these strengths to deliver enhanced economic and social outcomes for Australia.

So I don't intend to propose a radical solution, of either diminishing or substantially enlarging the powers of one or another constitutional actor.

Of course, the lawyers among you might first think of constitutional reform as the key to transforming Commonwealth–state relations for the better. That is certainly a conversation worth having.

As the Special Minister of State remarked in his speech for Constitution Day celebrations in July 2008, there was a strong case for updating what he described as the 'stump-jump plough' of constitutions.

However, I can only agree with Senator Faulkner's judgment that Australians on the whole are a sceptical lot who must be thoroughly convinced that any proposed changes will deliver practical and necessary improvements on the current system.

Where constitutional reform is concerned, that has always been a tough job. A number of ideas were put forward at the 2020 Summit for potential constitutional reform. The government is currently considering these proposals.

However, for those of us who deal in public policy, it is clear we have made enormous progress even without any fundamental change in the institutions to which the constitution gives rise.

We as Australians demand a great deal of ourselves and our governments. This has led to the continuous pursuit of practical but necessary improvements within the parameters of the current arrangements. And when challenges have arisen, we have worked constructively to find a way through.

The cooperative forces that forged the federation compact in the first place have continued to ensure that our country works. As greater fiscal power has moved to the Commonwealth, community attitudes have also changed.

Now there is broader acceptance of the Commonwealth taking an interest in a larger array of domestic government activity. But this is not to say the community wants outright Commonwealth control.

We have all come a considerable distance—but this is not to diminish the challenge still before us.

So in considering the future of Australian federalism, I would like first to discuss some recent research, the core challenges for the future and then turn to the ambitious program of reform that COAG currently has before it.

Griffith University's federalism project

One of the most striking findings to emerge from Griffith University's Federalism Project was that over two-thirds of Australians thought the current federal system was working quite well or even very well.

This might seem surprising, given the crowd's well-publicised reaction at the 2020 Summit when former Deputy Prime Minister Tim Fischer declared that his regional and rural stream had 'almost abolished the states'.

Almost 80 per cent of respondents agreed that the Commonwealth should intervene in cases where state governments had not resolved important issues.

And yet, over half of those surveyed also agreed with the principle of subsidiarity, that decision-making power should be devolved to the lowest competent level of government.

Clearly, the ways people view their relationships with governments are diverse and complex.

While some Australians did support wholesale abolition of one or more levels of government, almost one-third supported the addition of a new regional level. Almost 60 per cent, given the choice, said they would prefer to have three or more levels of government.

When asked to consider all current levels of government, 50 per cent of Australians rated the Commonwealth Government as the most effective at 'doing its job'.

In contrast, only 18.1 per cent rate the state level as the most effective, and 19.9 per cent rate the local level of government as the most effective.

Of course, views depended to some extent on the state the respondents called home. As a Victorian, I couldn't comment on the fact that almost two in five New South Welshmen said they would be happy to do away with state government altogether.

But it was heartening to learn that only one in four Victorians shared this view.

Twomey and Withers' federalist paper for the Council for the Australian Federation

There are undoubted benefits from federation. Professors Anne Twomey and Glenn Withers—whom you've heard from earlier at this conference—summarised the economic and social benefits of federalism in their first federalist paper.

They find that federalism:

- divides and limits power between different players in the system and protects the individual
- gives Australians a wider range of choices and allows policies and services to be tailored to meet the needs of communities
- spurs Australian governments, at all levels, to be more innovative and responsive to the needs of the community.

Victorian Skills Reform package

One example of this innovation is the Victorian Skills Reform package announced by the Brumby Government in August 2008. It is a perfect example of how state governments, with the assistance of the Commonwealth, can create and implement groundbreaking and far-reaching reforms, which will have a positive impact on the economy and future generations.

The centrepiece of the package is a redesigned investment model, which pursues two important reform agendas: a training guarantee and increasing market mechanisms.

The introduction of a training guarantee in post-compulsory education is a world first. In introducing this guarantee, the governments have committed to uncapped public funding for all Victorians in need of training, and it demonstrates an unparalleled commitment to developing a skilled workforce.

The package is one of the most significant microeconomic reforms introduced by a state government within the past 20 years. It creates structural change in the training market by:

- placing the purchasing power in the hands of the clients
- increasing contestability and introducing price competition
- aligning government funding to public benefit.

With the support of the Commonwealth Government, all students studying a diploma or advanced diploma will be able to access an income-contingent loan in the form of FEE-HELP.

This initiative will mean additional hundreds of thousands of Victorians accessing training related to employment in the next few years.

In Withers' technical analysis, he found that, depending on which statistical approach one took:

- for the past half-century, federations had a 15.1 per cent advantage in average income growth
- the average advantage of federations in their practise of fiscal decentralisation was 8 per cent
- the average federation benefit was 10.46 per cent.

On any of these figures, there is a distinct economic advantage to a federal system.

As compared with centralised unitary governments, federal nations such as Australia tend to have more efficient governments, higher rates of economic growth and higher income growth.

The reasons why we want and need to make federalism work better and enable it to reach its full potential are summed up in the six 'Cs' as presented by Twomey and Withers:

- a meaningful and effective federation is also a Check on power
- an effective federation offers Choice and diversity
- a federation provides Customisation of policies according to the different needs of states and territories.

At the same time, a federation instils healthy Competition, Creativity and, most of all, Cooperation.

Many of these elements underpin the approach to a reinvigorated COAG.

These perceived benefits have also guided significant devolution in France, Germany, Italy, Spain, Switzerland and the United Kingdom over the past decade.

However, when federalism is discussed, it is often about the inefficiencies of federal systems. Instead, we need to focus upon improving it to get the most out of it, socially and economically.

It is not impossible. In an increasingly competitive globalised world, we also need to undertake these reforms to position Australia competitively for the future.

So we currently face a paradox: the federation provides considerable benefits but it is also seen as the 'horse and buggy' of government arrangements.

It is easy to speculate on the reasons for this:

- there has been a deal of duplication and excessive levels of administrative burden at the state and the national level of government
- this directly or indirectly can result in a lack of coordination of services for the consumer and the community
- the blurring of lines of responsibility over time for clients can lead to frustration and inefficiency—and the related blurring of political accountability.

Taken together, these views might have contributed to a belief that the federation is an accident of history irrelevant to contemporary circumstances.

This is not a view to which I subscribe, but as I have already said, it does not mean that I do not see significant scope to improve the situation.

The Commonwealth Government has now been in office for a little over nine months.

In the Prime Minister's address to the National Press Club of 27 August, he outlined the government's long-term agenda for reform. Some of the particulars might have been overlooked in all the commentary surrounding his vision for an education revolution, but in essence, he set out the five key priorities for the government:

- building a more secure Australia, given the national security challenges we faced
- building a stronger Australia, with a successful economy to enable us to deliver on the needs of our people
- building a fairer Australia, based on equality of opportunity, a humane safety net and acting on disadvantage
- an Australia capable of meeting the significant new challenges of the twenty-first century, including climate change
- a new way of governing.

It is clear that in so many ways, the work of COAG is contributing directly to progressing these key themes.

In relation to the new way of governing, for example, COAG has a significant role to play, in improving the mechanisms for intergovernmental cooperation, clarifying roles and responsibilities and establishing a new financial framework.

It is not always possible, however, to reallocate functions on a 'clean lines' approach.

Sometimes power will need to be shared and, in such cases, needs will be reassessed in the best interests of good outcomes for the community, in redefining roles and managing these shared responsibilities.

Key challenges for the future

I turn now to the task of building a stronger economy and a fairer Australia, capable of addressing the challenges of the twenty-first century.

Whether it is climate change, an ageing population, long-term skill shortages, infrastructure bottlenecks or productivity growth, Australia continues to face major long-term challenges.

The Commonwealth can't tackle all these challenges on its own, nor does it want to. These challenges demand approaches that rise above traditional divides in the federation.

According to Michael Keating and Glyn Davis in their book *The Future of Governance*, [2] Australia's current economic success is, in part, the product of Commonwealth–state cooperation on competition policy in the 1990s.

Indeed, the Productivity Commission (April 2005) estimated that the National Competition Policy (NCP) and related reforms in the 1990s directly increased Australia's GDP by 2.5 per cent, or $20 billion.

I think the current COAG process has now reached a point where it is apparent that the total body of reform possibilities is broader and more substantial than all of the national competition policy reforms of the 1990s.

We need a bold approach to reform. And to achieve such reform, we need a new way of governing—in particular, increased cooperation between federal, state and local governments, businesses and community organisations.

A renewed belief in the possibility of reform was apparent at the 3 July 2008 COAG meeting. Leaders reaffirmed their commitment to the goals of the COAG reform agenda to address the challenges of:

- boosting productivity
- increasing workforce participation and mobility
- delivering better services for the community.

Reforms in these areas will in turn contribute to achieving broader goals of social inclusion, closing the gap on Indigenous disadvantage and environmental sustainability.

An overriding principle is that the key to building a strong economy is long-term productivity growth and participation in the workforce.

As the Prime Minister has said, the Commonwealth is committed to building long-term prosperity by investing in five key platforms for productivity growth:

- an education revolution—improving the qualitative and quantitative investment in the skills of the workforce
- an infrastructure reform program—kicked off by the government's establishment of the $20 billion Building Australia Fund
- investing in innovation and the industries of the future
- creating a seamless national economy through business deregulation
- finally, taxation reform.

The long boom has convinced many that prosperity is solving most problems. In truth, we cannot take prosperity for granted and the COAG reform agenda I have outlined above will be crucial for delivering long-term productivity growth to underpin a strong economy.

Creating a fairer Australia is also a key priority for the government. Disadvantage holds the economy back by reducing workforce participation.

The government's challenge is to bring these Australians back into the mainstream through a reform agenda of social inclusion.

The Commonwealth Government will be pursuing new ways of doing this including through COAG.

In March 2007, the Productivity Commission reported that the full implementation of reforms in human capital, competition and regulation would, over 25 years, grow the economy by 12 per cent (more than $100 billion a year) and bring great economic and social benefits to individuals, families, communities and businesses.

This is a substantial body of work and a tribute to the willingness of the state and territory governments to end the blame game in the interest of Australia and Australians.

COAG—a new reform framework

In December 2007, we all returned to the COAG table with renewed vigour and a comprehensive reform agenda for Australia. Four COAG meetings have been scheduled for 2008 to deliver a substantial body of work on the agenda.

Central to this is sweeping reform to the architecture of Commonwealth–state funding arrangements. Key elements of a new intergovernmental agreement on Commonwealth–state financial arrangements will be finalised by the end of 2008, following extensive work by treasurers and the COAG working groups.

The intention of this reform is that states will be able to deploy Commonwealth Specific Purpose Payments (SPPs) more effectively and creatively, with enhanced public accountability. New National Partnership (NP) agreements will sharpen the incentives for reform.

Specific Purpose Payment base funding has tended to be viewed in terms of funding shares provided by each level of government.

The new agreements for SPPs will replace input controls with a rigorous focus on the achievement of objectives, outcomes and outputs. That is, the agreements will focus on what services the states and territories can deliver, without prescribing how this is to be achieved.

The COAG working groups have been developing outputs, outcomes and performance measures for the new agreements in areas such as health, schools, vocational education and training, affordable housing and disabilities.

These new arrangements should lead to the greater choice, competition, creativity and customisation that I referred to earlier—and ultimately to delivery by the states and territories of better outcomes for people.

The new financial framework will result in fewer SPPs—many of the existing payments will be combined into a smaller number of new payments—but no reduction in total Commonwealth funding.

These reforms will better clarify roles and responsibilities, reduce duplication and provide greater flexibility for states and territories to put money into areas where they can produce the best outcomes for their communities.

The revised SPPs will be augmented by new NPs. These partnership arrangements will:

- provide funding for specific projects in areas of joint responsibility, such as in interstate transport
- provide payments to facilitate reforms to lift standards of service delivery
- reward states that deliver on nationally significant reforms.

This new Commonwealth–state financial arrangement will provide the platform for improving economic, social and environmental outcomes.

This architecture will also be crucial to improving performance in service delivery in the states. States and territories will have more flexibility to pursue different forms of service delivery that best suit their circumstances.

But the flip side is that in return for increased Commonwealth funding under NPs, the Commonwealth will expect improved delivery of services, key measurable outcomes and outputs.

The states and territories are important partners in this process. The Commonwealth Government's challenge to them is to commit to concrete, tangible reforms.

And our commitment is to match ambitious policy reform delivering better outcomes for people with new financial support. This bargain forms part of the government's upcoming negotiations for reform in the key areas of health, education and Indigenous affairs.

This is a significant development in managing Commonwealth–state relations and a step forward in improving government services to people. Let me talk about some of these in more detail.

Health

COAG has agreed that the new National Healthcare Agreement would be signed in December 2008 with new funding arrangements to commence on 1 July 2009.

This new agreement will go beyond previous agreements—and the current hospital system—to encompass primary health care, prevention and the acute and aged-care systems. And it will spell out the agreed accountability framework of all governments (Commonwealth, state and territory) for the objectives, outcomes and outputs in these areas.

Key priorities include reform and additional service provision in hospitals, preventative health, closing the Indigenous health gap and fixing the intersection of aged care, disability services and mental health roles and responsibilities.

The Commonwealth Government is willing to provide extra funding for health—but expects in return real reform in the sector and for more funding to result in the provision of more services.

Schools

In relation to schools, as the Prime Minister announced on 27 August, the three central pillars of reform that the Commonwealth aims to achieve through COAG this year are:

- improving the quality of teaching
- making school reporting properly transparent
- lifting achievement in disadvantaged school communities, including closing the gap between Indigenous and non-Indigenous students in terms of literacy and numeracy achievement, as well as year 12 (or equivalent) attainments.

A major thrust of the schooling reform agenda is to embed quality teaching. Raising teacher quality provides the platform for lifting student engagement and performance, as well as making progress on other school reforms.

A particular challenge for most education systems (including Australia's) is to attract quality teachers in 'hard-to-staff' schools.

In recent years, the United States and United Kingdom have implemented innovative and successful programs—the Teach for America and the Teach First programs—where highly talented graduates are given an accelerated pathway into teaching in difficult and challenging schools for two years.

These programs have given talented young graduates a taste of teaching—and many have made it their profession as a result.

One aim of the Commonwealth's new partnership with the states and territories, beginning in 2009, is to establish a similar scheme in Australia.

These are just some features of two streams of COAG work.

Better ways to deliver

The new financial framework and reforms being pursued through COAG are the result of creative experimentation and innovation.

We intend to keep monitoring how this innovation is working. The COAG Reform Council will be able to make an independent assessment of whether predetermined milestones and performance benchmarks have been met and it will also highlight examples of good practice and performance around the country.

In effect, it will provide continuous feedback on the success of the new financial arrangements in driving reform that leads to better outcomes for Australians in such important areas as health, education and closing the gap on Indigenous disadvantage.

Conclusion and looking forward to 2009 and beyond

The COAG meetings during the remainder of 2008 will focus on finalising policy reforms and the new financial arrangements, which will in turn reform Commonwealth–state relations; I am confident this will be for the better.

As well as a full policy agenda, addressing these key challenges will be a major focus of endeavour for COAG officials for 2009.

The new National Healthcare Agreement will set the groundwork for the first stage of health system reform.

The final report of the National Health and Hospitals Reform Commission in June 2009 will provide recommendations for a second round of reforms to address the interface between the public and private health sectors, the health workforce and integration of care across the health system.

We also need to reform service delivery with a 'citizen-centred' focus that can be more responsive to community needs.

As the Prime Minister said early in 2008, we must 'continue to reform the system of government and government service so that citizens lie at the centre, rather than the inflexible behemoths of official bureaucracy'.

I agree with the Prime Minister that government is not the repository of all wisdom, that there are limits to what governments can effectively do and that the private and community sectors have much to offer.

We look forward to working with groups across the community to improve the delivery of government services.

I believe the Commonwealth and state and territory governments have a great opportunity to reach agreement.

And I am also confident, given the evidence of goodwill that I have seen from states and territories and the Australian Local Government Association (ALGA), that we can achieve far-reaching reform.

From the Commonwealth's point of view, it marks just the beginning—the beginning of a period of long-term reform to tackle the nation's long-term challenges; we have to achieve this in order to ensure better outcomes for the people of Australia.

ENDNOTES

[1] This essay was originally presented as a keynote address at the ANZSOG Annual Conference on 12 September 2008.

[2] Keating, Michael and Davis, Glyn 2000, *The Future of Governance*, Allen & Unwin, Melbourne.

5. The reform imperative and Commonwealth–state relations[1]

The Hon John Brumby MP, Treasurer of Victoria[2]

More than 40 years ago, the late Donald Horne coined one of the most memorable phrases to describe our nation. He called Australia the 'lucky country'. As many of you no doubt realise, Horne was not singing Australia's praises. Rather, he was decrying Australia's complacency, its lack of innovation in important forms of industry and business and its failure to match the enterprise of other prosperous industrial societies. Horne believed that Australia owed its prosperity not to its native creativity and innovation, but rather to blind luck.

Horne warned that we were a nation taking it easy, that we were coasting along and drifting with the tide. While I don't agree with everything Horne argues in *The Lucky Country*, I do believe his message is as apt today as it was in 1964. Most importantly—as Horne cautioned 40 years ago—we need to remain focused on national reform and innovation if we are to prosper in the twenty-first century. While Australia's economic performance has been solid through the mid 1990s and in this decade, our productivity growth has stalled and our living standards are slipping in relation to comparable OECD countries. And, as I will address in some detail here, the challenges we face are not just economic.

In the health area, for example, the paradigm has changed dramatically. For the first time in our history, the impact of non-communicable diseases now exceeds that of communicable diseases. Yet our health system remains largely designed to treat injury and infections.

New solutions, new reforms and a recommitment to cooperative federalism are crucial to meeting the challenges facing our country.

The reform challenge

I want to talk here about how cooperative Commonwealth–state relations will be crucial in meeting the reform challenges ahead. In particular:

- human capital (the National Reform Agenda)
- regulation (the National Reform Agenda)
- innovation (the National Innovation Agenda)
- climate change and water
- Commonwealth–state financial relations.

The need for action

As I have mentioned, our productivity growth is stalled, the gains from past reforms are running out and we risk relying on blind luck yet again. Australia's first wave of reforms introduced by the Hawke Government in the mid 1980s saw the floating of the dollar, the deregulation of financial markets and the beginning of a phasing out of tariff barriers designed to protect Australian industry.

These reforms lowered the cost of imports as inputs into Australian industry, made exports more competitive and generally allowed the Australian economy to begin the process of aligning with the global economy.

Under the leadership of the Keating Government, the introduction of enterprise bargaining and the 1995 COAG agreement to implement a National Competition Policy (NCP) were central to a second wave of reform that sought to increase competition and productivity.

These measures were pivotal in boosting the competitiveness and growth of the Australian economy. The NCP was groundbreaking in the sense that all governments agreed to a common set of objectives, and it demonstrated what could happen when Commonwealth, state and territory governments had a common purpose and collaborated to implement major reforms.

Australia's current economic success owes as much to past reform efforts as it does to the resources boom. In the case of Victoria, for example, our leadership in implementing the NCP as well as other micro-reforms has meant our economic performance is much stronger than it otherwise would be. In fact, Access Economics in its most recent *Business Outlook* described Victoria's performance as 'magnificent' despite 'the onslaught of the $A, interest rates and drought'.

To ensure our prosperity in the future, Australians must take the next step in reforming our economy, and cooperative federalism—governments working together—is the best way to achieve these reforms.

Evolving federalism

Australia's federal system has both strength and weaknesses. To engender a more cooperative federalism, we need an overhaul of Commonwealth–state relations; and, as someone who has served in state and federal parliaments, I feel better qualified than many to draw that conclusion. I've seen Commonwealth–state relations from just about every angle: as a federal MP in the 1980s during the Hawke Government, as chief of staff to a cabinet minister in the early years of the Keating Government, as Leader of the Victorian Opposition for six years during the Kennett Government and as Victoria's forty-ninth Treasurer for the past seven years.

There's not much I haven't seen, heard or experienced about the often very volatile relationship between the Commonwealth, states and territories.

The causes of many of the problems in Commonwealth–state relations today stem from the fractious relations that existed between the states that voted for Federation in 1901 and the flaws in the constitution that they accepted as an article of federal union. More than a century later, we are lumbered with constitutional machinery that was intended to protect each state's prerogatives from each other and from the Commonwealth Government. This machinery has frequently made the pursuit of national reform a difficult and complicated endeavour.

Prior to federation, Australia's states maintained fierce tribal rivalries with one another. They levied customs excises on goods passing between their borders. They laid rail track with different gauges. Victoria even celebrated the date of its separation from the colony of New South Wales for nearly 50 years, prior to Federation. Not surprisingly, the founding fathers of Australia's constitution were concerned to protect state power and they anticipated the federation would function by allocating different responsibilities to the Commonwealth and the state governments so that each could act autonomously within their respective spheres of influence. However, despite these intentions, Australia has evolved rapidly into what has been termed a system of 'cooperative federalism', where the states and a federal government share responsibility for many areas of government and must cooperate to carry out these responsibilities.

The seeds of cooperative federalism were sown in the constitution itself. Section 51 of the constitution, which outlines the Commonwealth's powers, has always been defined expansively by the High Court, allowing the Commonwealth to assume powers that are implied or incidental to those powers. Section 96 of the constitution further enables the Commonwealth to make payments to the states on whatever conditions it determines. This has become the principal means by which the Commonwealth has influenced or mandated policy in what have traditionally been seen as state responsibilities.

Alfred Deakin was very prescient when he wrote, back in 1902, that the constitution had made the states 'legally free, but financially bound to the chariot wheels of the Central Government'.

Vertical fiscal imbalance

The extreme degree of fiscal imbalance in the Australian federal system leads to the need for substantial financial transfers from Canberra to the states. And Canberra cannot resist the temptation to control how these funds are spent. This undermines one of federalism's key strengths, by narrowing the scope for policy experimentation and innovation and restricting the capacity of states to respond to local needs and preferences. The current Federal Government has repeatedly used its control of the purse strings to impose ill-considered, ideologically driven compliance measures on the states' delivery of core services, such as education and health. These measures are typically focused on micro-managing the way states deliver core services, rather than on the big-picture outcomes that we are all striving to achieve.

As a result of vertical fiscal imbalance, and for many other reasons, a joint Commonwealth–state approach is important. I'd like now to turn to what it will be important for now and in the near future.

National Reform Agenda

Victoria has led the push for a new round of economic reform, by putting forward the National Reform Initiative in August 2005—a third wave of reform to ensure Australia's future prosperity. This culminated in the National Reform Agenda (NRA), agreed at COAG.

There are two broad dimensions to this new NRA. The first aims to improve the economic environment through further competition and regulatory reforms. The second and most important element of the reform agenda concerns human capital. Together, these reforms will increase our standard of living through raising economic productivity and workforce participation.

And the gains are significant: the Victorian Treasury has estimated that the potential impact of the NRA on GDP will be up to 5 per cent over the next 10 years and 14 per cent over the next 25 years. After 10 years, this translates to a fiscal dividend to the Commonwealth of up to $10 billion, with less than $3 billion shared between the states. After 25 years, this translates to a fiscal dividend to the Commonwealth of up to $35 billion, with less than $5 billion shared between the states. Even after one allows for the transfer of GST revenue from the Commonwealth, the states receive only 28 per cent of the total tax revenue in Australia, yet are responsible for the lion's share of service delivery. It is imperative to redistribute these fiscal dividends fairly to ensure that vertical fiscal imbalance is not further exacerbated and the states can afford real reform.

Reforms in human capital, or workforce incentives, education and health, are the areas that will produce the biggest economic gain and greatest benefits through participation and productivity. Skills and education have never been more important. We need to ensure that we are engaging people in learning throughout their lives to enable and motivate them to participate in the workforce more efficiently and for longer. And, of course, good health provides the foundation for economic and social participation.

Health

I mentioned in my introductory comments the new health paradigm. In the old days, people used to die from injury or infection, and we built whole health systems aimed at treating injury and infections, especially evident in our investment in drugs and acute-care hospitals. But now, the developed world has undergone an epidemiological transition. Now it is non-communicable or chronic disease that will kill most people; in fact, chronic disease now accounts for more than 80 per cent of mortality in Western countries and is rapidly encroaching on communicable disease as a major cause of illness and disability in the developing world also. By chronic disease, I mean diabetes, heart disease, hypertension and other health conditions directly related to the more affluent, inactive lifestyles of industrialised countries. In the twentieth century, we made rapid advances in longevity and health on the back of three fundamental health innovations: clean water, immunisation and antibiotics. Together they have saved millions of people from the scourge of waterborne infectious diseases, common infectious diseases like small pox, measles and polio and bacterial infections like tonsillitis and blood poisoning. In a sense, each one has been a magic bullet that has delivered better health for whole populations.

Today we don't have a box of magic bullets at our disposal. Paradoxically, our ill health is largely the result of social, economic and technological success; the 'epidemiological transition' has occurred as a direct result of social, economic and medical progress. Let me put more of this in a practical context. The Department of Human Services has estimated that more than $1 billion of income is lost by twenty-five to sixty-four-year-old Victorians per annum due to poor health associated with smoking, obesity and high blood pressure. This illustrates the enormous benefits of focusing on prevention. It's a simple concept: healthier people equal a more capable workforce—capable of participating in the workforce and capable of being productive by using the skills they have gained. However, estimates of the economic cost of poor health usually encompass only the financial costs of providing health care and the years of life that might be lost. Costs that are less often considered include lost employment and productivity resulting from poor health, but these are significant.

For example, new research from the Victorian Department of Treasury indicates the presence of Types 1 and 2 diabetes in females aged twenty to sixty reduces the probability of employment by about 12 per cent. The productivity effects of poor mental health are even more pronounced. For example, a female with a mild level of psychological distress is about 7.6 per cent less likely to be able to hold down a job as her healthy counterpart. A male with high levels of psychological distress is 36 per cent less likely to be able to do the same. To put this in context, a mild level of psychological distress might mean feeling tired, nervous, hopeless, fidgety and sad 'most of the time'. A high level of psychological distress might mean having these feelings 'all of the time'.

The economic cost of poor health is a real one—and, of course, the flip side is that good health provides the foundation for economic and social participation.

To address this issue, we need a national approach to shift the focus of our health system towards prevention rather than treatment, to reduce chronic disease and achieve a healthier workforce. We need a fair share of the fiscal dividends the Commonwealth is set to reap from the National Reform Agenda so that we can boost our investment in preventative care.

National Innovation Agenda

While it is imperative that we improve our health, education and training outcomes, this alone will not be enough to safeguard Australia's prosperity and productivity in the new century. The OECD estimates that in advanced industrial economies, innovation and the exploitation of scientific discoveries and new technologies have accounted for 50 per cent of economic growth. This is a fact recognised by global powerhouses such as the United States, which in 2006 released its American Competitiveness Initiative—a 10-year US$137 billion blueprint for investment in research and development capacity, skills and training.

This would be equivalent to the Australian Government providing about $860 million a year in additional investment in science and technology research and development. While Australia has no shortage of innovative and creative people, it lacks a cohesive and focused nationwide system to best translate their work into tangible economic gains.

Recently, the Australian Innovation Research Centre provided compelling evidence, if we needed it, that the lucky country's luck had just about run out. In a sobering assessment, the centre cautioned:

> Australian industry is no more innovative than it was a quarter of a century ago. We don't export a higher proportion of high-value goods, the proportion of our stock market comprised of [sic] technology companies hasn't grown, our companies introduce fewer new products and services than those of other countries, and our industries have significantly lower ratios of research and development to sales than comparable economies.

The NRA needs buttressing. This is why the Victorian Government will soon release a National Innovation Agenda (NIA), which will build on and extend the NRA.

Our vision for an NIA encompasses five critical areas:

- increasing incentives for business innovation
- building new innovation infrastructure
- developing new skills for the innovation economy
- creating a better regulatory environment for innovation
- forging better connections and collaborations.

The NIA will ensure that additional value, jobs and wealth are created from the NRA, as well as delivering significant economic and social returns in its own right.

The National Reform Agenda

The NRA reforms will help to ensure that we have a labour force with the skills business needs to innovate, even as population ageing and lower fertility rates place pressure on the labour force and the growth of highly skilled industries creates growing demand for skills.

Competition and regulation reforms will help to create a competitive regulatory environment—one that promotes the competitive pressures that drive innovation, and does not impede business as it responds to those challenges.

In this context, an NIA would complement and follow on from the NRA, encouraging business to be more innovative and to take advantage of human capital and competition and regulatory reform currently being pursued. So, for example, new innovation infrastructure should include a clear national plan for building the information and communications technology (ICT) infrastructure that is required to participate effectively in international business and research. The importance of such reform is illustrated by the evidence of Australia's high take-up of ICT equipment and the impact that take-up has had on the broader economy.

GST distribution

Our current Commonwealth–state financial relations impede progress on these vital challenges. I have already spoken about our extraordinary vertical fiscal imbalance (VFI). Additional problems are generated by our problems of horizontal fiscal equalisation (HFE).

In 2006–07, Victoria will receive only 87 cents of every dollar that Victorians pay in GST. Victorians pay about $1.24 billion more in GST than we receive (we pay $9.75 billion in GST and receive $8.51 billion back in General Purpose Payments). We subsidise other states by $242 a person.

Despite the emergence of a 'dual economy' in Australia, where Western Australia and Queensland are benefiting from high growth rates and booming mining royalty revenues, New South Wales and Victoria are still carrying most of the burden of HFE, with Queensland still a net beneficiary from HFE.

Now, the rationale for the redistribution of GST funding to the states becomes more arcane with the passing of the years. The assessment methodology for the redistribution comprises individual consideration of about 40 main expenditure categories, 13 revenue categories, as well as about 30 Specific Purpose Payment (SPP) categories. Then a further 350 expenditure component assessments and about 40 revenue component assessments are applied.

GST 'black box'

Without delving further into this 'black box', I'll simply point out that the redistribution system intrinsically acts as a disincentive for states to undertake reforms encouraging economic growth. Rather than seeing strong fiscal incentives for promoting development and growth, states operate in an environment in which direct revenue gains from public policy reforms are to a considerable extent 'equalised away' by the current HFE arrangements because revenue capacity growth is a key factor in assessments. There is a growing view among businesspeople, opinion leaders and the general community that we need fundamental reform of HFE in Australia. Victoria concurs and we are keen to open up dialogue with the Commonwealth and other states to find a better, simpler and more equitable way to distribute GST revenues.

Victoria supports the principle of equalisation and redistribution to those states with small economies, however, resource-rich states with substantial financial capacity, such as Queensland and Western Australia, should at a minimum be able to stand on their own, and potentially help those states in clear need of assistance.

Any reform model should be a simple and implementable approach that addresses the significant deficiencies of the current system, while retaining the core concept of horizontal fiscal equalisation based on the smaller states and territories continuing to get the support they need from the larger and stronger states.

To achieve this, Victoria proposes that more substantial HFE reform should be built around four pillars:

- protecting the fiscal positions of the smaller states and territories
- delivering greater certainty of GST revenues for all states in the medium to long term
- reducing the distortions and deadweight costs imposed by the current system
- managing the transition to the new model.

We are keen to open a dialogue, with the Commonwealth as an active partner, to find a better and simpler way to distribute GST revenues in order to provide greater funding certainty and remove the disincentive for states to pursue economic reform. We recognise that no model is likely to please everyone. But we know that without these or similar reforms, Australia's capacity to undertake the NRA and NIA and address our key challenges in developing our human capital, our competition and regulatory policy will be jeopardised. Doing nothing about HFE is simply no longer an option.

Today I can say that Victoria will be advocating a new model in the very near future.

Our environmental challenges

The other major challenges we face as a federation are environmental: water and climate change.

Climate change

In February 2007, the International Panel on Climate Change issued a report that said the scientific evidence was now 'unequivocal' that global warming was upon us and that the pace of climate change was due to human activity. While there will always be debate about the extent and rate of climate change, the reality is we must begin to act now to protect the environment and to provide a degree of certainty for industry in a carbon-constrained world.

The Victorian Government has long recognised the need for action on climate change. We have invested $1.8 billion in our Innovation Agenda since 1999, allocated $103.5 million for clean-coal technologies (through the Energy Technology Innovation Strategy), invested $30 million in the Centre for Energy and Greenhouse Technologies, contributed $50 million to building the world's largest solar power station of its kind in Victoria and instituted the Victorian Renewable Energy Target (which mandates 10 per cent renewable energy by 2016). In a number of these areas (clean coal and solar power), we have been able to work very constructively with the Federal Government.

As another initiative, the government is supporting the development of a bio-fuel industry and aims to manufacture more than 400 litres of ethanol or bio-diesel by 2010 with significant environmental benefits. Our aim is that by 2010, 5 per cent of all transport fuel will come from a bio source, leading to improved air quality in metropolitan areas and significant regional investment in country Victoria.

But it has long been clear that we also need a clear carbon price signal to bring forward commercial investment in clean-energy technologies. Only when firms and households face a clear price signal will the incentives be there to adopt more energy-efficient, less greenhouse-intensive technologies.

Uncertainty about greenhouse policy, and the lack of a clear price signal, is now becoming a significant impediment to needed new base-load investment in long-lived electricity generation assets. This was clearly brought out in discussion papers released in November 2006 by the COAG-commissioned Energy Reform Implementation Group, based on extensive stakeholder consultation within the energy sector. Our need for energy security alone tells us that we cannot allow this degree of investment uncertainty to persist.

We have been strong proponents of a national emissions trading scheme to send a clear price signal to energy producers and consumers and reward businesses that adopt less carbon-intensive technologies. While all greenhouse abatement options entail costs for energy consumers, it is becoming increasingly clear that the costs of inaction are likely to outweigh the cost of mitigation. And an emissions trading scheme is the most effective means of abatement because it provides real financial incentives for firms to reduce their emissions but leaves it up to the market to implement the lowest-cost form of abatement. The flexibility of permit trading means that the impacts on business and consumers can be minimised. A domestic scheme can also be designed in such a way to protect adversely affected companies and groups, and link in with international schemes.

Leaders of major corporations and businesses in critical energy industries are now breaking ranks with the Federal Government and calling for Australia's involvement in carbon emissions trading schemes. Recently, some of Australia's largest companies, including from the energy, resources and manufacturing sectors, have submitted their views to a state and territory task force examining a possible design for a national emissions trading scheme. Major companies such as BHP, Rio Tinto, Shell and Insurance Australia Group have joined calls for the implementation of an emissions trading scheme. Rio Tinto suggested that the lack of a global mechanism should not be used as an excuse for inaction on the domestic front.

Australia urgently needs national policy leadership on this vital issue; we cannot wait until the rest of the world solves the problem or it will be too late. The states and territories have done the groundwork in developing a workable design for a domestic national emissions trading scheme.

Key elements of the state and territory proposal are:

- the scheme will be a national 'cap-and-trade' scheme initially covering the stationary energy sector
- to provide certainty, investors will always have 10 years of firm caps, with a range of caps for the following 10 years; the range of caps for the second 10-year period provides the flexibility to respond to any changes in Australia's international obligations or circumstances
- it will have modest initial emission reduction targets (to be agreed) to allow a gradual transition for the economy
- assistance will be provided to adversely affected generators and energy-intensive trade-exposed industries (most likely through a free allocation of permits)
- the scheme will be able to be linked to international schemes in the future.

Now it is time for Canberra to accept the states' longstanding offer to join them in implementing a scheme as soon as practicable. I hope the Prime Minister's Task Group on Emissions Trading seriously considers the benefits of an early domestic scheme to prepare Australia for a future carbon-constrained world, when it releases it discussion paper.

Water

To take another example, let's take the currently very topical issue of water management—one of Australia's most significant national challenges.

If you believed the Prime Minister, you'd think the states had been doing nothing to reform our water management framework or to protect our water assets. This is far from the truth.

Victoria has been leading the nation on water reform for 20 years. In the past couple of years, we unveiled our blueprint for securing Victoria's water future for the next 50 years, *Our Water Our Future*, which led to a more sustainable balance between consumption and environmental uses of available water supplies, a more robust system of water property rights and a more dynamic and efficient water market than anywhere else in Australia.

Ultimately, however, it is likely to be beyond the efforts of any state acting alone to resolve future water supply and demand imbalances in the most cost-effective way. The Commonwealth has called for a transfer of powers over the Murray-Darling Basin in order to accelerate the pace of water reform. Yet Canberra's record on water management does not stack up too favourably. In *The Age* newspaper in February 2007, Andrew Macintosh described the Federal Government's $10 billion water plan as 'a bad remake of Groundhog Day, only without the happy ending'. Macintosh notes that the Commonwealth 'has made too many similar announcements in the past for it to be credible that this one will solve the nation's water problems'. In the past 10 years, no fewer than 12 such announcements have been made by the Commonwealth. None of them has 'solved our water woes or even put our rivers on the path to restoration'. Nor is there much real evidence of 'reform' in what the Commonwealth is proposing.

Our national vision should be for a secure set of diversion limits to ensure a sustainable level of environmental flows and the allocation of all non-environmental water through water markets. This calls for a water grid of interconnected systems within South-East Australia facilitating the broadest practicable basis of trade in water entitlements. Only in this way can we ultimately secure a sustainable and efficient allocation between agricultural, industrial, residential and environmental uses.

Let me be clear. Victoria will support a plan that acts in the national interest to protect and preserve our most precious resource. Securing our water resources for the future is one of the biggest challenges Australia has ever faced. The best way to meet that challenge is to come up with new solutions:

• that are properly thought out

- that are developed in consultation with the community, industry experts and relevant government departments
- that are properly costed
- that do not raise more questions than they answer
- that cannot be addressed by the Prime Minister issuing a media release announcing his plan and then following that up a few days later with a letter to the leaders of each state and territory.

This is unacceptable—unacceptable because you can't unwind 100 years of constitutional control of the river system with a media release and a letter. That is why the Victorian Premier, Steve Bracks, has set three preconditions regarding John Howard's plan for the Murray-Darling:

- Victorian farmers and irrigators are not disadvantaged
- we want assurances from the Prime Minister and Malcolm Turnbull that this is not privatisation of our water resources by stealth
- we want to see the existing federal $1.8 billion fund for water projects actually flowing into projects that have been waiting for months for Canberra's approval.

Premier Bracks, together with the other premiers, is attending a meeting called by the Prime Minister to discuss the $10 billion water package. Victoria had already asked for such a meeting. We now go to that table wanting to see details of the Prime Minister's proposal, because—as far as I can see—there are no details. Indeed, key federal departments including Treasury, finance and the environment were left out of the process of formulating the package—unorthodox at best; arrogant at worst.

I can tell you that our officials have examined the Prime Minister's proposal. And they have raised more than 40 significant issues that need to be resolved. Steve Bracks has today written to the Prime Minister outlining those issues. Issues around:

- the scope of the proposed arrangements
- the time line
- governance
- funding
- river operations
- water entitlements and trading
- flood-plain management
- water-quality management
- land-use planning
- urban water supply within the basin
- irrigators' existing property rights
- metering and monitoring

- implications for the Murray-Darling Basin Agreement
- any other further work.

These are serious considerations.

We are not talking about a modest medium-term state-based water-saving project. The Prime Minister has proposed a $10 billion plan that dramatically reshapes federal–state responsibilities. So how will that work?

Tell us about the funding model proposed for water reform and infrastructure projects.

How will flows from the Snowy Hydro Scheme be accounted for and managed?

Will the National Water Commission have an ongoing role?

What is the process for determining the level of environmental flows?

And how do we find a balance between these and the entitlements of irrigators?

Does the Commonwealth propose to manage urban water supply in urban centres around the basin.

Will the Commonwealth claw back flood-plain harvesting activities in the Darling and other catchments?

The Victorian Government has been working hard for years putting in place the right plans and projects to secure the state's water resources for the future. We understand there is more to be done. We also understand Victoria is not facing this challenge in isolation.

Conclusion

I began by suggesting that while reform of Commonwealth–state relations might not appear to be an exciting subject for discussion, it is absolutely crucial to national economic and social planning for the next generation and beyond.

While Australia is adequately served by its constitutional arrangements that are now more than 100 years old, we must recognise that we have failed to achieve the right balance of shared responsibility and fiscal discretion between our state and federal governments.

In addition, we must heed Donald Horne's nearly 50-year-old call to action, to realise that the days of the lucky country are well and truly numbered and that substantive action is required if we are to become the clever country, or the innovative country, or the prosperous country.

For this to occur, a joint approach between the Commonwealth and the state governments is crucial to laying the groundwork for our future prosperity—implementing the National Reform Agenda and the National Innovation Agenda and meeting out water and climate change challenges.

ENDNOTES

[1] This essay was originally presented as an ANZSOG Public Lecture on 6 February 2007.

[2] John Brumby assumed the office of Premier of Victoria on 30 June 2007, after the resignation of Steve Bracks.

6. Fostering creativity and innovation in cooperative federalism — the uncertainty and risk dimensions[1]

Mark Matthews[2]

Policy narratives in OECD nations are now starting to stress the importance of 'innovation' as a public sector objective. On one level, this reflects efforts to align thinking with a wider discourse on innovation, arguably in an effort not to be left out of the picture. For example, Geoff Mulgan[3] has argued persuasively that, contrary to some common assumptions, the public sector has a longer history of innovation than the private sector. Indeed, public sector innovation created the modern world—an operating environment in which private sector innovation per se has flourished.[4]

In this essay, I focus upon a particular objective of innovation in the public sector: the management of uncertainty and risk. In this context, following Knight (1921), 'risk' applies to cases in which a probability of occurrence can be assigned. Uncertainty refers to situations in which it is not possible to assign such probabilities. The critical distinction is that the ability to assign probabilities allows various other formal estimates related to risk and its consequences to be estimated.[5] I argue that governments place too great an emphasis on the 'management of risk' and not enough emphasis on the 'management of uncertainty'. A greater emphasis on the management of uncertainty, in turn, helps us to understand what public sector innovation is—and why it is so important.

This perspective applies a line of inquiry previously developed in relation to innovation in the private sector to the specific issues faced in the public sector.[6] In so doing, it also draws upon previous efforts to define a new 'realist' agenda for science and innovation policy that addresses the distinctive role of the public sector in providing the 'prescience and preparedness' for dealing with potentially damaging future events.[7] The essay also seeks to relate this treatment of the public sector innovation challenge to the issue of cooperative federalism. This is a particularly important issue when the uncertainties and risks governments must address cross jurisdictional boundaries—as many do.

The theoretical underpinning for this policy-oriented discussion is that there is much to be gained from exploring how our policy narratives can be informed by drawing upon the 'Austrian' tradition in economics associated with Von Hayek and others. For a flavour of this work, see Kirzner[8] and Littlechild[9] for a discussion of markets as processes. One can extract some very useful insights from such thinking without necessarily subscribing to the full gamut of liberalist stances associated with that body of work. As I set out to show, certain insights in this 'subjectivist' tradition in economics are particularly useful for helping us to develop strategies for effective innovation in the public sector.

Somewhat paradoxically, reframing key aspects of the policy narrative along neo-Austrian lines in terms of the 'management of uncertainty' rather than the 'management of risk' does more to *re-enforce* the importance of the State than undermine it. The trick is to recognise that whilst most of the discussion on the management of uncertainty and risk in current policy narratives focuses on the management of *risk*, the management of *uncertainty* is in fact what governments spend more of their time actually grappling with. For instance, in 2007 the Australian Public Service Commission moved to highlight the challenge posed by 'wicked problems'—complex intractable challenges with uncertainty over causes and effects and also a likelihood of damaging unintended consequences arising from policy interventions, see Australian Public Service Commission (2007).[10] Indeed, vast swathes of public expenditure (notably funding for basic science) seek to translate uncertainty into risk. This is the essence of the process of 'discovery': delving into the unknown to make it less threatening and easier to live with—whether we are talking of diseases, near-Earth objects or climate change.

Framing public sector innovation objectives as a response to handling uncertainty and risk

A key difference between public sector innovation and private sector innovation is that market-based selection mechanisms play a different role in the innovation process. In the private sector, by definition, the litmus test for attempts at innovation is market success. Not all innovations prevail in the market, and indeed various other factors mean that the 'best' solutions might not become the dominant solutions. However, markets do enforce selection processes that tend to eliminate less-competitive solutions. Competing firms therefore do their best to second-guess what will prevail in the market, often applying rigorous structured decision-making processes (such as stage-gate methods) to weed out less-promising concepts and solutions.

However, in the final analysis, it is the market, and the social and cultural preferences that are reflected in markets, that will decide which innovations succeed and which do not. The academic and policy literature on how these processes work (and do not work) is well developed and full of useful insights. These insights work backwards from market processes into the research and development and demonstration stages that drive new product introduction. They also work forwards into how market processes drive the incremental innovations that continue once new products have been introduced into the marketplace.

In a public sector context, the relationship between innovation and markets (as selection mechanisms) is significantly different. Governments deal with the uncertainties and risks that markets cannot handle. This requires innovations in what governments seek to do. But, crucially, governments cannot rely on market processes to play the critical 'weed-out' stage in the innovation process by eliminating solutions that do not align well with the preferences expressed in markets and encouraging those that do. Rather, governments need to try to mimic this aspect of the functionality of market-based selection processes without the recourse of relying on markets to actually carry out this selection process. This requires that the public sector draws heavily upon external and internal expertise to weigh-up complex risks, often using large amounts of evidence. When there is no market-based 'short cut' available, the sheer weight of evidence that might need to be assessed poses major challenges and raises important questions about whether 'hierarchies of evidence' are required to deal in a rational way with the sheer quantity and complexity of information available.[11]

The point here is similar to that made by Mary Kaldor in relation to trajectories in the advance of military technologies. 'Baroque' (overly complex) military technologies evolve because the only real test of superiority is a 'symmetrical' war in which weapon systems with comparable missions are pitted against each other. If there are no wars of that type—that is, no wars or only so-called 'asymmetrical' conflicts—then there is no 'market-like' test of technical superiority. Technologies evolve—but not necessarily in ways that make them 'fit for purpose'.[12]

As an illustration, consider what the recent government responses to the global financial crisis have entailed. Governments have been grappling with the need to act innovatively (over particularly tight time frames) in order to mitigate severe failings in how financial markets have been operating. Rather than simply seeking to miminise the risk of introducing an uncompetitive new product or service into the market (the far simpler challenge faced by a company), governments have been forced to address a far more severe challenge. If the innovative market interventions attempted by governments fail then the global economy could fail—dramatically. Rather than one or a few corporations failing, whole industries could go out of business with catastrophic social and national security impacts.

In short, the consequences of incorrectly judging what will and won't work when seeking to innovate are disproportionately greater for this type of public sector innovation than for private sector innovation.

Furthermore, when private sector innovation goes wrong—for example, a new drug that has unforeseen and terrible side effects—it is governments that bear the responsibility by virtue of their regulatory roles. This is why, in comparison with the private sector, public sector decision-making processes can appear cumbersome, risk averse and time consuming. The unintended consequences of getting it wrong are far too severe to rely on the market to correct problems—as in the private sector. The far greater complexity of what governments do generates great uncertainty over *what* to do in response to challenges. The extraordinarily damaging potential associated with unintended consequences necessitates robust risk-averse decision making. I find it far more helpful to view the role that central economic ministries play in setting public intervention guidelines from this perspective rather than to critique them for being too risk averse by (incorrectly) viewing them from a less-demanding private sector risk-management perspective.

Given this, it is important to deploy a practice-oriented classification of public sector innovation that highlights this aspect of risk exposure in the public sector. Some aspects of public sector innovation are comparable with, indeed might be almost identical to, aspects of private sector innovation (examples are business processes improvements and many aspects of ICT—e-government—and so on). However, as the arguments above highlight, there are other aspects of public sector innovation, particularly those associated with policy innovation, for which governments must bear responsibilities that greatly outweigh those born by the private sector (national security, counter-terrorism, pandemic preparedness and the like).

As discussions of public sector innovation evolve, it could therefore be useful to draw a clear distinction between those aspects of public sector innovation that are comparable with what is found in the private sector and those aspects that are distinctive and far more severe in terms of the damaging consequences of getting things wrong. There is a tendency for the literature to focus more heavily on areas of public sector innovation that are similar to private sector innovation (often in terms of 'importing' concepts and practices from the private sector). There is less emphasis in this discourse on the most challenging types of public sector innovation—the areas in which the consequences of getting things wrong are far more severe than in the private sector. This is a shortcoming that it is essential for current policy narratives on public sector innovation to address.

In this context, it is not surprising that the uncritical acceptance of private sector norms and business processes can potentially wreak havoc in the public sector. Whilst it might suit some elements in the private sector to point to costly and cumbersome decision-making processes in the public sector (usually as a marketing-driven justification for emulating and eventually purchasing private sector products and services), it is dangerous for governments to react to such criticism defensively. Rather, the reaction should be to stress the sort of points made above: governments handle the uncertainties and risks that markets can't cope with. Creativity and innovation in the public sector are by necessity more challenging and more critically important activities than private sector innovation—not, as some would have us believe, activities with a lamentable track record.[13]

By implication, senior officials in the public sector would be wise to articulate far more clearly than at present the nature and extent of the differences between public sector innovation and private sector innovation—especially in regard to the far more severe consequences of getting things wrong when attempting to innovate.

The prevailing emphasis in the literature on public sector innovation at present is on areas of commonality with private sector innovation. This results in part from efforts to import principles and practices from the private sector, with relatively little emphasis on grasping what makes the public sector innovation context significantly *different*.[14] The treatment of risk is symptomatic of this prevailing emphasis. There is far more discussion of the internal project management-type dimension to risk taking—that is, when and how to take risks in order to try something new—than of the external matter of the role that public sector innovation plays in managing the uncertainties and risks that markets either cannot cope with or (as recent experience in banking demonstrates) generate themselves.

Similarly, there is much discussion of the use of information and communication technology (ICT) in the public sector (e-government, customised service delivery, and so on) and of how innovation is required to produce more 'joined-up' government. The discussion of innovation cycles and processes also frames risk fairly tightly in relation to concepts of product and service development imported from the private sector.[15] Whilst such work is useful, it essentially amounts only to providing a first step toward developing a more comprehensive and appropriate framework for encouraging effective public sector innovation. Unless these internal considerations (how best to make decisions about public sector innovation) are related in practical ways to the wider external concerns of governments, the guidance available to public servants will be biased—and perhaps even dangerous. A 'realist' perspective on government's role in handling uncertainty and risk should help to bring these two aspects of the public sector innovation challenge together. In order to do this, the appropriate conceptual tools must be available and must be used effectively.

Choosing the best conceptual tools

One aspect of intellectual history that is relevant to understanding public sector innovation is the way in which the study of innovation in the private sector originated, in part, in a reaction against the difficulties faced by neo-classical economics in explaining technological advance. If one assumes a world of perfect information and a state of equilibrium in which markets are operating in a stable manner then technological advances must be treated as externally originating deviations from these equilibrium conditions—processes of disruption to which the economic system must respond and adapt. The finding that long-run productivity growth had a large 'residual' element that could not be explained by increases in the standard factors of production (capital and labour, and so on) stimulated a large and productive line of investigation that eventually led to the 'innovation studies' work that currently informs thinking on public sector innovation. As innovation studies has evolved, it has moved away from economic theory and econometrics and toward more managerial approaches—with a particular (and useful) emphasis on documenting and understanding real practices in business.

Inevitably, this emphasis on how businesses *do* innovation in practice leads to a focus on how firms accumulate and exploit proprietary knowledge and capabilities, how they seek to exploit intangible assets that their competitors do not have. The emphasis is on *differences* between firms' capabilities—on how innovation drives markets in such a way that they are in continual evolution, rarely in states of equilibrium. It should be of little surprise that the management of uncertainty and risk features strongly in this perspective on innovation.

By evolving in this manner, work on innovation studies now has the (largely unrealised) potential to converge with another stream of thinking in economics known as 'Austrian' or subjectivist economics. This stream of thinking is distinguished from neo-classical economics in some fundamental ways—and ways that are highly relevant to understanding public sector innovation.

Rather than a world of quantitative uncertainty, the Austrian economic perspectives describe a human condition in which creativity is a necessary response to qualitative uncertainty (effectively ignorance) over what the future has in store—both good and bad. In some circumstances, there are no probabilities to assign to future states of the world, but rather the necessity to act *creatively* in order to generate parameters that can be assigned probabilities (and hence managed 'rationally'). The resulting competition is *inherently* a process of discovery and innovation. From this standpoint, markets are inherently *exploratory* and *innovative* collective endeavours that operate via selection.

If we think about markets in this more analytical way—as exploratory processes and selection mechanisms—then it is easier to understand their limitations and, hence, grasp why public sector innovation is so important in helping us to manage uncertainty. Markets can cope with risk (quantifiable likelihoods) but they cannot cope with uncertainty as easily.

This is why governments spend vast amounts of taxpayers' money on translating uncertainty into risk. Many scientific and technological inventions are driven by the fundamental human desire to transform ignorance into uncertainty and risk. There are whole rafts of imaging technologies (x-ray, ultrasound and magnetic resonance imaging, microscopes, particle accelerators, telescopes, seismic analysis, magnetic anomaly analysis, and so on) that provide us with data that we would not otherwise have access to—that is, that translate ignorance into indications and likelihoods. Much scientific theory is concerned with translating ignorance into risk—that is, the analysis of complex data sets in order to generate patterns of risk—such as crop planting strategies in the face of unpredictable weather patterns. In short, investments in scientific instrumentation and pattern recognition are, collectively, investments in translating ignorance into risk. We are very rarely certain of what might happen, particularly in complex situations such as human health, but we collectively prefer to have more information than less information to guide our decision making.

Another dimension to science and innovation policy that is relevant to understanding innovation in the public sector relates to prescience and preparedness. In previous policy work, I have sought to highlight why it is important for governments to be more explicit than they are at present about how their spending on public science generates useful outcomes that need not require innovation or research commercialisation per se.[16]

In an uncertain and risky world, public science plays a critically important role in 'prescience': identifying risks and associated costs that we might have to face in the future (climate change being an excellent example). The widespread dissemination of this information to business and the general community could (eventually) help to change behaviours—and in turn changes what the future might actually have in store for us. The objectives for innovation are driven by this prescience—for instance, the rationale for investing in research and development on lower-emission technologies.

Consequently, the benefits generated by this type of outcome from public science tend to be reflected in less unfavourable futures than would otherwise be the case. As the *Stern Report* seeks to stress, the economic value of mitigating risks in this manner is massive. Preparedness reinvigorates the traditional concept of capability building by highlighting the uncertainty and risk dimensions.

When these ideas were submitted to the Productivity Commission as part of its 2006 Review of Public Support for Science and Innovation, the approach gained traction and the preparedness dimension featured strongly in their report.[17] This momentum was, however, lost in the subsequent Review of the National Innovation System in 2008, which sought to reinforce the link between innovation policy and industry policy rather than seeking to explore new avenues for articulating the benefits generated by public science.

The discovery-based perspective is also reflected in emerging views on how to conduct public policy innovation. Charles Sabel has sought to promulgate an 'experimentalist' approach to innovation in US public policy. This work, which draws upon innovation management experience in the automotive industry, stresses the ways in which, in an uncertain decision-making environment, managers in the public sector are better off explicitly adopting exploratory and experimental approaches in which goals and intended outcomes are fairly fluid, efforts are redirected as learning advances and overly hierarchical command and control systems are avoided.[18] Interestingly, as Ian Marsh[19] points out, contemporary commentaries on public sector reform tend to overlook this useful strand of work.

Implications for cooperative federalism

The proposed policy narrative seeks to articulate a far more explicit and proactive focus on managing uncertainty (rather than risk per se) as an objective for public sector innovation. The public sector needs to be innovative because it holds stewardship over the challenge of managing uncertainty.

I think it could be useful to think about the implications that such a policy narrative would have for federal–state relations in Australia. Federal and state/territory governments must cooperate in managing many major areas of uncertainty and risk. When this comes to budget negotiations, this can be contentious.

In this context, one of the more interesting public sector innovations that emerged from the Blair Government in the United Kingdom was the 'Invest to Save Budget' (ISB). This was initially a joint HM Treasury–Cabinet Office (subsequently just a Treasury) initiative aimed at providing 'venture capital for oiling the wheels of government'. The ISB set out to provide risk finance to allow innovative partnership-based projects to be piloted and demonstrated in order to make it easier for new and improved public services to be rolled out. By 2007, 487 partnerships had been funded at a total cost of £460 million.

The ISB has evolved through an explicitly 'experimentalist' process of learning-by-doing based upon a series of fairly robust independent and internal Treasury evaluations that have led to significant changes in how the ISB works.[20] There is now a far stronger emphasis on supporting local and community projects than at the launch of the ISB.

What makes the ISB interesting and significant is the notion that, in order to generate net budget savings, central economic ministries should be willing to sanction explicitly experimental partnership-based projects. The series of reviews and evaluations of the ISB has highlighted how difficult it is for project proponents to specify the risk taking they propose. Indeed, in the early phase of the ISB, most tended to outsource the risk-based benefit–cost estimates that

HM Treasury required them to provide—leading to 'boiler-plate' project appraisal submissions provided by management consulting and accounting firms. These problems would have been avoided if the ISB had opted for an uncertainty management rather than a risk management-based approach. Hence one lesson from the ISB experience is that it is much easier to implement experimentally based public sector innovation programs if they are framed in terms of managing uncertainty rather than just in terms of managing risk. Many partnerships sought funding in order to work out what the risks would be: they set out to translate ignorance into risk.

Another lesson from the ISB experience was that whilst HM Treasury took the view that a successful ISB project that demonstrated that a new approach was superior would lead to widespread adoption of the piloted approach, this tended not to be the case in practice. Simply providing the information that a new approach is better does not address the bureaucratic impediments to adopting innovations—particularly those requiring partnerships. Hence evaluators' recommendations that the innovative new concepts demonstrated by the ISB would still need active 'innovation adoption championing' by powerful people or teams found it hard to gain traction in a central economic ministry context. The assumption tended to be that information would flow freely and that rational decision making would lead to the adoption of innovative approaches.

The United Kingdom's experience might be pertinent to federal–state cooperation in Australia because it points the way towards a program that would explicitly fund uncertain and risky experimental projects targeting cross-jurisdictional concerns—especially those addressing major uncertainties in policy and service delivery.

In this context, the 2008 Review of the National Innovation System proposed that:

> Experimentation in innovative policy and administration should be a major theme of the current refashioning of federal relations. States and Territories should be able to bid for federal funds to pioneer innovative approaches and to have their innovations properly and independently evaluated. This could be taken up within the COAG National Partnership Rewards payments currently being negotiated.[21]

Perhaps it would be preferable for this sort of experimentation to be approached as ISB-type partnership-based projects crossing federal–state jurisdictions, involving mutual interests in addressing the major uncertainties and risks that the state governments and the Federal Government need to address (such as what climate change might have in store). This would help to generate consensus and would avoid the contentious situation in which states/territories bid for federal funds as the solution to their problems. An 'Innovative Australian

Federation' scheme of this type could require a minimum of two states and one federal partner—thus seeking to mitigate the other problem in cooperative federalism: interstate rivalry.

Conclusions

If we are to avoid making serious mistakes in articulating how best to achieve creativity and innovation in the public sector then it is essential to make clear why the innovation imperative for government is significantly different from that in the private sector. We should avoid approaching public sector innovation as a form of downgraded private sector innovation game that overlooks critical differences between the two sectors. Instead, we should define a robust account of the distinctive and vitally important nature of public sector innovation and actively promote this narrative. A focus on the ways in which governments must handle the uncertainties and risks that markets cannot cope with provides a key element in this evolving policy narrative.

This perspective could help those who work in the public sector to better articulate why innovation in policy and service delivery (and particularly the former) involves balancing the costs and consequences of not attempting to innovate with the costs and consequences of *misjudged* attempts to innovate. Too little public sector innovation is a problem. However, innovation for innovation's sake, in an attempt to emulate private sector norms without due regard for what makes the public sector *different* with regard to the unintended consequences of risk taking, can also be a problem.

It would therefore help if public sector and private sector innovators had access to a better-developed framework for relating risks and uncertainties to *both* 'rewards' (upside considerations) and 'punishments' (downside considerations)—rather than simply framing things in terms of a simplistic risk–reward relationship.

There are important trade-offs between the rewards and the punishments faced when seeking to achieve private sector innovation. Innovation exploits the risk–reward relationship, whilst failures to innovate can be punished through business failure (though as consumer preferences for older vintages of technology over newer vintages, such as handmade bespoke clothing, illustrate, this is by no means inevitable).

In the public sector, these trade-offs still exist but, thanks to the nature and extent of the unintended consequences, there is arguably far more emphasis on the punishments that arise through misjudged attempts to innovate (particularly via the ballot box and through litigation).

There is also the inter-generational equity issue to consider. The private sector applies relatively high discount rates when valuing possible future states of the world—that is, it avoids worrying about the very long term. It is the prerogative of governments to concern themselves with being fairer to future generations (balancing the needs of current generations against the needs of generations to come). These low discount-rate objectives can amplify the consequences of misjudged attempts to innovate. It is also inherent in governments' role that they must deal with the long-term consequences of damaging failures in private sector innovation (such as chemically induced birth defects inherited by future generations). Either way, the public sector must handle the punishments created by misjudged innovations and the damaging unintended consequences of past innovations.

This means that governments require superior methods for evaluating uncertainties and risks—the consequences of slavishly emulating private sector practices are far too severe. Now that innovation is becoming an explicit part of the public sector reform agenda perhaps the time has come for the public sector to define the nature and extent of its distinctive and vital role in the evolution of modern innovative societies better than it does at present. We can start by ceasing to talk about the 'management of risk' quite so much and start to spend a lot more time talking about the 'management of uncertainty'.[22]

In a cooperative federalism context, who bears primary responsibility for managing risk is something that can be wrangled over endlessly. The challenge of managing uncertainty is different: it encourages a more collective approach based upon mutual interest and less scope for 'passing the buck', or, as Keynes[23] observed, 'The social object of skilled investment should be to defeat the dark forces of time and ignorance which envelop our future'.

ENDNOTES

[1] This paper was originally presented at the ANZSOG Annual Conference on 11 September 2008.

[2] I would like to thank Dave Marsh, John Wanna, Bradley Smith and Grahame Cook for useful comments, and Bev Biglia and John Butcher for proofreading and editorial contributions. Thanks are also due to SQW Consulting in the United Kingdom and Geoff White in particular, for stimulating and supporting exploratory thinking on the role of risk and uncertainty in public sector settings several years ago. Thanks also to the Federation of Australian Scientific and Technological Societies (FASTS) for funding the science and innovation policy work on uncertainty and risk that is reflected in this paper and also to The Australian National University's new Centre for Policy Innovation for more recent support for this line of research.

[3] Mulgan, Geoff 2007, *Ready or not?: taking innovation in the public sector seriously*, National Endowment for Science, Technology and the Arts (NESTA) Provocation 03, April.

[4] Many key aspects of the physical, legal, financial, scientific and cultural infrastructures that have enabled private sector innovation to flourish and grow in prominence rely on, and stem from, public sector innovations—for example, patent protection regimes, dual-use export controls, ways of organising public science, and so on.

[5] Knight, Frank (1921), *Risk, Uncertainty and Profit*. H Mifflin: Boston.

[6] See Hartmann, G. and Myers, M. 2001, 'Technical risk, product specifications, and market risk', in L. Branscomb and P. Aursweld (eds) *Taking Technical Risks: How innovators, executives, and investors manage high-tech risks*, MIT Press, Cambridge, Mass. pp. 30–43; and also a detailed case study in Matthews, Mark and Frater, Robert 2007, 'Capacity building and risk management in commercialisation: lessons from the Radiata experience', *Innovation: Management, policy & practice*, vol. 9, no. 2, pp. 170–80.

[7] Matthews, Mark 2006, *Managing uncertainty and risk in science, innovation and preparedness: why public policy should pay more attention to financial and geopolitical considerations*, Discussion paper commissioned by the Federation of Australian Scientific and Technological Societies, Howard Partners, August, Canberra.

Kirzner, Isreal 1973, *Competition and Entrepreneurship*, University of Chicago Press, Chicago; Kirzner, Isreal 1979, *Perception, Opportunity and Profit*, University of Chicago Press, Chicago.

[9] Littlechild, Stephen 1989, 'Three types of market process', in Richard Langlois (ed.), *Economics and a Process: Essays in the new institutional economics*, Cambridge University Press, Cambridge.

[10] Australian Public Service Commission (2007), *Tackling Wicked Problems: A Public Policy Perspective*. Australian Public Service Commission: Canberra.

[11] Leigh, Andrew 2009, 'What evidence should social policymakers use?', *Economic Roundup*, 2009, no. 1, pp. 27–43.

[12] Kaldor, Mary 1983, *The Baroque Arsenal*, Abacus Books, London.

[13] As a recent call for papers in one journal intending to devote a special issue to public sector innovation framed the issues: 'its innovation record is often weak and its innovation processes are regularly dysfunctional' ('Call for papers', *Innovation: Management, policy & practice*, <http://www.innovation-enterprise.com/archives/vol/12/issue/1/call/>). What might appear to be weak and dysfunctional in comparison with private sector norms could in fact be entirely appropriate to decision making on innovation in which the unintended consequences will far exceed simply the failure of one company.

[14] For an example of work exhibiting this weakness, see Bessant, John 2005, 'Enabling continuous and discontinuous innovation: learning from the private sector', *Public Money & Management*, vol. 25, pp. 35–42.

[15] See Mulgan, Geoff and Albury, David 2003, *Innovation in the Public Sector*, Strategy Unit, Cabinet Office, London; and Albury, David 2005, 'Fostering innovation in public services', *Public Money & Management*, vol. 25, pp. 51–6.

[16] See Matthews, *Managing uncertainty and risk in science, innovation and preparedness*.

[17] See Productivity Commission 2007, *Public Support for Science and Innovation*, Productivity Commission Research Report, March, Australian Government.

[18] See Sabel, Charles 1994, 'Learning by monitoring: the institutions of economic development', in Neil Smelser and Richard Swedberg (eds), *Handbook of Economic Sociology*, Princeton University Press and Russell Sage Foundation, Princeton, pp. 137–65; Sabel, Charles 2006, *Beyond Principal-Agent Governance: Experimentalist organisation, learning and accountability*, Columbia Law School, New York; Sabel, Charles and Zeitlin, Jonathan 2003, Active welfare, experimental governance, pragmatic constitutionalism: the new transformation of Europe, Paper presented at the International Conference of the Hellenic Presidency of the European Union, The Modernisation of the European Social Model and EU Policies and Instruments, Ioannina, Greece, May.

[19] Marsh, Ian 2009, *Pragmatist and Neo-Classical Policy Paradigms in Public Services: Which is the better template for program design*, Australian Innovation Research Centre, Hobart, viewed 6 March 2009, <http://www.airc.net.au/extras/935.926.ExperimentalistPolicyDesign.pdf>

[20] See SQW Ltd 2002, *Programme Evaluation of the Invest to Save Budget*, Report to HM Treasury, SQW Ltd, London; National Audit Office 2002, *The Invest to Save Budget*, Report by the Comptroller and Auditor-General, HC 50 Session 2002–2003, 22 November; HM Treasury 2007, *A Review of the Invest to Save Budget: An innovation fund for public services*, HM Treasury, London.

[21] Cutler and Company 2008, *Venturous Australia: Building strength in innovation*, Review of the National Innovation System commissioned by the Minister for Innovation, Industry, Science and Research, Cutler and Company Pty Ltd, North Melbourne, Victoria, < http://www.innovation.gov.au/innovationreview/Pages/home.aspx http://true/truewww.innovation.gov.au/trueinnovationreview/truePages/truehome.aspx >, Recommendation 10.5.

[22] For a useful treatment of some of these issues, see Strategy Unit 2002, *Risk: Improving government's capability to handle risk and uncertainty*, Cabinet Office Strategy Unit Report, London.

[23] As cited in O'Driscoll, Gerald P. and Rizzo, M. J. 1985, *The Economics of Time and Ignorance*, Basil Blackwell, Oxford, p. 1.

Part 2. Reflections on policy and politics

7. Cabinet government: Australian style[1]

Patrick Weller AO

So Tony Blair has gone. It is said of Tony Blair that he killed the cabinet in Britain, that he held a few meetings that didn't last very long and that in any one year there were about half a dozen decisions made by cabinet—in a year, not in a meeting. Gordon Brown will come into office and change the way the decisions get made in Britain. Not because he needs to, but because he has to, in order to illustrate that he is a different sort of leader. So the shape of cabinet will change, even if the outcomes might not, or at least it will change initially, because leaders can shape cabinets to their own style and their own preoccupations. Brown will be different. His former head of department called him a Stalinist, or said that he was Stalinist in the way that he approached decision making, allowing no opposition, no debate. It will be interesting to see if he tries to run the English government as Prime Minister the same way as he acted when he was Chancellor.

But if the British system of organising and running cabinet is compared with the Australian style, it's really quite different. Cabinet here still appears to exist. The ministers meet regularly, they have a formal agenda, a working committee system and a process by which the majority of issues are at least discussed in cabinet, even if some of the decisions might have been preordained and decided beforehand.

I want to talk about the contrasts between the British and the Australian system. As Rudyard Kipling said, 'What can they know of England who only England know?' If we actually look only at the Australian cabinet, we take for granted so many things that are surprising about the way the cabinet works. A comparison with Britain encourages us to look at the things that happen here and ask why they don't happen in Britain. Then it is possible to understand better the dynamics that push the Australian system.

It is also useful to ask how Australia has changed. By instinct, I'm a historian, so I look at the contrasts, at the different ways in which prime ministers have operated cabinets, at the different pressures on cabinet that have existed over the hundred or so years of our federal politics. We know it has changed and will change. We know that if Howard goes some time between now and the year 2015, the new Prime Minister, whether it be Costello, Rudd or somebody not yet in the Parliament, will run the cabinet differently, in part to show that they're an individual. But they will be operating in Australia with the constraints that have been created by 100 years of history, just as in Britain Gordon Brown will have to take account of the long history of England in how he chooses to operate the system there. Comparisons across nations and across time help us understand something about the way cabinet works.

Peter Shergold has said that only Australia maintains the true traditions of cabinet government. Only Australia believes in collective decision making, in contrast with Canada and Britain. In Canada, cabinet has been called a focus group. The cabinet committees will meet to discuss new proposals and, at the end of the day, they decide to support them or not support them. But there's no money attached, and they are effectively put in a folder. Around one budget time, the British Prime Minister, the Minister for Finance (our Treasurer) sent out a questionnaire to ministers saying, you have agreed to fund 50 programs, please nominate your top 10. As ministers filled out the questionnaire, there was a little bit of game-playing about, 'well, they're going to fund that one anyway, so I'll choose another one'. The Privy Council Office tallied up the results, but never told the ministers what the outcome was. The Minister for Finance just announced in the budget what was going to be funded. The stories are that in Britain, Tony Blair at one cabinet meeting begged Gordon Brown to tell him what was in the budget. I can't quite imagine John Howard and Peter Costello working that way. The traditions, it seems to me, are very different and essentially much more collective still in this country than elsewhere.

So what is it that we're looking at? Cabinet government is an arena, not a set of rules by itself, not a simple institution. It's a process by which people work. At one stage, I asked senior officials in three countries to say what cabinet government was. Let me give you their replies.

> Canada: Cabinet government is the arrangements the Prime Minister makes to ensure that decisions are made in the interests of the general, rather than the individual minister, with a view to presenting a unified program for legislation and supply.

> Britain: Cabinet government is a shorthand term for the process by which governments determine their policy and ensures the political will to implement them.

> Australia: Cabinet government is collective government and must establish a coherent set of policies consistent with its strategic directions; it needs policy coherence and political support.

They are all public service views, but they touch on what seem to be the two key components of what cabinets do: gain political support and get some level of policy decision or policy coherence. It's politics and it's policy; it's not one or the other. It's the place where the political, the policy and the administrative interests intersect. People who argue that cabinet spends too much time on politics seem, to me, to miss the point that that's very much what they're about the whole time.

The other point about those interesting definitions is that, even though they come from public servants, they are effectively process neutral. They tell you what you must do; they make no suggestions how you must do it. There's no instruction about the way cabinets ought to operate, just what the outcomes will be. And that's because it's difficult to find any coherent view about the best way to operate. It's a question I'll come back to.

One of the questions that is often posed is: should things be discussed by cabinet? Probably yes. Then by whom should they be discussed? What is 'the cabinet' in these situations? Is it a full cabinet, a cabinet made up of all the ministers or all the cabinet ministers, since most countries have a distinction between who's in cabinet and who is not? Or something less? Every system will agree, but perhaps not all the ministers. Every system has a war cabinet when there's a fight on. Every system has reduced to small numbers the people whom it wants to discuss strategic and military decision making. So Australia in 1941 had a war cabinet consisting of seven or eight people who took most of the crucial decisions. It was briefed by the military. It was briefed by senior public servants. It had the advantage of maintaining a small group of people with some sort of strategic view. It also had the political advantage for John Curtin that he didn't have to put Eddie Ward and Arthur Caldwell in there, so that he could run it without fearing they were going to leak the whole time. So it served a political and a suitably administrative purpose at the same time.

Australia has had 20 years' experience of the Expenditure Review Committee process, by which a small group of ministers examines budgetary proposals each year, supported largely by the Department of Finance. It's regarded as a sort of inner-expenditure cabinet, which can make the tough decisions. Howard instituted a National Security Committee, which is responsible currently for overseeing the way that issues in Iraq and Afghanistan and other security problems are taken into account and it incorporates its own supporting organisation of senior staff. So there's never been an occasion when a particular forum or a particular group alone constitutes 'the cabinet'. It's organised by prime ministers on different occasions in a way that they can best ensure the job is done.

Structures are devices to reach sensible decisions and maintain the necessary support for the decisions that you're going to make; it's a combination of power and good information. Getting support for good policies is significant because good policies without support go nowhere.

If we go back to 70 or 80 years ago, we see process even then. There is nothing new about a national security council or national security committee. It has a lineage that goes back quite a long time. It always raises questions about the power of prime ministers in contrast to the power of cabinets. The critics talk about the presidentialisation of the prime ministership, as though it reflects an increase in the Prime Minister's power. That is really a silly term, since most American presidents would dearly love to have the same power as any Australia prime minister. They would love to have the guaranteed support that exists within the Parliament and the cabinet for what they wish to do.

The presidentialisation concept raises questions about individual power; we're much better talking about centralisation of power. Even then a sense of history will quickly destroy any notion of trends towards greater authority for Australian prime ministers. Billy Hughes went overseas for 15 months while he was Prime Minister. He left in about April 1918 and came back in August 1919, which would be difficult to do today. He ran the country by telegram, which meant of course that the messages had to be coded, sent, decoded, read, considered by cabinet, coded, sent back, decoded and considered by the Prime Minister. At one stage, Hughes said, 'I don't want Cabinet to make any decisions without consulting me first.' The then Acting Prime Minister, a careful, methodical person called W. A. Watt, exploded. He said, 'You can't run a country if everything has to go to and from Britain.' Watt said, 'I sent you the details of the last meeting in a telegram' to America; it cost £100 to send that telegram, in 1918 values. Only later came the wonderful contraption of the overseas telephone. When Joe Lyons was in London, he arranged a phone call to the cabinet in the cabinet room. It took three days to organise. Hughes used to make decisions; Watt used to complain that cabinet found out what the Australian Government had decided by reading the newspapers (shades of CNN 100 years later). Hughes was announcing decisions to the press and then the Australian cabinet was asked to respond to them. Billy Hughes was maverick, individualistic; he had a crazy way of running cabinet and he had more power than any Australian prime minister has ever had before or since in terms of getting away with what he wanted to do because he scared the hell out of all his colleagues. He was quite a character, when you actually look at the way that he chose to operate.

But there's another way of operating, another way in which you can run cabinet from the prime ministership, and let me quote about a prime minister who did it by a very different strategy. He said, 'We adopted the idea of a definite agenda and the circulation of papers by Ministers in respect to any item they put down.' He had an arrangement that any minister with an item listed had to see the Prime Minister before the meeting. This, he argued,

> worked admirably…Notwithstanding the provision that the papers had to be circulated by the Minister, it was obvious at Cabinet meetings that the majority of his colleagues had not read them. With our system, however, that wasn't frightfully material. I always allowed a discussion for half an hour, or some limited period, and then came into the ring

myself, being fully informed in the matter by reason of my private conversation with the Minister concerned beforehand. The weight of the Prime Minister definitely on the side of the Minister, in the face of the rest of the Cabinet—the majority of whom had not read the paper and did not know what it was all about—proved it practice to be quite decisive and we got through a great deal of work in minimum time.

So who was this Prime Minister who ran a very collective system, in which everyone was permitted to talk, everyone was permitted to participate and he decided in advance exactly what was going to happen? That was Stanley Bruce, who came into office in 1923 with the inclinations of a businessman to try to run government efficiently, although eventually of course his cabinet got into more and more political trouble and it collapsed. I suspect that's the more common feature of prime ministers in cabinet. It's not a choice between the individual and the collective; it's how the individual uses the collective.

When I went to see Malcolm Fraser to talk to him about writing a book on the way he ran his government, he said to me, 'Why do you want to write the book?' I said, 'Well, your image is of a totally dominant prime minister, but everyone I talk to emphasised how much you consulted.' He laughed. He said, 'Just because I consulted, it didn't mean I didn't dominate, you know.' And, of course, that's precisely how he chose to run his cabinet; he consulted exhaustively, he consulted until people were prepared to accept his particular proposals. When he didn't like what they were proposing, he would put it off, he'd ask for another paper, he'd argue that time was needed to think about this a bit more, he would decide to call a meeting later that day. There was a whole range of tactics that he produced to ensure that his views were actually heard, but he worked through the cabinet in a way that many of his equivalents in other countries never felt the obligation to do.

What's happened of course since the days of Hughes and Bruce is that the circumstances have changed—not only the political circumstances, but all those other things: the media, the access to prime ministers, the notion that anything a prime minister says, whether deliberate or otherwise, can rapidly be circulated right around the country within seconds on the Internet, or by other mechanisms. A prime minister can be asked questions on any item at any time. Opinion polls tell them what people think rather than them relying on their backbench or other people to report on how the government is going. Imagine what Billy Hughes would have done with those advantages. Imagine how he would have manipulated the media. Imagine how he would have controlled the flow of information. Imagine how, in his own, I suspect, unique way, he would have managed to use the mechanisms to be just as dominant as any prime minister possibly could be in the past, or in the future.

Centralisation depends on style, on the different ways of running things. But I suspect when we talk about the greater information for prime ministers and greater support for prime ministers, some of it at least is a case of running hard to keep up, not to get ahead. Prime ministers need to understand the immediacy of the pressures that are landing on them rather than operating some time in the future. Robert Menzies came out once from a meeting with the US President, he had a press conference and somebody said to him, 'Mr Menzies, you've had private conversations with the President?' 'Yes.' 'Can you tell us what you talked about?' He said, 'Son, you've answered your own question.' The reporter said, 'What do you mean?' Menzies said, 'They were private conversations. Do you expect me to tell you before I tell the Australian Parliament?' He could get away with it then; it would be much harder to do so now.

So how has the Australian cabinet changed over this period? First, there's one distinct line that is continuous: the bureaucracy surrounding cabinet has grown more complex and more distinct over 100 years. At those first meetings of cabinet, the Prime Minister used to keep the minutes; he used to write down on one side of the minute book the topics, across the top the people who turned up and the decisions on the opposite page—'delayed', 'deferred', 'agreed', or something. And that was the only record; we've still got some of those notebooks. Occasionally, we can see the frustration: conciliation and arbitration, deferred, deferred, discussed, discussed, and after about 10 meetings, it says, 'Kingston resigns, decision finalised at last' underlined. A huge sigh of relief springs out of the page. But gradually prime ministers start formalising the process of government. Eventually cabinet received the support that occurred in Britain in the First World War. The first official to sit in cabinet sat in the war cabinet in 1939–40. The first secretary to sit in the full cabinet was Frank Strahan in 1941. Gradually, official numbers moved from one to two to three to four, as officers sat there to take notes of what was being decided. The handbooks, the rules of cabinet, started at half a page, half a page in which Bruce actually discussed with the head of cabinet what would happen, what would go in and how it would be done. There are now two or three handbooks, as people add to the rules that define the way that cabinets work and seek to maintain some sort of control of the processes. It works to some extent but not always.

Sometimes mavericks can never be controlled. Let me read one cabinet submission in 1936—hazard a guess about what it might be discussing.

> We are faced with a situation which demands serious thinking and courageous action. What is the greatest problem of nations today? We are faced with world unrest which is causing great anxiety. We have fierce economic wars between countries. We have the piling up of armaments and behind all these we have the separation of peoples into political camps of the most extreme kind.

Armaments? Defence expenditure? Foreign affairs? No, Billy Hughes was Minister of Health and was proposing the introduction of school milk. How you make the connection, I've really no idea.

But there were different times, of course, in which others again tried to add to the rules. Let me quote a comment from John Bunting about how cabinet should be run. There was particular concern in the late 1950s that the cabinet load was becoming too onerous, even if by modern standards it was scarcely onerous at all. He particularly objected to the number of papers being presented by the Treasury, and he wrote this to his superior:

> These papers either waste time or the Cabinet gallops through them. And galloping, once started, becomes the fashion. They are then apt to gallop when they should work...I don't want to pose as a reformer. For one thing, there are certain virtues, from the point of view of the Prime Minister and Treasurer, for example, in the confusion.

There is a recognition the cabinet is not about getting things right, it's about getting things done. A prime minister can appreciate that no-one except himself and the Treasurer is probably briefed on what they're discussing and thus has some genuine advantages with which he likes to operate. So an examination of the rules provides some idea of why they're put there and for what purpose they're being applied. To quote Sir John Bunting, I like the slightly paternalistic view of Menzies, who says to Bunting at one stage when he is proposing new rules (you can imagine Menzies, can't you?):

> Lad, the thing is, if you're taking over from someone, to assume that he knew what he was doing. You can disagree later if you want to and make a change, but if you're wise about it, you will discover his reasons for his actions before you disagree. You may find those reasons convincing. In any case it's always a gross error to assume that your predecessor was a species of a fool.

There is a linear line of the organisation of cabinet, which makes it much more bureaucratised than it's ever been before. The informality of the early cabinet, when you had nine people sitting around a table arguing without the benefit of papers on a range of items, has now largely disappeared.

A second question, though, is how could you do it better? There's been a struggle for 100 years to work out how best to organise cabinet to get the best results. We tend to assume that cabinets know what they're doing; I suspect the closer you get to cabinet, the more you appreciate the difficulties that cabinet has of understanding the issues, and understanding exactly what it is that they're trying to decide.

Hugh Heclo used a lovely notion of governments 'puzzling'—the government is a sort of collective puzzlement on society's behalf. I think that's largely true in many of the issues that come before cabinet. When they were starting to introduce satellites, there were 36 meetings of cabinet or its committees to try to work out what on earth this meant. What were their implications? They couldn't understand them because nobody really knew what they were. So on a range of issues, there have been 100 years of attempts to sort out how to deal with information. How do ministers absorb it? How do they come up with sensible decisions? The first cabinet committees were set up in 1903; cabinets have been setting them up ever since as ways of allowing people to look at particular problems. The basic problems are systemic: a lack of time, a lack of capacity to absorb information or occasionally a reluctance to read too much material. There is no single solution that can satisfy those sorts of issues, so prime ministers are constantly looking at different ways, different committees, larger and smaller cabinets, supporting groups of officials, strategic cabinets—all of these have been attempted at different times. None of them by themselves has solved the problems, because it's basically an insoluble problem, which is going to be readjusted to suit the individuals and particularly the Prime Minister's style and interests.

The third point about cabinet has never changed. It's a political forum in which ministers contest not only the items, but for their own position. Cabinet, someone said, is a bull ring, in which everyone has their place and ensures they aren't knocked off too often. In those first years, Kingston and Forrest couldn't stand the sight of each other and fought long and bitterly over the conciliation and arbitration bill; their animosity was reflected time and time again in cabinets in which people fought tense battles for the sake of the policy and for the sake of their own careers.

Cabinet is a tough forum in which people are operating all the time. That cannot change. Our system of government is one of the few in which the Prime Minister's putative successors are probably sitting around the table, all conscious of the fact that they want to make sure that some day in the future they get there.

So there is a long history of fights in cabinet, which can get dramatically bitter—for example, over conscription. Also in the Great Depression, the Scullin Government fragmented and cabinet was constantly buffered between a Senate that would pass nothing and a caucus that would approve nothing. The image of cabinet tick-tacking endlessly and fruitlessly with caucus is an illustration of how badly cabinet government can sometimes work.

The question is: why, given all those problems, do we still have the system of cabinet government in Australia, which exists in a much more collective style than is true in Britain? What are the dynamics in Australia that keep cabinet discussing things collectively, whereas in Britain it's been handled much more through committees and bilaterally and in Canada it has become little more than a focus group?

Three or four reasons can explain. First, cabinet still, in Australia, has some sort of representational role. We are a federation that requires that state voices still be heard or at least not be excluded too often. So we've always had different states represented in the ministry and nearly always in the cabinet.

Second, there's an egalitarian tradition that I suspect is cautious of giving too much power to leaders—dramatically so in the case of the Labor Party. The Australian Labor Party, from a very early stage, decided that ministers were the delegates of caucus and could be instructed by caucus. In the battles that went on between 1910 and 1913, 1914 and 1915, 1929 and 1931, there were occasions when the demands of caucus effectively destroyed the government. Curtin and Chifley, better politicians than Hughes and Fisher, were able, to some extent, to work through the party in order to maintain the controls that they needed. Not until the Hawke/Keating Government did the caucus gradually fall into a more submissive role, accepting that if they wanted to stay in Parliament, they could not constantly seek to direct cabinet.

But even in the Liberal Party, even in coalition governments, there was long a tradition that people would listen in party committees. Even prime ministers attend party committees. In 1941 in particular, Menzies had a constant battle with his party room about whether he should stay in Australia or whether he should go back to Britain, eventually to the extent that they drove him out of the Prime Minister's job. So there's an egalitarian tradition that doesn't accept the royal prerogative as readily as happened, certainly, in Britain.

Third, there's location. Everyone works out of Parliament House. They meet each other on a regular basis. There's a much greater notion of a group activity in the Australian Parliament, whereas in Britain they are spread around Whitehall. They see each other less often. They talk to each other less frequently. There's a hothouse atmosphere in Canberra that requires that people know what's going on.

But the key factor that maintains cabinet collective government in Australia is the method by which parties select and remove leaders. From a very early stage, the tradition was accepted that the caucus selected the leader and the caucus could remove the leader. In Canada, since 1925, all Canadian leaders have been elected by convention. As it takes a convention to elect a leader and a convention to remove a leader, prime ministers there would say to their colleagues, 'You didn't elect me and you can't get rid of me'. The only way a Canadian prime minister can be removed is through the calling of a leadership convention and a vote of no confidence; that process will destroy the government so critics are more restrained. In Britain, for a long time, conservative leaders 'emerged', but now in both parties there is an external convention that elects them—a conference that is broader than the parliamentary party. So for a prime minister to be removed, critics have to organise…well, no prime minister has been removed by party revolt since the franchise was widened. Thatcher lost because the selection then, at a particular moment, was in the hands of the parliamentary party. No longer. It's virtually impossible to get rid of a British prime minister without destroying the government. Why did Gordon Brown wait for so long? Because he had no choice.

When it comes to removing a prime minister in Australia, ask Paul Keating. When he had the numbers, he used them. Ask Peter Costello. If he had had the numbers, he would have used them. Look at the strategies of the three potential leaders in the past 15 years across three countries. In the Canadian Chrétien Government, Paul Martin was the leader in waiting. He became frustrated; after 10 years, Chrétien wouldn't go. In fact, Chrétien said, 'If you start campaigning, I'll stay in office longer' and there was nothing the critics could do about it. Paul Martin left the Parliament and campaigned for the leadership in the party outside. After he won the party leadership at a convention, he had to win a seat and only then take up his position as Prime Minister. He left and campaigned. Gordon Brown didn't have a mechanism for removing Blair. He had to wait him out or start a revolt in the party and the cabinet, which was full of Blairites because Blair had chosen them. He had to stay in the House of Commons to be eligible when Blair eventually resigned. So he stayed and fumed.

Keating and Costello conspired and hoped to assassinate, at least potentially, because the mechanism was there. If aspirants have the numbers within the party, they can take the Prime Minister out on any occasion. Now turn that position around on its head. If that is the way that the system works, what do prime ministers need? And the answer is: the continuing positive support of their senior colleagues. They need the continuing support of cabinet colleagues to ensure that their position remains strong. They have to keep talking to the parliamentary party because they're the ones who elected them in the first place. Australian government becomes collective because that is a matter of survival for prime ministers. The party chooses, the party can remove, the party can replace. The dynamics of the party make collective cabinet essential, because otherwise a prime minister finds himself at odds with the most powerful people, including his potential successor.

The consequence is that no prime minister in Australia will ever try to operate again the way that Billy Hughes did, unless they are highly confident of their position (and eventually of course even Hughes fell foul of the Country Party). I suspect that, although his party claimed to be prepared to support him, they weren't that sorry to see him go. No prime minister now could survive spending as much time overseas or could act continually in as arbitrary a fashion without consultation with the cabinet.

So it's the dynamics of the party and the dynamics of government; it's the history of politics and administration and the rules of succession that underpin the notions of a collective cabinet process in Australia. As long as the position continues that members of cabinet and their supporters in the party can make or break prime ministers, the prime ministers will be conscious of those rules and make sure that that happens as seldom as possible. So maintaining the party's support, working with cabinet, maintaining a degree of contentment in cabinet, consulting ministers even if only for the sake of going through the processes, ensuring they know what's happening—that's all part of the process. It's that mixture of politics and policy that makes cabinet government significant.

John Howard commented in his dark days of opposition:

> One of the tensions I find as a senior minister in the Fraser government [is] the balance between the political role and the administrative role. The extent to which too frequent a number of Cabinet meetings and too cumbersome an administrative procedure can paralyse one's political activity and one's political effectiveness, it's a real constraint.

Too much policy discussion in cabinet and the politics can get forgotten. Too much politics and the administration can decline. Getting that balance right is one of the constant challenges for cabinets in Australia.

ENDNOTES

[1] This essay was originally presented as an ANZSOG Public Lecture on 16 May 2007.

8. Consumers and small business: at the heart of the Trade Practices Act[1]

Graeme Samuel AO

Thirty-four years ago when the *Trade Practices Act* was but a twinkle in the Parliament's eye, the then Attorney-General Senator Lionel Murphy accurately summed up the state of the marketplace in his second reading speech introducing the *Trade Practices Act*:

> Restrictive trade practices have long been rife in Australia. Most of them are undesirable and have served the interests of the parties engaged in them, irrespective of whether those interests coincide with the interests of Australians generally. These practices cause prices to be maintained at artificially high levels. They enable particular...groups...to attain positions of economic dominance which are susceptible to abuse...[and] allow discriminatory action against small businesses.

'Protecting the interests of Australians generally' is the fundamental principle at the very heart of the ACCC and the *Trade Practices Act*. We're here to promote the welfare of all Australian consumers, all 21 million of us in all our activities: when we buy things from a retailer, when we compete in a marketplace of goods and services, when we run a small business and deal with myriad suppliers.

Small business is an important and integral part of the economy. There are two million small firms in Australia today and they account for nearly half of our workforce and provide about one-third of our GDP. Small business is a vital part of vigorous competition and, for the most part, the interests of small business are consistent with those of consumers overall.

A fair and competitive marketplace *is* in all our interests; whether we are consumers or small businesspeople, it is paramount and, to achieve this, we must protect competition, not individual competitors.

The structure of the ACCC reflects the critical importance of these two areas, with deputy chairs each having a specific focus: Peter Kell in Consumer Protection and Michael Schaper in Small Business.

I started with the history of the *Trade Practices Act* from 1974. Let me take you back now to the 1600s. In Simon Schama's *A History of Britain*, he recounts with great colour the period when James I opened up trade between his newly united kingdoms of Scotland and England:

> Once a ferocious border policing commission was in place and had started to catch, convict and hang the gangs of rustlers and brigands who had

made the Borders their choice territory, cross-frontier trade took off. Fishermen, cattle drivers and linen-makers all did well. Duty-free English beer became so popular in Scotland that the council in Edinburgh had to lower the price of the home product to make it competitive.

Although these days we have different ways to deal with those wishing to restrict competition or inhibit trade, the benefits stemming from a highly competitive but fair marketplace are just as relevant in Australia today as they were to Scottish beer drinkers in the early 1600s.

The economic reforms of the past 25 years have seen the floating of the Australian dollar, the introduction of new players in previous monopoly industries and Australia's strong participation in the global marketplace. As a result, the nation has become more efficient, more flexible, more productive and, above all, more competitive.

And while the opening up of the Australian economy to greater competition internally and from overseas has produced immense rewards, it has also provided great benefits to consumers.

Vigorous competition provides consumers with:

- choice
- all the information to make that choice rationally
- convenience
- higher quality and lower prices for goods and services.

Business, too, is a beneficiary of competition policy. Competition—and this includes intense and, at times, incessant price competition—benefits those businesses that are able and motivated to take advantage of the powerful forces driving their particular market.

The corollary, of course, is that those businesses unable or unwilling to respond to the often-daunting challenge of competition will languish behind and might ultimately fail.

But this is the essence of an open market economy.

As the story about the Scottish beer drinkers demonstrates, free-enterprise economies have operated in one form or another for hundreds of years. It is just the intensity and speed of change that are different.

I have no doubt that when that duty-free English beer first crossed the border, the local beer makers appealed for some sort of protection. But ultimately what was regarded as unfair by those who benefited from the previously closed beer market was seen by the consumers who benefited from the end of that monopoly as vigorous and fair.

And they were right, because the purpose of competition policy must be to benefit consumers—not competitors. The question to be asked must always be what is in the long-term interest of consumers.

The principles of competition policy enshrined in the *Trade Practices Act* and the National Competition Policy emphasise the primary purposes of a vigorous competitive economy and the protection of the interests of consumers.

In this context, businesses that are motivated to take advantage of the competitive marketplace will thrive. And, for the most part, small business is able to respond to the rigours of competition more quickly and with more flexibility than many of its larger competitors. As stated previously, the corollary is that businesses that are unable or unwilling to respond to the challenge of competition will languish and might ultimately fail.

In short, an open competitive economy is the best environment for small business to flourish.

This message has greater significance against the backdrop of the current turmoil in global financial markets, where we are seeing governments take strong and often interventionist approaches in the interests of stability. It is important to consider the impact of that priority and how it relates to competition and policy development.

To a certain extent, government intervention in a particular industry can cushion it from some of the realities of the marketplace. Earlier this month, for example, the Australian Government committed to invest $6.2 billion over the next 13 years in the car industry under the New Car Plan for a Greener Future.

Whatever one's view as to that commitment, one cannot but agree wholeheartedly with the comments of Prime Minister, Kevin Rudd, and the Minister for Innovation, Infrastructure, Science and Research, Senator Kim Carr, that the future of the car industry is dependant on research, innovation and global integration rather than protection, quotas and tariffs. If the car industry does not heed these calls, it simply won't survive.

Similarly, the ACCC has been fielding calls in recent times from sectors of small business about 'giving them a fair go'. However, if government did intervene to shield small business from some of the competitive rigours of the marketplace, the result would not in fact be giving small business 'a fair go'; it would be artificially changing the dynamics of an open and competitive marketplace by giving one player added protection that others do not have.

As a result, consumers overall would be given an 'unfair go' as a less competitive marketplace invariably leads to higher prices and a poorer standard of goods and services, as Attorney-General Murphy pointed out back in 1974.

But such a solution also ignores the numerous and significant advantages that small business has in the marketplace. However, they involve a lot of hard work, perseverance and the ability to 'think outside the square'.

Small business has the capacity to innovate—to adapt quickly to changing market needs, provide personalised service and develop niche markets.

These qualities must be harnessed by small business to remain competitive in the marketplace and benefit all Australian consumers. Governments and regulators have an ongoing challenge in striking a balance that promotes vigorous, lawful competitive behaviour that is likely to lead to significant and sustained benefits for consumers, while preventing unlawful anti-competitive behaviour that is likely to disadvantage us as consumers.

This is a task that needs to be undertaken independently, rigorously, transparently and objectively to ensure it remains focused on the interests of consumers. But this cannot result in the insulation of certain sectors of business from normal competitive disciplines.

Now that is theory and it has been endorsed by the Dawson Committee Review into the Competition Provisions of the *Trade Practices Act* and the Senate committee considering the effectiveness of the act in relation to small business.

The *Dawson Committee Report* summed up the issue as follows:

> The Committee does not favour the introduction of competition measures specifically directed to particular industries to respond to perceived shortcomings in the relevant markets. Often the complaint when analysed is not about reduced competition, but about the structure of the market which competition has produced.

> Concentrated markets can be highly competitive. It may be possible to object to the structure of such markets for reasons of policy (the disappearance of the corner store, for example), but not on the grounds of lack of competitiveness.

> Of course, concentrated markets should attract scrutiny to ensure that competition is maintained, but the purpose of the competition provisions of the Act is to promote and protect the competitive process rather than to protect individual competitors. The competition provisions should not be seen as a device to achieve social outcomes unrelated to the encouragement of competition. As a matter of policy those outcomes may be regarded as desirable, but the policy will not be competition policy.

> Nor should the competition provisions seek the preservation of particular businesses or of a particular class of business that is unable to withstand competitive forces or may fail for other reasons.

Those are matters which may legitimately be the subject of an industry policy, but that is not a policy which is to be found in the competition provisions in Part IV of the Act.

The Senate committee considering the effectiveness of the *Trade Practices Act* in relation to small business noted:

[T]he Committee considers that while the objects of the Act refer to enhancing competition, these objects implicitly require—or at least prefer—the existence of an effective number of competitors.

Having stated this, the Committee recognises that there is a significant difference between protecting competitors, and protecting particular competitors. The entry and exit of competitors from the market is a normal part of vigorous competition. Market efficiency is often enhanced by driving inefficient competitors from the market.

To summarise the Committee's views on this issue, the purpose of the Act is to protect competition. This can best be achieved by maintaining a range of competitors, who should rise and fall in accordance with the results of competitive rather than anti-competitive conduct. This means that the Act should protect businesses (large or small) against anti-competitive conduct, and it should not be amended to protect competitors against competitive conduct.

These findings are consistent with the purpose of the *Trade Practices Act* as outlined in Section 2: 'The object of this Act is to enhance the welfare of Australians through the promotion of competition and fair trading and provision for consumer protection.'

But while the theory is easy to state, it is not so clear that the principles are either well understood or applied in practice. For while it is now widely accepted that the purpose of competition policy is to promote competition in the interests of consumers and not to protect competitors from the rigours of competition, in practice the distinction between these objectives is confused and sometimes leads to conclusions that are inherently anti-competitive in nature.

Competition policy regulators are required to deal with two issues. The first is to analyse whether in the context of any particular market there exists a course of behaviour that will have the effect or be likely to have the effect of substantially lessening competition in that market. This requires rigorous, economic analysis of the market and the likely impact of the behaviour of competitors in that market. Then if that analysis reveals a likely anti-competitive consequence, competition policy requires regulators to intervene to prevent it.

It might or might not be the case that to protect and nurture competition in a market it is necessary to take steps to protect competitors or a class of competitors in that market from substantial damage or indeed elimination as a result of a course of behaviour by another competitor. The provisions of Part IV of the *Trade Practices Act* are designed to permit that intervention by competition regulators to take place.

What is not clear, however, in the claims and counterclaims that are made by small and big business respectively in relation to these matters, is whether the primary case has been made for regulatory intervention. That is to say, it is not apparent that a course of behaviour by one or more competitors in those markets will lead to a substantially anti-competitive (and thus anti-consumer) impact.

If such an analysis leads to the conclusion that there is likely to be a substantial lessening of competition in the relevant market, then of course the competition regulator should intervene.

But if the analysis merely leads to the conclusion that some competitors in the market might suffer damage or indeed be eliminated, but that competition in the market will still be vigorous with consumer benefits, then there is a dubious case for intervention by the competition regulator.

The difficulty in this area is that so often those who seek regulatory intervention have failed to first demonstrate the case for it. Indeed, in some cases, they have been reluctant to have the relevant market, and the course of behaviour complained of, subjected to an independent rigorous analysis to determine whether there is justification for intervention.

The point is, if we intervene too soon and without transparent, open and independent analysis, we might be acting to protect competitors at the expense of vigorous, lawful competitive behaviour and, as a consequence, disadvantage the consumer.

Having spent 12, at times difficult, years undertaking an independent and robust process of examination and reform of anti-competitive regulations pursuant to National Competition Policy, I suggest policy makers need to be continually on the alert that they are not drawn back by private interests to protect specific sectors of business from the competitive environment.

No better example of this can be seen in the area of petrol. You might recall the recent campaign directed towards government by some independent small petrol retailers around Australia, calling for what they describe as a 'fair go'. These small retailers want the same wholesale pricing as Coles and Woolworths and want the supermarkets' shopper dockets petrol discount schemes outlawed.

Now I know that my response to this is not going to be popular with these small independent petrol retailers or with parts of the media, but the truth is that those small independent petrol retailers will find it very difficult to respond to the price-competitive pressure that Coles, Woolworths and the large independent chains such as United, Liberty, Gull and Matilda can provide.

What is being sought is not a levelling of a playing field. It is a request for protection against the rigours of the marketplace. In fact, the ACCC petrol inquiry reported that the emergence of shopper docket schemes had not had an anti-competitive effect but had delivered discounts to consumers and promoted competition among retailers. And despite all the media hype about petrol prices, consumers are voting with their wallets in support of any discount schemes that offer cheaper petrol.

In these circumstances, the interests of small business are at odds with the interests of Australia consumers. However, rather than lessening competition, a better approach would be finding ways to make the petrol sector, at the source of supply, more competitive, which of course is also in the interests of small business.

The situation as it stands in Australia is that there are four major players in the petrol market—BP, Shell, Mobil and Caltex—and they are responsible for refining and importing 98 per cent of our petrol. This is why the ACCC's focus is on the wholesale petrol market, where we see an opportunity to expand competition. Petrol Commissioner, Joe Dimasi, is working hard to see whether new players can enter the Australian wholesale market and, if this happens, the new wholesalers will need petrol outlets, which is where the independents could come into their own.

Moving onto another contentious issue—groceries—it has long been claimed that if smaller retailers are not protected from competition from the major retailers, a market duopoly of Coles and Woolworths will result. This necessitates, it is claimed, policy and regulatory intervention, for example, to retain discriminatory shop trading hours, to limit the acquisition of additional market share by the major retailers and to prevent price discrimination by suppliers to, and price discounting—claimed to be predatory pricing—by, the major retailers.

In early 2008, the ACCC conducted an inquiry into the competitiveness of retail prices for standard groceries and, overall, it found supermarket retailing is 'workably competitive'.

However, there are a number of factors that bear closer examination, including high barriers to entry for large-format supermarkets, a lack of incentives for Coles and Woolworths to compete strongly on price and limited price competition from the independent sector. It is our opinion that the appropriate response for policy makers is to lower barriers to entry and expansion in retailing and wholesaling to independent supermarkets and potential new entrants. As always, the ACCC will continue to examine the acquisitions of existing supermarkets as well as site acquisitions and leases for new supermarkets.

To that end, in May 2008 we issued a *Statement of Issues* concerning a proposed lease of a new supermarket site in Wallaroo, South Australia, by Woolworths.

In that statement, the ACCC expressed its preliminary view that the proposed lease might constitute a substantial lessening of competition—on the basis that if the lease did not proceed, it was likely that another non-Woolworths operator would acquire the lease to operate a supermarket in competition with an existing Woolworths supermarket in an adjacent locality. The ACCC is seeking the views of interested parties to assist it in reaching a final decision on this matter.

The lack of incentives for Coles and Woolworths to compete strongly across the board on price reflects the high level of concentration in the industry and frequent monitoring of competitors' prices. But despite this, Aldi has had a significant impact on grocery retailing. Where Aldi stores are present in an area, Coles and Woolworths have reduced prices. Aldi represents a new type of retailing, which has overcome some of the barriers in place, and this innovative approach is what small business needs to consider. Their strategy might well be summed up as: 'If I can't win the game under the current conditions, why not play a different type of game?'

Aldi has shown that a new player does not have to be a full-service supermarket to generate a significant competitive reaction from Coles and Woolworths. The entry of grocery retailers with differentiated business models poses a competitive threat to the major supermarkets and benefits Australian consumers. Without a doubt, retail groceries and petroleum have been experiencing, and will continue to undergo, rapid change. Now supermarkets are four to five times their previous size; service stations are fewer in number but significantly larger, located on major highways and directly linked with substantial convenience stores, car washes, fast-food outlets and even hotels.

These changes are driven by consumer preferences, and businesses operating in these markets will continue to undergo rapid change. But those which do adapt will survive, indeed thrive, while those unable to adapt or resting on the belief that governments or regulators will step in to protect them will languish and might ultimately fail.

I repeat, it is not the job of the *Trade Practices Act* or the ACCC to protect competitors; it is our job to protect competition and the welfare of Australian consumers. Let us not forget, however, that businesses are also consumers. Every opportunity to reduce costs and increase choice, service and availability of goods helps businesses as well, and allows them more options for innovation.

Protection of small business under the *Trade Practices Act*

This is not to say that small business has no protection under competition policy, for competition policy is about encouraging lawful, vigorous, competitive behaviour to benefit consumers—that is to say, the public interest.

The ACCC interacts on a number of levels with small business:

- working with them towards voluntary compliance—by far the best outcome for all parties involved
- educating and informing them of their obligations under the *Trade Practices Act* with advice and publications
- providing measures to protect them from anti-competitive behaviour.

And, as part of this process, our outreach officers get beyond metropolitan Australia to regional and rural areas to ensure small business and other operators in those areas are aware of the *Trade Practices Act*.

Let me now illustrate how the *Trade Practices Act* and the ACCC actively protect the interests of small business, while remaining consistent with the principles of promoting the interests of Australian consumers in protecting competition.

Franchising

The ACCC plays a significant role in working with small business through the Franchising Code of Conduct and the *Trade Practices Act*.

You might be surprised to learn that Australia is one of the most franchised nations in the world. We have three times as many franchises per capita as the United States, with about 1100 business-format franchise systems, up from 693 in 1998, which amounts to 71 400 individual franchises. Franchising employs an estimated 413 500 people and contributes $130 billion to the Australian economy each year.

The code and the *Trade Practices Act* provide a range of protections for franchisees and prospective franchisees in their dealings with franchisors. These include:

- ensuring prospective franchisees receive key information about a franchise before making a financial commitment and entering into a franchise system
- ensuring that franchisees have certain rights in their ongoing franchise relationship.

When disputes occur between franchisors and franchisees, there is capacity under the code to resolve these effectively.

The ACCC uses a variety of tools to achieve this, including direct liaison with affected parties, the Office of the Mediation Adviser and the various legal powers of the ACCC. Similarly, in securing compliance, the ACCC considers a range of measures that involves:

- consultation and liaison with, and education for, industry participants
- consideration of franchisee complaints
- detailed investigation, enforcement action or litigation.

However, neither the laws nor the ACCC can guarantee that all franchised businesses will thrive.

Franchised businesses can and do fail for reasons other than franchisor wrongdoing. It is a part of the ACCC's task, when assessing complaints, to determine whether the cause of concern flows from conduct contravening the law or whether the harm is the result of other factors. The ACCC has made recommendations to the Parliamentary Inquiry into Franchising including:

- a review of mediation under the franchising code
- a review of the requirements for disclosure under the franchising code
- the introduction of civil pecuniary penalties for breaches of parts IVA (unconscionable conduct), IVB (breach of the code) and V (consumer protection) of the *Trade Practices Act*.

We strongly believe these changes will bolster the Franchising Code of Conduct and the *Trade Practices Act* in providing greater clarity for franchisees and those considering entering into franchise agreements.

Small business and Section 46

Now I'd like to speak about s.46 of the Act and how it can help protect small business from the misuse of market power by larger competitors.

Effective misuse of market power provisions are an important part of any competition law. They deal with situations where a firm has substantial market power and uses that power to damage competitors or to prevent new firms from competing. These provisions are an important adjunct to the other main pillars of an effective competition law: the restrictions on the accumulation of market power through mergers and acquisitions and anti-competitive agreements between competitors.

These provisions are just as important to small business if they are targets of a misuse of market power by a larger business. In this situation, the commission will act to protect the small businesses involved. We do this not to protect a particular business merely because it is a small business, but to protect competition where small businesses are being targeted for anti-competitive reasons by a more powerful firm.

While it is true that in the past the ACCC's ability to litigate misuse of market power allegations has been hampered by the High Court's narrow interpretation of the concept 'take advantage' in judgments such as Melway, Boral, Safeway, NT Power Generation and Rural Press, this will no longer be the case.

Amendments to s.46, which became law in May 2008, clarify that if a corporation's market power drives its conduct then that is sufficient to prove it has taken advantage of its market power. And then there is, of course, s.46(1AA) or the so-called Birdsville amendment, dealing with predatory pricing. Much has been claimed and counterclaimed in relation to this amendment.

Only time and the courts will tell which of the claims are correct. Suffice to say, the amendment introduces some new concepts into the competition provisions of the *Trade Practices Act*, which will require interpretation by the courts before business, big and small, can derive any certainty as to its implications.

The ACCC is closely examining the recent amendments to the *Trade Practices Act* with respect to predatory pricing. We will be reviewing the operation of this section in light of our own determinations, any litigation—whether instituted by the ACCC or private litigants—and senior legal advice.

The ACCC plans to issue general guidance about the likely interpretation of the terms in s.46(1AA), but this guidance will be qualified, as the ultimate interpretation will be up to the courts and will take place on a case-by-case basis. Nevertheless, we will enforce s.46 and its components with the utmost vigour, wherever our legal advice tells us we have reasonable grounds to do so. However, a word of caution: small business should not place undue reliance on the misuse of market power provisions.

It needs to be understood that these provisions require conduct that is damaging, or potentially so, to competitors and for this conduct to be intended to, or to have the purpose of, damaging specific competitors. It is not enough to point to the fact that competitors, even small competitors, are being damaged by the actions of a larger, more powerful business. Normal, even aggressive competition is not on its own a misuse of market power. The conduct of the larger business needs to be targeted or intended to damage particular competitors.

The misuse of market power provisions are not a panacea for the concerns of business, and to achieve any outcomes the commission will require the assistance of business.

The commission will investigate properly alleged instances of abuse of market power and use its statutory powers to do so.

Unconscionable conduct

Many of the complaints received at the ACCC from small businesses do not relate to concerns about direct competition with large businesses; the majority are about their commercial relationships with large businesses. In these situations, the more relevant provisions that apply are the unconscionable conduct laws, particularly the statutory unconscionability provision, Section 51AC.

One business cannot use its power or influence over another for unconscionable purposes. A business in a position of power threatening to withhold the supply of products, especially where those products cannot be sourced elsewhere, in order to impose harsh and oppressive conditions will likely breach the unconscionable conduct provisions of the act.

In the Simply No Knead case, the ACCC under s.51AC made it clear to franchisors that they could not hold their franchisees to ransom with unreasonable terms and conditions. The franchisor in this case withheld essential supplies unless the franchisees bowed to a range of unreasonable conditions, including making them pay for advertising that did not even include their stores' details and forcing them to buy many years worth of product at a time.

At one point, the franchisor demanded the surrender of diaries containing details of current customers, while setting up his own businesses that competed directly with his franchisees. The franchisor demanded unreasonable conditions, such as refusing to consider meetings unless the request was received by mail, and refusing joint meetings, when the franchisees tried to discuss their concerns with him.

The court declared that the conduct of the franchisor was unconscionable, in breach of the act and that the managing director of the franchise was involved in the contraventions. The conduct of this franchisor beggared belief and the franchisees in this case had no way forward in running their businesses.

The unconscionable conduct provisions seek to protect parties from unfair dealing such as this, particularly where one of the parties is especially vulnerable. Businesses should not take unfair advantage of a person in a vulnerable position by entering into commercial arrangements without ensuring that the person has full knowledge of its terms and effects.

The cases that the ACCC has pursued with regard to unconscionable conduct all have an unscrupulous factor. It is more than tough negotiating. For a matter to be regarded as unconscionable by the courts, a business must have crossed the line and engaged in conduct that is not tolerated in a normal commercial relationship.

It is important to reiterate that the law does not exist to inhibit businesses from advancing their own legitimate commercial interests. The law will not apply to situations where a business has merely driven a hard bargain, nor does it require one business to put the interests of another party ahead of its own.

However, the ACCC has long recognised that when it comes to negotiating with big business the playing field is far from level for small business in some contexts.

Collective bargaining

This leads me to the area where significant changes have been made to assist small business—that of collective bargaining. Normally, where groups of competing businesses come together to collectively negotiate terms and conditions and, in particular, prices, this is likely to raise concerns under the *Trade Practices Act*.

The ACCC and the Act, however, explicitly acknowledge that it is sometimes fairer to enable a relative mismatch in bargaining power to be evened up by enabling small business to come together to bargain collectively. This is legitimised under the authorisation process.

Through authorisation, the ACCC has the power to authorise protection from court action for otherwise anti-competitive conduct where those proposing to engage in that conduct can demonstrate that there is a net public benefit.

In 2007, changes were made to the process for small business seeking collective bargaining authorisations. These changes were designed to make it easier for businesses to access these authorisations through a new notification process.

While having many of the same characteristics as authorisation, the notification process provides automatic immunity within 28 days from the date of notification unless the ACCC is satisfied that the proposed collective bargaining arrangements are not in the public interest. A notification also provides a three-year immunity period from the date the notification is lodged. Another benefit of this process is the low cost in submitting an application, which is currently $1000.

While we have encouraged, indeed exhorted, small business operators to contemplate collective bargaining, and to contact the ACCC for guidance and assistance on this matter, it is a constant source of frustration to us at the ACCC that many small businesses which might benefit significantly from a collective bargaining arrangement have shown a reluctance to proceed down that path.

National consumer law

Thus far I have focused my comments on the protections afforded by the *Trade Practices Act* for small business. But, as has been emphasised by successive reviews of the act, its primary intent is to enhance the welfare of all Australian consumers.

So while the small business sector will concentrate on its status under the act, 21 million consumers will be keenly observing what can best be described as a revolution that will bring Australia's consumer laws into the twenty-first century. I am talking about the adoption of a national consumer law, from which all Australians will benefit.

Agreed to by the Ministerial Council on Consumer Affairs in August 2007, the new national consumer law will operate in all states and territories.

This will provide consistency and certainty as consumers will no longer have to consider whether federal or state law is relevant to their issue. It will also mean if consumers move interstate, they will be covered by the same law, which will no doubt boost confidence in the national consumer law system.

Compliance costs should also reduce substantially for business as the national consumer law will replace consumer laws across nine jurisdictions. In fact, the Productivity Commission estimated a national consumer law could save consumers and businesses up to $4.5 billion each year. It is pleasing that the national consumer law will be based on the consumer protection provisions of the *Trade Practices Act* as well as incorporating amendments reflecting best practice in state and territory legislation.

There will also be a provision dealing with unfair contract terms. The Commonwealth will be the lead legislator, through an application legislation scheme, and enforcement of the national consumer law will be shared jointly with the ACCC and state and territory fair trading offices. This is an important achievement in harmonisation, which is very clearly in the public interest. We eagerly await formalisation of the national consumer law in an intergovernmental agreement, and anticipate that the national consumer law will be fully implemented by 2011.

Summary

As I have described, it is not the role of competition policy, the *Trade Practices Act* or the ACCC to favour one sector over another. Our role is to promote the welfare of Australian consumers through a fair and competitive marketplace; we're not here to protect competitors, we protect competition.

The benchmark test for competition regulators is whether a course of conduct is likely to lead to a substantial lessening of competition in a specific market for goods or services.

One of the difficulties is that there is not a wide understanding of the difference between protecting competitors and promotion of competition.

And while small business will seek the focus of competition policy to tend towards greater protection of competitors, ostensibly in the interests of competition, the voice of the consumer will be constant in urging that the focus remain on the promotion of competition for the benefit of consumers.

The interests of consumers rest with consumer groups, governments and regulators such as the ACCC to ensure that competition is muscular and lawful, even if this implies that it be aggressive and potentially damaging to some players in the market. For this is the way consumers derive the advantages of choice, quality and price to which they are entitled and we ensure that our economy is best able to adapt to maximise productivity and growth, especially in challenging economic times.

The commission cannot interpret its responsibility to promote competition to mean the protection of individual companies and the outlawing of vigorous, legitimate competition—even where that competition causes difficulties for individual firms.

As I stated earlier, an open competitive economy is the best environment within which small business can flourish.

Vigorous competition is not market failure and it is not the job of the ACCC to preserve competitors or protect any sectors of the economy from competition.

The role of the ACCC and the *Trade Practices Act* is fundamentally to enhance the interests of Australian consumers by promoting fair, vigorous and lawful competition, whether it is between businesses big, medium and/or small.

ENDNOTES

[1] This essay was originally presented as an ANZSOG Public Lecture on 26 May 2008.

9. Constitutional litigation and the Commonwealth[1]

David Bennett AC QC

As a rule, Australians tend to be ignorant, perhaps blissfully so, of the existence, terms and effect of the *Constitution of the Commonwealth of Australia*. A 1987 survey indicated that only about half of the population was aware that Australian had a written constitution.[2] A 1994 survey of people aged fifteen years or over indicated that only 13 per cent felt that they knew something about what the constitution covered and only 18 per cent actually showed some degree of understanding of what the constitution covered.[3]

Of course, participants in, and keen observers of, Australian politics would be well aware of the potential impacts of the courts' decisions in constitutional cases. An obvious example of a case that has attracted considerable attention in this community is the High Court's decision in the Work Choices case. This decision has stimulated vigorous debate on the future of the federal arrangement provided for by the constitution. However, the manner by which the disputes that give rise to these decisions are conducted in the courts is, perhaps, not well understood by many politicians and political scientists, let alone lawyers. Potentially, the topic is both very broad and very technical. However, I will confine myself to outlining the manner by which the Commonwealth participates in, and thus influences the outcome of, constitutional cases before the courts. When I refer to 'the Commonwealth' I refer, in a general sense, to the Australian Government. Specifically, my essay will address the following questions:

- How do constitutional cases come before the courts?
- How does the Commonwealth become aware of constitutional cases?
- By what power is the Commonwealth able to participate in constitutional cases?
- How does the Commonwealth participate in constitutional cases?
- What are the advantages of the way the Commonwealth participates in constitutional cases?

How do constitutional cases come before the courts?

A court does not express its view on a question of law unless it has jurisdiction in relation to a dispute between parties. And, by the word 'dispute', I do not mean a dispute merely concerning what the law is—for example, a dispute over what is the proper interpretation of a particular provision of the constitution. Generally speaking, for a federal court to have jurisdiction in relation to a dispute between parties relating to a constitutional issue it is necessary, at least, that there be a 'matter'—that is, 'some immediate right, duty or liability to be established by the determination of the Court'.[4] Thus, a constitutional dispute must be real, not merely hypothetical or academic, before the courts will consider it.

As some provisions in the constitution tend to be more productive of disputes about the existence of relevant rights, duties or liabilities than others, the courts have had the opportunity to consider and express their views on some provisions in the constitution more than others. It is important to note that constitutional litigation does not always, or even generally, arise between polities—that is, the Commonwealth, the states and territories—or their officers, and so on. Constitutional litigation may arise as a result of a disputed right, duty or liability affecting only natural persons or corporations. There are many examples of such cases. One example is *Smith vs ANL Ltd* ([2000] 204 CLR 493), which concerned an employee who argued that he was entitled to assert his common law right to sue his employer for damages for personal injury sustained during his employment, despite the existence of a Commonwealth act that appeared to bar him from doing so. The employee argued that the act was invalid to the extent that it had the effect of acquiring the employee's existing right of action without providing just terms contrary to s.51(xxxi) of the constitution. The employer argued that the act did not infringe s.51(xxxi). The High Court agreed with the employee. The Commonwealth was not initially a party to the proceeding, as it was not involved in any way on the facts. However, the Attorney-General did intervene in the case in order to argue in support of the validity of the Commonwealth act. (I discuss what is meant by the concept of 'intervention' below.)

Another, more recent, example is *Australian Pipeline Ltd vs Alinta* ([2007] 159 FCR 301), which concerned a provision of the *Corporations Act 2001* that allowed the Takeovers Panel to make a declaration that 'unacceptable circumstances' existed in relation to the affairs of a company in relation to a proposed takeover bid. Having made a declaration of unacceptable circumstances, the panel could then make various orders in relation to the circumstances. Failure to comply with the orders was a criminal offence, and the panel could apply to the court to seek to enforce its orders. The dispute arose between companies involved in the proposed takeover. Again, the Commonwealth was not initially involved; however, the Attorney-General intervened in order to argue in support of the validity of the provision. The Full Court of the Federal Court held that the relevant provision was invalid, on the basis that it purported to confer judicial power on an administrative body. The judgment was then appealed to the High Court, which came to the opposite view.

How does the Commonwealth become aware of constitutional cases?

Obviously, where the Commonwealth is a party to a case that involves a dispute about the meaning or application of a provision of the constitution then it is aware of that fact. The more interesting question is how the Commonwealth becomes aware of constitutional cases to which it is not (originally) a party.

The effect of s.78B of the *Judiciary Act 1903* is that, whenever a proceeding in a federal or state court raises a constitutional question, the court hearing the matter cannot proceed unless it is satisfied that a notice of this fact has been provided to the attorneys-general of the Commonwealth, the states, the Northern Territory and the Australian Capital Territory. The purpose of the provision is to give the attorneys-general the opportunity to 'intervene' in the proceeding or to apply to the High Court to have the proceeding removed into the High Court under s.40(1) of the same act. Incidentally, s.78B contains a trap for young players seeking to comply with it. It requires the notices be given to the attorneys-general of 'the states'. The Act defines 'states' for this purpose as including the Australian Capital Territory and the Northern Territory.

By what power does the Commonwealth participate in constitutional cases?

Obviously, where the Commonwealth has initiated a proceeding that involves a constitutional issue, or where it is a defendant or respondent in such a proceeding, it is able to participate in the proceeding. Again, the more interesting question is: by what power does the Commonwealth participate in other constitutional cases?

Section 78A of the *Judiciary Act* confers on the Attorney-General of the Commonwealth the power to 'intervene' in a proceeding before a court if the proceeding raises a constitutional question. As an intervener, the Attorney-General is taken to be a party to the proceeding, with the effect that the Attorney-General is able to address arguments to the court in relation to that question, even though the Commonwealth's rights, duties and liabilities might not be directly affected by the outcome of the case. As an intervenor, the Attorney-General is also able to appeal from a judgment given in the proceeding.

There are a number of factors that can influence the Attorney-General's decision whether to intervene in a constitutional case, including:

- whether the matter involves an attack on the validity of a Commonwealth law (as was the case in *Smith vs ANL* and *Australian Pipeline Ltd vs Alinta*, the cases referred to above, where the Attorney-General intervened)

- whether the constitutional principles involved are well established by decisions of the High Court, or are the subject of a reserved judgment of the High Court
- the level of the court (that is, lower court or superior court, single judge or appellate court)
- whether there is likely to be an appeal from the judgment of the court
- whether a Commonwealth party is already involved in the matter
- whether the applicant is represented, and whether the applicant's constitutional argument is well conceived.

How does the Commonwealth participate in constitutional cases?

If the case is one to which the Commonwealth is not a party, the first step is for the Attorney-General to decide whether to intervene. Generally, s.78B notices are received in the Attorney-General's office, which forwards the notice to the Constitutional Litigation Unit of the Australian Government Solicitor (AGS). AGS is a law firm owned by the Commonwealth. Pursuant to the *Legal Services Directions 2005* (which are made under the *Judiciary Act*), generally speaking, and subject to my role as the Solicitor-General, constitutional work can be performed only by AGS and the Attorney-General's Department.

AGS forms a view on whether the Attorney-General should intervene. In doing so, AGS consults with the Solicitor-General, the Constitutional Policy Unit of the Attorney-General's Department and any other area of the department or other department that has a policy interest in the subject matter of the notice (for example, if the constitutional issue is the validity of a Commonwealth law, AGS consults with the department that administers that law). If AGS and the Solicitor-General agree that there should be no intervention, the Attorney-General is not further consulted and there is no intervention.

If the Attorney-General approves intervention, generally, AGS acts for the Attorney-General in the conduct of the matter, but briefs counsel to appear for the Attorney-General at the hearing. Generally, AGS will brief one senior and one junior barrister. The pool of talent from which counsel are selected includes the Solicitor-General, senior constitutional lawyers employed by AGS (for example, AGS's Chief General Counsel, Henry Burmester) and private barristers with expertise in constitutional law. Generally, where the matter is of significant importance to the Commonwealth, or where the matter is particularly complex, AGS will brief the Solicitor-General to appear, along with a junior barrister. The Attorney-General has issued guidelines on briefing the Solicitor-General.

What are the advantages of the way the Commonwealth participates in constitutional cases?

In my view, the way that the Commonwealth handles constitutional litigation allows it to present its arguments to the court in a way that ideally combines the experience and expertise of the public sector as well as private practice.

AGS and the Attorney-General's Department employ outstanding constitutional lawyers, many of whom have careers advising, and acting for, the Commonwealth in relation to constitutional matters. This deep well of experience and expertise is obviously invaluable to the Commonwealth in the conduct of its cases. AGS and Attorney-General's Department lawyers and advisers generally have strong relationships with, and the trust of, the government. These lawyers have finely honed skills in constitutional law and policy, as well as long memories of cases won and lost in the past and a good sense of some of the reasons why.

However, by also involving private counsel, the Commonwealth is able to draw on the particular skills and attributes of the private bar.

Whereas the public sector brings the advantages of specialist expertise in public law, private barristers bring specialist expertise in advocacy. Advocacy is as much a specialisation as constitutional law; a person who does something all the time will tend to do it better than someone who does it only occasionally.

Second, private barristers offer the attribute of independence. As sole practitioners bound by the cab-rank rule to act for all who come to them regardless of their personal views, private barristers tend to practice on both sides of the record. That is, leading private barristers in Australia with expertise in constitutional law will have acted for the Commonwealth and its emanations, the states and territories and their respective emanations, corporations, citizens and others over the course of their careers at the bar. They will have argued for and against the validity of Commonwealth legislation. A barrister who represents all sides over time is better able to advise his or her client at any particular time; he or she tends to have a broader view of the law than a solicitor who acts only for or against the Commonwealth.

Third, by retaining private barristers to appear for it, the Commonwealth enhances its capacity sensibly to cooperate with opponents in the conduct and, occasionally, settlement of cases. Almost universally, private barristers with expertise in constitutional law trust one another. These barristers represent a small pool of lawyers who regularly appear with, and against, each other. These circumstances facilitate a highly respectful and cordial professional culture that is amenable to the smooth conduct of litigation.

In many respects, the Solicitor-General (who, incidentally, is neither a solicitor nor a general!) tends to have a combination of these various skills and attributes. The Solicitor-General is a statutory office-holder, appointed by the

Governor-General for a term (see the *Law Officers Act 1964*). The functions of the Solicitor-General are: a) to act as counsel for the Commonwealth and its emanations, and so on; b) to advise the Attorney-General on questions of law referred to him by the Attorney-General; and c) to carry out such other functions ordinarily performed by counsel as the Attorney-General requests. As a matter of practice, the dominant function of the Solicitor-General has been to appear on behalf of the Commonwealth in important constitutional cases.

Thus, like AGS and Attorney-General's Department lawyers, the Solicitor-General tends to possess the skills that arise from appearing in the area of constitutional law over time. However, the Solicitor-General has generally been selected from the pool of private barristers with expertise in constitutional law. Thus, the Solicitor-General also tends to bring with him (so far, the eight solicitors-general since Federation have all been male) the skills developed over a long career as a specialist advocate at the bar, representing many interests over that career and forging many strong relationships with fellow barristers. Finally, there is an advantage in the Solicitor-General appearing in almost all the major constitutional cases because of the importance of the Commonwealth not putting submissions in one case that are inconsistent with its submissions in another and the desirability of not giving an answer to a question from the Bench in one case that might be used against the Commonwealth in another. This is not a problem when one appears for a private litigant.

Conclusion

I have attempted to demonstrate that the ways in which the Commonwealth conducts constitutional litigation enable it to combine the best aspects of constitutional legal experience in the public sector with the specialist skills and knowledge of the private bar. Hopefully, from this mix of expertise, we are better able to advance the public interest.

ENDNOTES

[1] This essay was originally presented as an ANZSOG Public Lecture on 16 July 2008.

[2] *Final Report of the Constitutional Commission. Volume One*, 1988, p. 43.

[3] ANOP Research Services Pty Ltd (1994), referred to in Patapan, Haig 1994, 'The forgotten founding: civics education, the common law and liberal constitutionalism in Australia', *Griffith Law Review*, vol. 14, no. 1, p. 91.

[4] The Advisory Opinions case (1921) 29 CLR 257.

10. Evidence-based policy making: what is it and how do we get it?[1]

Gary Banks AO

In an address sponsored by the Australia and New Zealand School of Government, I thought a couple of quotes about government itself might be a good place to start. P. J. O'Rourke, who is scheduled to speak in Australia in April 2009, once said, 'the mystery of Government is not how it works, but how to make it stop'. In an earlier century, Otto von Bismarck is famously reported to have said, 'Laws are like sausages: it's better not to see them being made.'

Those witty observations have become enduring aphorisms for a reason. They reflect a rather cynical and widespread view of long standing about the operations of government. Also, let's face it, within government itself, many of us today find ourselves laughing knowingly at the antics of *The Hollowmen*, just as we did with *Yes, Minister*; and perhaps also cringing in recognition at how a carefully crafted policy proposal can be so easily subverted, or a dubious policy can triumph with little real evidence or analysis to commend it.

The idea for *The Hollowmen* was apparently conceived, and the first few episodes developed, under the previous government. That said, a change of government did not seem to reduce the program's appeal, or its ratings. No doubt that is because it contains some universal realities of political life—notwithstanding which party happens to be in power. And, indeed, notwithstanding the greater emphasis placed by the current government on evidence-based policy making, as reflected in a variety of reviews and in new processes and structures within the Commonwealth and COAG.

Thus, we have seen considerable public debate about the basis for a range of recent policy initiatives. These include: the 'alco-pops' tax, the change in the threshold for the private insurance surcharge, the linkage of Indigenous welfare payments to school attendance, Fuel Watch, Grocery Watch and the Green Car Innovation Fund. There was similar public debate under the previous government about the basis for such initiatives as the Alice-to-Darwin rail link, the Australia–US Free Trade Agreement, the Baby Bonus, the banning of filament light bulbs, Work Choices and the National Water Initiative, among others.

Moreover, where public reviews inform such initiatives, they have themselves been subjected to considerable criticism—in relation to their make-up, their processes and the quality of their analysis. This too is obviously not a new phenomenon, but it illustrates the challenges of properly implementing an evidence-based approach to public policy—and of being seen to have done so, which can be crucial to community acceptance of consequent policy decisions.

Advancing further reforms will be challenging

It is as important that we have a rigorous, evidence-based approach to public policy in Australia today as at any time in our history. Australia faces major long-term challenges—challenges that have only been exacerbated by the economic turbulence that we are struggling to deal with right now. When the present crisis is over, we will still have the ongoing challenges of greenhouse, the ageing of our population and continuing international competitive pressures. We should not underestimate the significance of these challenges, which place a premium on enhancing the efficiency and productivity of our economy.

The good news is that there is plenty of scope for improvement. COAG's National Reform Agenda embraces much of what is needed—not just the completion of the old competition agenda, but getting further into good regulatory design and the reduction of red tape, efficient infrastructure provision and the human capital issues that will be so important to this country's innovation and productivity performance over time. The Productivity Commission's modelling of the National Reform Agenda indicates that the gains from this 'third wave' of reform could potentially be greater than from the first and second waves.[2] The problem is that there are few 'easy' reforms left. The earlier period had a lot of low-hanging fruit that has now been largely harvested.

Even in the competition area, rather than further deregulation, we are confronting the need for regulatory refinements that are quite subtle and complex to assess. In the new agenda to do with enhancing human capital, complexities abound. We don't know all the answers to the policy drivers of better health and educational outcomes, for example, let alone to the pressing goal of reducing Indigenous disadvantage.[3]

These are all long-term issues. They also have an inter-jurisdictional dimension, bringing with them the challenge of finding national solutions to problems that have been dealt with by individual states and territories in the past. This has 'upped the ante' on having good analysis and good processes to help avoid making mistakes on a national scale, which previously would have been confined to particular jurisdictions.

In an address to senior public servants in April last year, the Prime Minister observed that 'evidence-based policy making is at the heart of being a reformist government'.[4] I want to explore why that is profoundly true, what it means in practice and some implications for those of us in public administration. In doing so, I will draw on the experience of the Productivity Commission—which, with its predecessors, has been at the heart of evidence-based policy making in

Australia for over three decades[5] —to distil some insights into what is needed across government generally if we are to be successful.

Why we need an evidence-based approach

I don't think I have to convince anyone of the value of an evidence-based approach to public policy. After all, it is not a novel concept. (I read somewhere that it is traceable to the fourteenth century, motivated by a desire to discipline the whimsical rule of despots.) Its absence in practice, however, has been long lamented. Over a century ago, for example, Florence Nightingale admonished the English Parliament in the following terms: 'You change your laws so fast and without inquiring after results past or present that it is all experiment, seesaw, doctrinaire; a shuttlecock between battledores.'[6]

The term 'evidence-based policy making' has been most recently popularised by the Blair Government, which was elected on a platform of 'what matters is what works'. Blair spoke of ending ideologically based decision making and 'questioning inherited ways of doing things'.[7]

Of course, 'inherited ways of doing things' meant to the Blair Government the ways of the previous Thatcher administration! The advent of a new government is clearly a good time to initiate an evidence-based approach to public policy, especially after a decade or more of a previous one's rule. I think that resonates too with the take-up in Australia of these 'New Labour' ideas from the United Kingdom, commencing with the Bracks Government in Victoria.

But, again, evidence-based policy making is by no means new to this country. Probably the oldest example, or the longest-standing one, would be tariff making, which for many years was required under legislation to be informed by a public report produced by the Tariff Board and its successor organisations (notably the Industries Assistance Commission). The nature of those evidence-based reports changed dramatically over time, however, from merely reporting the impacts on industries under review to also reporting the effects on other industries and the wider economy.

Other key economic policy reforms that have drawn heavily on evidence-based reviews/evaluations include the exchange rate and financial market liberalisation of the 1980s, the National Competition Policy reforms of the 1990s and the shift to inflation targeting in monetary policy in 1993. Examples from the social policy arena include the Higher Education Contribution Scheme (HECS) in its initial configuration and the introduction of 'Lifetime Community Rating' provisions in private health insurance regulation.

The tariff story illustrates the crucial point that the contribution of an evidence-based approach depends on its context and the objectives to which it is directed. Evidence that is directed at supporting narrow objectives—a particular group or sector, or fostering use of a particular product or technology—will generally look quite different to that which has as its objective the best interests of the general community. Of course, this depends on having the analytical tools to enable such a broad assessment to be undertaken. Developments in this area were also an important part of the story on tariffs, as well as in other policy areas.

While the systematic evaluation and review of policy have not been pervasive—and arguably have been less evident in the social and environmental domains than the economic—Australia's experience illustrates its potential contribution. It also reveals the sterility of academic debates about whether evidence can or should play a 'deterministic' role in policy outcomes. It will be clear to all at this gathering in Canberra that policy decisions will typically be influenced by much more than objective evidence or rational analysis. Values, interests, personalities, timing, circumstance and happenstance—in short, democracy—determine what actually happens.

But evidence and analysis can nevertheless play a useful, even decisive, role in informing policy makers' judgments. Importantly, they can also condition the political environment in which those judgments need to be made.

Most policies are experiments

Without evidence, policy makers must fall back on intuition, ideology or conventional wisdom—or, at best, theory alone. And many policy decisions have indeed been made in these ways. But the resulting policies can go seriously astray, given the complexities and interdependencies in our society and economy and the unpredictability of people's reactions to change.

From the many examples that I could give, a few from recent Productivity Commission reviews come readily to mind:

- in our research for COAG on the economic implications of Australia's ageing population,[8] we demonstrated that common policy prescriptions to increase immigration, or raise the birth rate, would have little impact on the demographic profile or its fiscal consequences (indeed, higher fertility would initially exacerbate fiscal pressures)
- our report into road and rail infrastructure pricing[9] showed that the presumption that road use was systematically subsidised relative to rail was not borne out by the facts (facts that were quite difficult to discern)
- in our inquiry into waste management policy,[10] we found that the objective of zero solid waste was not only economically costly, but environmentally unsound
- our inquiry into state assistance to industry showed that the bidding wars for investment and major events the state governments engaged in generally constituted not only a negative sum game nationally, but in many cases a zero sum game for the winning state[11]

- our recent study of Australian's innovation system[12] reaffirmed that, contrary to conventional opinion, the general tax concession for research and development acted mainly as a 'reward' for research that firms would have performed anyway, rather than prompting much additional research and development
- our recent draft report on parental leave[13] indicated that binary views in relation to whether child care was a good or a bad thing were both wrong, depending on which age group you were looking at, and that there were many subtle influences involved.

To take a separate example from the education field—which is rightly at centre stage in COAG's National Reform Agenda—the long-term policy goal of reducing class sizes has received very little empirical support. In contrast, the importance of individual teacher performance and the link to differentiated pecuniary incentives are backed by strong evidence, but have been much neglected. (That illustrates not only a lack of evidence-based policy in education, where social scientists appear to have had little involvement, but the influence over the years of teachers' unions and other interests.)

Among other things, policies that haven't been informed by good evidence and analysis fall more easily prey to the 'law of unintended consequences'—in popular parlance, Murphy's Law—which can lead to costly mistakes. For example, the commission found, in a series of reviews, that the well-intentioned regulatory frameworks devised to protect native flora and fauna, and to conserve historic buildings, were actually undermining conservation goals by creating perverse incentives for those responsible.

Our report for COAG, *Overcoming Indigenous Disadvantage*,[14] is littered with examples. One of the first field trips that I did as part of establishing that process was to Alice Springs, where I learnt of one instance of an unintended consequence that would be amusing if the issues weren't so serious. It involved children taking up petrol sniffing so that they could qualify for the various benefits and give-aways in a program designed to eradicate it. That this might happen no doubt would not have occurred to any of us in Canberra, but it could well have occurred to some of the elders in the community if they had been asked.

But, as Noel Pearson and other Indigenous leaders affirmed, perhaps the most calamitous and tragic example of all was the extension of 'equal wages' to Aboriginal stockmen in the late 1960s. Despite warnings by some at the time, this apparently well-motivated action led to the majority losing their jobs, driving them and their extended families into the townships—ultimately subjecting them to the ravages of passive welfare, with liberalised access to alcohol as the final blow. Good intentions, bad consequences; very, very difficult to remedy.

Now I am not saying that policy should never proceed without rigorous evidence. Often you can't get sufficiently good evidence, particularly when decisions must be made quickly. And you can never have certainty in public policy. All policy effectively is experimentation. But that does not mean flying blind; we still need a good rationale or a good theory. Rationales and theories themselves can be subjected to scrutiny and debate, and in a sense that constitutes a form of evidence that can give some assurance about the likely outcomes. Importantly though, all policy experiments need to be monitored and evaluated and, over time, corrected or terminated if they turn out to be failures. These are things that governments typically find hard to do—particularly the termination part.

Arguably the biggest-ever case of policy making under uncertainty is the contemporary challenge posed by global warming. With huge residual uncertainties in the science, economics and (international) politics, there can be little confidence that anyone can identify a uniquely 'correct' policy prescription for Australia at this point. The only sensible way forward, therefore, is to start gradually, to monitor, to learn by doing as we develop institutions and see the effects of carbon pricing on our economy and community, and as we wait for others to come to the party—in other words, an adaptive response. That appears to be broadly the strategy that the government has ultimately adopted in its recent white paper.[15] That said, the success of such a strategy still depends on judgments about the most appropriate timing and extent of action by Australia, and indeed the particular form of the policy action itself—notably, the mechanism for pricing carbon, its coverage and compensation provisions. These remain subject to ongoing debate.

Conditioning the political environment

Complexity and uncertainty would make policy choices hard enough even if they could be made purely on technical grounds. But policies are not made in a vacuum. Rather, they typically emerge from a maelstrom of political energy, vested interests and lobbying. Commonly, those with special interests will try to align their demands with the public interest. The average person (voter) rationally doesn't do the hard work necessary to find out whether that is correct or not, but often feels intuitively supportive.

In that *realpolitik*, evidence and analysis that are robust and publicly available can serve as an important counterweight to the influence of sectional interests, enabling the wider community to be better informed about what is at stake in interest groups' proposals, and enfranchising those who would bear the costs of implementing them. Tariff reform again provides a classic instance of evidence being used to galvanise potential beneficiaries from reform in the policy debate. In Australia, the losers under the tariff regime were the primary exporting industries—the farmers and the miners—who started to appreciate, with help from the Industries Assistance Commission, the extent of the implicit taxes and costs they were bearing; and they soon became a potent force for tariff reform. The National Competition Policy has seen a similar political role being discharged through evidentiary processes.

To take a quite different example, the gambling industry got a lot of political support for deregulation essentially based on a myth—namely, that it would generate many jobs but have only minor adverse social impacts. The commission's report showed the reverse to be true.[16] Gambling did not (and could not) generate significant additional jobs in the long term and had very substantial social impacts. Establishing that gave community groups a stronger platform to push for reforms to gambling regulation and the development and funding of harm-minimisation measures.

My point is that good evidence can ameliorate or 'neutralise' political obstacles, thereby making reforms more feasible. That is part of the reason why, as the Prime Minister has said, a reformist government needs to have an evidence-based approach at centre stage.

The essential ingredients

For evidence to discharge these various functions, however, it needs to be the right evidence; it needs to occur at the right time and be seen by the right people. That might sound obvious, but it is actually very demanding. I want to talk briefly now about some essential ingredients in achieving it.

Methodology matters

First, methodology. It's important that, whatever analytical approach is chosen, it allows for a proper consideration of the nature of the issue or problem, and of different options for policy action. Half the battle is understanding the problem. Failure to do this properly is one of the most common causes of policy failure and poor regulation. Sometimes this is an understandable consequence of complex forces, but sometimes it seems to have more to do with a wish for government to take action regardless.

A contemporary example that has received a bit of airplay as a consequence of the commission's report on waste management is the move to ban the ubiquitous plastic shopping bags from our supermarkets. This initiative drew much support from the alleged problems that these bags posed for the litter stream and for marine health. But closer investigation by the commission soon exposed gross inaccuracies and overstatements in those claims. Indeed, some of what passed for 'evidence' was contrary to commonsense and some was outright hilarious. (A Regulation Impact Statement soberly cited media reports from India that a dead cow on the streets of New Delhi had 35 000 plastic bags in its digestive system!)[17]

In situations where government action seems warranted, a single option, no matter how carefully analysed, rarely provides sufficient evidence for a well-informed policy decision. The reality, however, is that much public policy and regulation are made in just that way, with evidence confined to supporting one, already preferred way forward. Hence the subversive expression 'policy-based evidence'!

Even when the broad policy approach is clear, the particular instruments adopted can make a significant difference. Thus, for example, economists overwhelmingly accept the superiority of a market-based approach to reducing carbon emissions, but they differ as to whether a cap-and-trade mechanism or an explicit tax (or some combination of the two) would yield the best outcomes. Australia's apparent haste to embrace the trading option remains contentious among some prominent economists, illustrated by recent public advocacy by Geoff Carmody[18] (in support of a consumption-based tax) and Warwick McKibbin[19] (in support of a 'hybrid' scheme, with trading and taxation components).

How one measures the impacts of different policies depends on the topic and the task—and whether it's an ex-ante or ex-post assessment. There is a range of methodologies available. There is also active debate about their relative merits. Nevertheless, all good methodologies have a number of features in common:

- they test a theory or proposition as to why policy action will be effective—ultimately promoting community wellbeing—with the theory also revealing what impacts of the policy should be observed if it is to succeed
- they have a serious treatment of the 'counterfactual'—namely, what will happen in the absence of any action
- they involve, wherever possible, quantification of impacts (including estimates of how effects vary for different policy 'doses' and for different groups)
- they look at direct and indirect effects (often it's the indirect effects that can be most important)
- they set out the uncertainties and control for other influences that might impact on observed outcomes
- they are designed to avoid errors that could occur through self-selection or other sources of bias
- they provide for sensitivity tests
- importantly, they have the ability to be tested and, ideally, replicated by third parties.

Australia has been at the forefront internationally in the development and use of some methodologies. For example, we have led the world in 'general equilibrium' modelling of the 'direct and indirect effects' of policy changes throughout the economy. Indeed, the Industries Assistance Commission, with its 'Impact Project' under Professors Powell and Dixon, essentially got that going.

But Australia has done relatively little in some other important areas, such as 'randomised trials', which can be particularly instructive in developing good social policy.[20] We seem to see a lot more (proportionately) of this research being done in the United States, for example.

Most evidence-based methodologies fit broadly within a cost–benefit (or at least cost-effectiveness) framework, designed to determine an estimated (net) pay-off to society. It is a robust framework that provides for explicit recognition of costs and benefits and requires the policy maker to consider the full range of potential impacts. But it hasn't been all that commonly or well used, even in relatively straightforward tasks such as infrastructure project evaluation.

The head of Infrastructure Australia's secretariat recently commented in the following terms about many of the infrastructure proposals submitted to that body: 'the linkage to goals and problems is weak, the evidence is weak, the quantification of costs and benefits is generally weak.'[21]

It is very welcome, therefore, that Infrastructure Australia has stressed that any project that it recommends for public funding must satisfy rigorous cost–benefit tests.[22] It is particularly important, as Minister Anthony Albanese himself has affirmed, that this includes quantification of the more 'subjective' social or environmental impacts, or, where this proves impossible, that there is an explicit treatment of the nature of those impacts and the values imputed to them.[23] In the past, this has proven to be the Achilles heel of cost-benefit analyses for major public investments: financial costs are typically underestimated, non-financial benefits are overstated.

Rubbery computations of this kind seem to be endemic to railway investment proposals, particularly 'greenfield' ones, which rarely pass muster on the economics alone. It is disquieting to observe, therefore, that rail projects feature heavily among the initial listing by Infrastructure Australia of projects warranting further assessment, totalling well over $100 billion. Among these we find such old chestnuts as a light rail system for the Australian Capital Territory and a very fast train linking Canberra with Sydney and Melbourne. (The rail proposals are not alone in evoking past follies, however. I note that expansion of the Ord River Scheme is also on the list.)[24]

It is undoubtedly challenging to monetise some of the likely costs and benefits associated with certain areas of public policy. But often we don't try hard enough. There are nevertheless some examples of creative attempts. These include work by the Productivity Commission in areas such as gambling, consumer protection policy and even animal welfare.

The key is to be able to better assess whether benefits are likely to exceed costs, within a coherent analytical framework, even if everything cannot be reduced to a single number, or some elements cannot be quantified. Thus, in our gambling and consumer policy reports, for example, we could provide estimates only of net benefits within plausible ranges. In the analysis required under the National Competition Policy of the ACT Government's proposal to ban trade in eggs from battery hens, we quantified the likely economic costs and identified the potential impacts on the birds.[25] However, we drew short of valuing these, as such valuations depend on ethical considerations and community norms that are best made by accountable political representatives.

Good data are a prerequisite

A second essential ingredient, of course, is data. Australia has been very well served by the Australian Bureau of Statistics and the integrity of the national databases that it has generated. But in some areas we are struggling. Apart from the challenges of valuing impacts, and disentangling the effects of simultaneous influences, we often face more basic data deficiencies. These are typically in social and environmental rather than economic domains, where we must rely on administrative collections—or indeed there might be no collections at all.

Data problems bedevil the National Reform Agenda in the human capital area. Preventative health strategies and pathways of causal factors are one example. Indigenous policy provides another striking one, involving myriad problems to do with identification, the incidence of different health or other conditions and their distribution across different parts of the country—all of which are very important for public policy formation. In the crucial education area, obtaining performance data has been an epic struggle, on which I will comment further. In the COAG priority area of early childhood development, a recent survey article from the Australian Institute of Family Studies concludes: 'The dearth of evaluation data on interventions generally…makes it impossible to comment on the usefulness of early childhood interventions as a general strategy to sustain improvements for children in the long-term.'[26]

Data deficiencies inhibit evidence-based analysis for obvious reasons. They can also lead to reliance on 'quick and dirty' surveys or the use of focus groups, as lampooned in *The Hollowmen*. A colleague has observed that a particular state government in which he had worked was a frequent user of focus groups. They have a purpose, but I think it is a more superficial one, better directed at informing marketing than analysing potential policy impacts.

The other risk is that overseas studies will be resorted to inappropriately as a substitute for domestic studies. Sometimes this is akin to the old joke about the fellow who loses his keys in a dark street, but is found searching for them metres away under a lamppost, because that is where there is more light. Translating foreign studies to Australia can sometimes be perilous, given different circumstances and the scope for misinterpretation.

One topical example is the celebrated work by James Heckman[27] in the United States demonstrating the benefits of preschool education based on the Perry Program. That work has become a policy touchstone for advocates of universal intensive preschool education in Australia. While that policy could well prove to be sound, Heckman's work does not provide the necessary evidence. As he himself clearly acknowledged, the Perry Project was confined to disadvantaged children. And the main gain from the intensive preschool treatment that those kids got came from reduced crime. So if there is relevance for the Perry work in Australia, it might be mainly confined to areas where there is concentrated disadvantage.

A major failing of governments in Australia, and probably worldwide, has been in not generating the data needed to evaluate their own programs. In particular, there has been a lack of effort to develop the baseline data essential for before-and-after comparisons. As an aside, I should note that quite often even the objectives of a policy or program are not clear to the hapless reviewer. Indeed, one of the good things about having reviews is that they can force some clarification as to what the objectives of the policy should have been in the first place. Examples of policies with unclear objectives from the Productivity Commission's current work program include the Baby Bonus, drought assistance and the restrictions on the parallel importing of books.

In the commission's first gambling inquiry, we had to undertake a national survey to get a picture of the social impacts, as there were no good national data around. We recommended that, in future, consistent surveys should be undertaken periodically, but this has not happened; the field has become a bit of a shemozzle, and we seem to be confronting the same problems again in revisiting this topic 10 years on. Moreover, while in this time there has been a multitude of harm-minimisation measures introduced by different jurisdictions around the country, very few of these have been preceded by trials or pilots to assess their cost effectiveness or have been designed with the need for evaluation data in mind.

In the Indigenous field, even the much-anticipated COAG trials lacked baseline data. The only exception, as I recall, was the Wadeye trial, but those data were derived from a separate research exercise, which took place before the trials commenced. More generally, we don't even know how much money has been spent on Indigenous programs, let alone how effective those programs have been. (There is currently an initiative under way to remedy that, through a new reporting framework involving all jurisdictions, with secretariat support from the Productivity Commission.)

Overall, we are seeing funding for data collection actually being cut. This is partly a consequence of the so-called 'efficiency dividend' in the public sector and the blunt way it is imposed. A consequence is that in agencies that have responsibility for collecting data, vital survey information and other data collections are being jeopardised. This seems particularly perverse at a time when governments are seeking to promote evidence-based policy making!

In contrast, Australia has made great strides in assembling comparable performance data across jurisdictions through the Government Services Review.[28] (This is currently being reviewed by a COAG senior officials group.) Foreign government officials visiting Australia have often expressed astonishment at what we have achieved. And international agencies such as the OECD and the United Nations have praised the *Blue Book* and *Overcoming Indigenous Disadvantage* reports.

But Australia could and should have done a lot more to take advantage of its federal system as a natural proving ground for policy learning across jurisdictions. Indeed, in some cases, rather than encouraging data provision to enable comparisons across jurisdictions, the basis for such comparisons has actually been suppressed. I mentioned earlier a lack of data on school learning outcomes. Such data are better now than in the past, but it has been a real struggle. And the data we have managed to collect and publish are highly aggregated. It certainly hasn't got down to the level of individual schools and involves very weak tests that don't reveal much about comparative learning outcomes across the country. The OECD's PISA data have generally been more revealing as well as more timely—despite being collected internationally.

Andrew Leigh from The Australian National University has published an interesting paper with a colleague, analysing the impact of individual school performance on literacy and numeracy.[29] But his research had to be confined to Western Australia, which was the only jurisdiction that released school data. Even then, the data were only revealed implicitly in charts. Leigh was obliged to digitise the charts to get the numbers to allow him to do his novel analysis.

So I think there is an opportunity, under the new federalism banner, to fund the evidence base that we need to compare policy performances across our federation, and thereby to devise better national policies where national approaches are called for. An important recent initiative in this direction is the allocation of additional funding, as part of a $3.5 billion education package, for a new performance reporting framework for schools. The minister, Julia Gillard, in endorsing the new framework, stated, 'It is my strong view, that lack of transparency both hides failure and helps us ignore it...And lack of transparency prevents us from identifying where greater effort and investment are needed.'[30]

Real evidence is open to scrutiny

This leads directly to the third area that I want to talk about: transparency. Much policy analysis actually occurs behind closed doors. A political need for speed or defence against opportunistic adversaries is often behind that. But no evidence is immutable. If it hasn't been tested, or contested, we can't really call it 'evidence'. And it misses the opportunity to educate the community about what is at stake in a policy issue, and thereby for it to become more accepting of the policy initiative itself.

Transparency ideally means 'opening the books' in terms of data, assumptions and methodologies, such that the analysis can be replicated. The wider the impacts of a policy proposal, the wider the consultation should be—not just with experts, but with the people who are likely to be affected by the policy, whose reactions and feedback provide insights into the likely impacts and help avoid unintended consequences. Such feedback in itself constitutes a useful form of evidence. The commission's processes are essentially based on maximising feedback. I cannot dwell on this much here, other than to say that, in a range of areas, we've learned a great deal through our extensive public consultation processes, particularly in response to draft reports. If you compare the drafts with our final reports you will often see changes for the better—sometimes in our recommendations, sometimes in the arguments and evidence that we finally employ.

Transparency in policy making helps government too, because it can see how the community reacts to ideas before they are fully formed, enabling it to better anticipate the politics of pursuing different courses of action. So the signs of a greater reliance again on green papers by the Australian Government, as advocated by the Regulation Taskforce, are very welcome.[31] For example, the policy-development process for addressing global warming clearly benefited from an elevated public debate after the green paper was released.

Evidence building takes time

Transparency can have its downsides. In particular, it 'complicates' and slows the decision-making process; transparency involves time and effort. That is what appears to have militated against draft reports in a number of the recent policy review exercises. This was a shame, especially for the major industry policy reviews last year, which contained recommendations with important ramifications for the community and economy. There is an obvious clash between any government's acceptance of the need for good evidence and the political 'need for speed'. But the facts are that detailed research, involving data gathering and the testing of evidence, can't be done overnight. As already noted, in some cases, the necessary data will not be available 'off the shelf' and might require a special survey. In other cases, data needed for program evaluation might be revealed only through pilot studies or trials with the program itself.

On a number of occasions in the past decade I have been approached about the possibility of the commission undertaking an attractive policy task, but in an amount of time that I felt was unreasonable for it to be done well, particularly in view of the time people need to make submissions and give us feedback. When the commission does something, people rightly expect to be able to have a say. As a consequence, those tasks have more often than not ended up going to consultants. (And in most cases the results have vindicated my position.)

Good evidence requires good people

The fifth area of importance is capability and expertise. You can't have good evidence and you can't have good research without good people. People skilled in quantitative methods and other analysis are especially valuable. It is therefore ironic that we appear to have experienced a decline in the numbers with such skills within the Public Service at the very time when it has been called upon to provide an evidence-based approach that relies on them. Again, that's been largely a consequence of budgetary measures over a long period. Research tends to be seen as a more dispensable function when governments and bureaucracies are cut back.

Several manifestations of the consequential reduction in capability have struck me. One is the lower calibre of some of the departmental project teams that I have observed trying to do review and evaluation work. Second, there appears to be increased poaching of research staff within the public sector, or at least pleas for secondments.

We are also seeing major new initiatives to train staff. One significant example is the Treasury's sponsorship of a new program, to be run by Monash University, to teach economics to non-economists. (We have seen shrinkage of the recruitment pool of economics graduates in recent years and I wonder whether the study of economics might be turning into a niche discipline in our universities.)

We've also seen a major increase in the contracting of policy-related research outside the Public Service. A lot of those jobs have gone to business consultants rather than to academics. This contrasts with the experience in the United States, where the academic community seems to be utilised much more by government.

Contracting out is by no means a bad thing (some of my best friends are consultants!). It has been happening progressively for decades. But it does seem to be changing in character more recently. The focus seems to be broadening from provision of inputs to policy making to preparation of outputs—the whole package. This gained public prominence last year through media reports of the Boston Consulting Group working up an 'early childhood policy' and developing a business plan for the 'global institute' for carbon sequestration. Also, KPMG seems to have become active in the infrastructure policy area.

There are clear benefits to government from using professional consultants: new ideas, talented people, on-time delivery, attractive presentation and, possibly, cost—although some of the payments have been surprisingly large. But there are also some significant risks. Consultants often cut corners. Their reports can be superficial. And, more fundamentally, they are typically less accountable than public service advisers for the policy outcomes.

Whether academics could be drawn on more is a key issue. In an earlier era, the involvement of academics was instrumental in developing the evidentiary and analytical momentum for the first waves of microeconomic reform. Examples from the trade and competition policy arena alone include Max Corden, Richard Snape, Fred Gruen, Peter Lloyd, Bob Gregory, Ross Garnaut, Fred Hilmer, among others. Where are the new academic generation's equivalents in support of the 'third wave'? Only a few names come to mind, for example, of academics making a notable public contribution to policies bearing on human capital development.

Such involvement is of course a two-way street—with both demand and supply sides. The supply side seems to have been diminished over time, partly as promising academic researchers have sought more attractive remuneration elsewhere and partly as their time has been increasingly consumed by their 'day jobs'. On the demand side, one sometimes hears senior public servants complain that academics can be very hard 'to do business with' or that they are too slow or lack an appreciation of the 'real world'. There might be some validity in these perceptions, though I suspect that they also reflect an unrealistic view of how much time is needed to do good research—and perhaps a lack of planning. Perhaps also a desire for greater 'predictability' in the results than many academics would be willing to countenance. As Brian Head from Queensland University has observed: 'Relatively few research and consulting projects are commissioned without some expectation that the reports may assist in upholding a certain viewpoint.'[32] (As I recall it, Sir Humphrey Appleby's maxim—akin to Rumpole's first law of cross-examination—is that 'one should never commission a study without knowing what the answer will be'.)

Independence can be crucial

Evidence is never absolute, never 'revealed truth'. The choice of methodologies, data, assumptions, and so on can all influence the outcome, and they do. Anyone who did first-year statistics at university probably read Darryl Huff's book *How to Lie with Statistics*, which was an early indication of the potential and the problems. Given the unavoidable need for judgment in evaluation, evidence is more likely to be robust and seen to be so if it is not subjected to influence or barrow pushing by those involved. Good research is not just about skilled people, it is about whether they face incentives to deliver a robust product in the public interest.

Some years ago, following a talk that I gave at a gambling conference in Melbourne, an American academic came up to me and said that the Productivity Commission's report was being used extensively in public debate in the United States. I expressed surprise, given the extent of home-grown research there. She said, 'Yes, but we don't know what to believe.' That appears to be because research is polarised in that country between that sponsored by community and church groups and that sponsored by the industry. And there is suspicion that 'he who pays the piper calls the tune'.

Independence is even more important when dealing with technical research than with opinions. People are better able to judge opinions for themselves, but the average person is naturally mystified by technical research. They look for proxies to help them know whether the results of such research are believable. The status of the researcher (or whoever is paying for the research) is one such proxy. Economic modelling is replete with these sorts of issues. Any model comprises many assumptions and judgments, which can significantly influence the results. For example, the Productivity Commission and industry consultants used similar models recently to estimate the economic impacts of reducing tariffs on cars. The commission found that there would be significant economy-wide gains from maintaining scheduled tariff reductions. The other modellers, using different (and some less conventional) assumptions, projected net losses—with the current tariff rate coincidentally turning out to be 'optimal'.

You might also recall that in modelling the potential gains to Australia from a mooted free trade agreement with the United States, the Centre for International Economics, in work commissioned by the Department of Foreign Affairs and Trade, obtained a significant positive result, whereas separate work by ACIL Tasman projected negligible gains at best. More recently, modelling of the Mandatory Renewable Energy Target in conjunction with an emissions trading scheme either found it to impose substantial additional costs on the economy or to yield substantial benefits, depending on the modeller and the sponsor.[33] (COAG's final decision to implement a 20 per cent target nationally essentially favoured the latter estimates. However, Productivity Commission researchers found the sources of gains in that modelling difficult to justify.)[34]

A 'receptive' policymaking environment is fundamental

We come to the final and most important ingredient on my list. Even the best evidence is of little value if it's ignored or not available when it is needed. An evidence-based approach requires a policymaking process that is receptive to evidence, a process that begins with a question rather than an answer, and that has institutions to support such inquiry.

As has been found through the work of the Office of Regulation Review, and now the Office of Best Practice Regulation, often we see the reverse, especially for more significant proposals. The joke about 'policy-based evidence' has not been made in the abstract—we have long observed such an approach in operation through the lens of regulation making in Australia.

Ideally, we need systems that are open to evidence at each stage of the policy-development 'cycle': from the outset when an issue or problem is identified for policy attention to the development of the most appropriate response and subsequent evaluation of its effectiveness.

The ongoing struggle to achieve effective use of regulation assessment processes within governments, which I describe in more detail elsewhere,[35] tells us how challenging that can be to implement. These arrangements require that significant regulatory proposals undergo a sequence of analytical steps designed first to clarify the nature of the policy problem and why government action is called for, and then to assess the relative merits of different options to demonstrate that the proposed regulation is likely to yield the highest (net) benefits to the community.

These steps simply amount to what is widely accepted as 'good process'. That their documentation in a regulation impact statement has proven so difficult to achieve, at least to a satisfactory standard, is best explained by a reluctance or inability to follow good process in the first place. I admit that an evidence-based approach undoubtedly makes life harder for policy makers and for politicians. Lord Keynes, who seems to be well and truly back in vogue, said in the 1930s: 'There is nothing a Government hates more than to be well-informed; for it makes the process of arriving at decisions much more complicated and difficult.'[36]

I think we can see what he meant. But against this are the undoubted political benefits that come from avoiding policy failures or unintended 'collateral damage' that can rebound on a government, and from enhancing the credibility of reformist initiatives.

Some implications for the Public Service

I will conclude now with some observations about how those of us in the Public Service can help advance the cause of evidence-based policy making. We begin with the considerable advantage of explicit endorsement by the Prime Minister and senior ministers for an evidence-based approach to public policy. In his speech to the Senior Executive Service last year, Kevin Rudd[37] declared, 'we cannot afford a Public Service culture where all you do is tell the Government what it wants to hear'. We've also heard from the head of the Public Service, Terry Moran, that 'for civil servants, a capacity to analyse problems rationally and empirically and to advance options for action by Governments is a basic ethical duty'.[38]

What both are talking about, in old parlance, is 'frank and fearless' advice: robust advice that does not second-guess the politics or the politicians. So the first suggestion I have for advancing evidence-based policy making is for us to be frank and fearless. That doesn't mean being a loose cannon, or acting contrary to a government's broad objectives, but using the opportunity of such political support to strengthen the bureaucracy's capacity to provide evidence-based advice—and delivering that advice, even if it is against the current or not confined to a minister's or government's favoured position (which often aren't set in concrete anyway).

Making better use of existing processes

There exist currently vehicles and frameworks within government that can be used more effectively to this end. Indeed, the recently upgraded regulation assessment requirements are ready-made for that purpose. As noted, these are based on a best-practice 'policy cycle', with explicit provision for evidence to be utilised at each step. With the recent introduction of higher analytical hurdles, including greater quantification of benefits and costs, in conjunction with stronger sanctions for inadequate compliance, the line of least resistance for the bureaucracy should be moving in favour of an evidence-based approach. The extent to which this is happening remains unclear. Relatively high overall compliance rates under the new system, as recorded by the Office of Best Practice Regulation in its annual report,[39] appear promising; though, as in the past, the compliance record is worse for the more significant regulatory proposals.

In relation to spending programs, there is also likely to be scope to enhance some of the requirements, particularly to strengthen ex-ante evaluation and to make explicit provision for ex-post review. This might be assisted by the financial crisis. For example, Finance Minister, Lindsay Tanner, observed recently: 'Every government dollar wasted on a poor program is a dollar that a working person doesn't have to spend on groceries, health care and education. It is also a dollar that the Government does not have available to spend on its policy priorities.'[40]

A heightened sense of the trade-offs has become apparent, for example, in some of the advocacy for publicly funded paid parental leave, with questions being raised about the relative pay-off from expenditure on industry support programs. Integral to advancing an evidence-based approach are the processes and institutions within government that enable different perspectives and information to be brought to bear at the 'pointy end' of a policy decision. These are well described by Meredith Edwards in her book *Social Policy, Public Policy*.[41] Crucial elements are the proper functioning of interdepartmental committees, the cabinet submission process (with 'coordination comments' on policy proposals by all relevant agencies) and, ultimately, well-informed discussions within cabinet itself.

Effective COAG arrangements

At the COAG level, we have a new working group structure, which is well placed to advance an evidence-based approach to public policy, given sufficient space and lead time. That said, these arrangements in themselves represent an experiment. Their novel design, in which state department CEOs essentially report to Commonwealth ministers, faces obvious challenges. More problematic, in my view, are the time constraints imposed on COAG processes under the punishing dictates of the quarterly cycle of meetings. The seeming imperative for bureaucrats around the country to be constantly preparing for these meetings appears to be displacing some of the work that should be done to inform decisions. After all, those meetings are at the highest level and decisions need to be made to justify them. While the frequency of meetings might have initially been good for pressure and momentum, if maintained, it could prove self-defeating for evidence-based policy making. It is to be hoped, therefore, that over time we might see a return to a more measured approach, which retains, or even strengthens, the new framework of working groups behind the scenes, but involves more time between meetings of COAG itself and thus for the gathering of the evidence that decisions require.

Building greater institutional capacity

Building capacity—or rebuilding it—is also very important. But it can't happen overnight. For one thing, we need to be recruiting into the Public Service more graduates in the social and economic sciences. The United Kingdom saw a doubling in the number of researchers in the civil service in one decade under the Blair Government. (There is some irony in the fact that many of those at the top of the bureaucracy began their careers in the Public Service as research officers and probably remain more highly skilled analysts today than many of their current subordinates.)

Any agency that is serious about encouraging an evidence-based approach needs to develop a 'research culture'. Establishing dedicated evaluation units, achieving a critical mass of researchers, strengthening links with academic and other research bodies are all integral to this. There is also the broader question of 'institution building' to underpin better evaluation generally across government. Some initiatives have developed out of the foreign aid programs and literature that might be instructive. These include 'evaluation clubs' or forums that promote cross-fertilisation, peer support and learning about 'what works'—in relation to methodologies and policy approaches themselves. We could think of developing comparable institutions as centres of excellence to foster greater inter-jurisdictional learning in Australia—a kind of 'Cochrane Collaboration'[42] in the policy arena. Government/COAG sponsorship for such institution building is worth considering. Indeed, it could be contemplated as a useful extension of the role of ANZSOG, given its 'ownership' by all governments in Australia and New Zealand.

Better use of external contracting

When it comes to the (inevitable) use of external contractors, I think we need to give far more attention to defining the task and to identifying how contractors can best help us to make good public policy. Choosing the contractor—getting the right consultant for the task—is obviously fundamental. I would suggest that in many cases, it is better to go directly to the experts rather than to the big jack-of-all-trades management consulting firms that might be willing to tackle anything, but have an indifferent performance record in policy-related work (to say the least). Such firms often rely on subcontractors anyway, so why not go directly to those with a reputation in the field?

Part of the challenge, if consultants are to become contributors to a truly evidence-based approach, is to limit their tendency to 'second-guessing', which can compound bureaucrats' own tendencies in this direction. As noted previously, this might be less of an issue for academics, who typically do not rely on such sources of income, than for business consultants, who do. An evidence-based approach ideally requires contractual arrangements that create neutral 'incentives' for the researcher to make robust findings—for example, by making it clear that his or her work will be peer reviewed.

More generally, monitoring and reviewing the quality of such external work are crucial and, again, academic specialists would seem particularly well placed to help with that, as well as helping agencies choose which consultant to use in the first place. Peer review can also be very worthwhile for the research that is done within government, but this is not common practice. It is especially valuable where political sensitivities require secrecy during the policy-development phase, but where there might be significant downside risks for the community from 'getting it wrong'.

Resourcing evaluations properly

We need to ensure that all government programs are designed and funded with future evaluation and review in mind. That includes data needs, especially baseline data, and making explicit budgetary provision for that. We should be pushing harder for more and better data generally, particularly in the social and environmental areas. Instead of being seen as an extra or a luxury, data for policy evaluation need to be recognised as a necessity—and a funding priority right now if we are serious about developing an evidence-based approach.

As already emphasised, we also need to be building in more time, where it is needed to come up with robust evidence that is adequately tested. In a crisis situation such as the present, time is of the essence, of course, and some decisions need to be made quickly. That is inevitable. But it is important that we lay the groundwork now to evaluate the consequences of those measures later, so the inevitable problems can be detected and timely adjustments made.

In the current context, this is particularly important for spending initiatives motivated by short-term demand management objectives, which could have an ongoing impact, or create a sense of entitlement and political pressure for their retention. For example, increased assistance to an industry—by strengthening its ability to withstand foreign competitors in a recessionary market—might initially help to shore up that industry's workforce. But this selective support will tend to weaken job retention in other local industries and, if sustained, inhibit overall job creation and productivity growth in the longer term.

Bottom line

In conclusion, the goal of evidence-based policy making is unquestionably important, and it is encouraging that it has received vocal support at the highest political levels. However, measured against the various ingredients for an effective approach, it seems clear that current practice continues to fall short. Addressing this is now largely up to the Public Service. Not only is there a need to improve the capacity of the Public Service to deliver evidence-based policy advice, there is a need for it to improve political understanding of what that entails. If we fail, it won't just vindicate the public's cynicism about *The Hollowmen* syndrome; it will compromise government's capacity to implement the beneficial national reforms that this country needs for the long term.

ENDNOTES

[1] This essay was originally presented as an ANZSOG Public Lecture on 4 February 2009. Early versions of this paper were presented to an Australian Public Service Commission Leader-to-Leader seminar in October 2008 and as a keynote address to the Annual Conference of the Economics Society in August 2008.

[2] Banks, G. 2008. *Riding the Third Wave: Some challenges in national reform*, Productivity Commission, Melbourne, March.

[3] Banks, G. 2007, Overcoming Indigenous disadvantage in Australia, Presentation to the second OECD World Forum on Statistics, Knowledge and Policy: Measuring and fostering the progress of societies, Istanbul, Turkey, 29 June.

[4] Rudd, K. Address by the Prime Minister to Heads of Agencies and Members of Senior Executive Service, Great Hall, Parliament House, Canberra, 30 April.

[5] Banks, G. and Carmichael, W. B. 2007, Domestic transparency in Australia's economic and trade reforms: the role of 'the commission', Paper for the Lowy Institute and Tasman Transparency Group Conference Enhancing Transparency in the Multilateral Trading System, Sydney, 4 July; and Productivity Commission 2003, *From Industry Assistance to Productivity: 30 years of 'the commission'*, Melbourne.

[6] Karl Pearson, 1924, *The Life, Letters and Labours of Francis Galton*, Cambridge University Press, Vol. 2, p. 418.

[7] Blair, T. and Cunningham, J. 1999, *Modernising Government*, Prime Minister and Minister for the Cabinet Office, London, United Kingdom; Wells, P. 2007, 'New Labour and evidence based policy making: 1997–2007', *People, Place and Policy Online*, vol. 1, pp. 22–9.

[8] Productivity Commission 2005, *Economic implications of an ageing Australia*, Research Report, Canberra.

[9] Productivity Commission 2006, *Road and rail freight infrastructure pricing*, Report No. 41, Canberra.

[10] Productivity Commission 2006, *Waste management*, Report No. 38, Canberra.

[11] Banks, G. 2002, Interstate bidding wars: calling a truce, Speech to the Committee for Economic Development of Australia, Brisbane, 6 November.

[12] Productivity Commission 2007, *Public support for science and innovation*, Research Report, Canberra.

[13] Productivity Commission 2008, *Paid Parental Leave: Support for parents with newborn children*, Draft Inquiry Report, Canberra.

[14] Steering Committee for the Review of Government Service Provision 2007, *Overcoming Indigenous Disadvantage: Key indicators 2007*, Productivity Commission, Canberra.

[15] Department of Climate Change 2008, *Carbon pollution reduction scheme: Australia's low pollution future*, White Paper, Canberra, December.

[16] Productivity Commission 1999, *Australia's gambling industries*, Report No. 10, Canberra.

[17] Environment Protection and Heritage Council, 2008, *Decision Regulatory Impact Statement: Investigation of options to reduce the impacts of plastic bags*, April.

[18] Carmody, G. 2008, 'User pays key to climate', *The Australian*, 29 August.

[19] McKibbin, W. 2009, 'Five problems to fix in a flawed policy', *Australian Financial Review*, 15 January.

[20] Boruch, R., De Moya, D. and Snyder, B. 2002, 'The importance of randomized field trials in education and related areas', in F. Mosteller and R. Boruch (eds), *Evidence Matters: Randomised trials in education research*, Brookings Institution Press, Washington, DC.

[21] Deegan, M. 2008, Presentation given at the Industry Leaders' Luncheon, Sydney, 9 October, <http://www.infrastructureaustralia.gov.au>

[22] Infrastructure Australia 2008, *A Report to the Council of Australian Governments*, Sydney, December.

[23] Albanese, A. 2008, Address to Australian Davos Connection Infrastructure Summit 21 by the Minister for Infrastructure, Transport, Regional Development and Local Government, Brisbane, 7 October.

[24] Infrastructure Australia, *A Report to the Council of Australian Governments*.

[25] Productivity Commission 1998, *Battery eggs sale and production in the ACT*, Research Report, Canberra.

[26] Wise, S., Silva, L., Webster, E. and Sanson, A. 2005, *The efficacy of early childhood interventions*, Research Report No. 14, Australian Institute of Family Studies, Canberra, July.

[27] Heckman, J and Masterov, D. 2007, The productivity argument for investing in young children, Paper presented at Allied Social Sciences Association annual meeting, Chicago, 5–7 January; Donohue, J. 2001, *The search for truth: in appreciation of James J. Heckman*, Working Paper No. 220, Stanford Law School, July.

[28] Steering Committee for the Review of Government Service Provision 2009, *Report on Government Services 2009*, Productivity Commission, Canberra.

[29] Leigh, A. and Thompson, H. 2008, 'How much of the variation in literacy and numeracy can be explained by school performance?', *Treasury Economic Roundup*, Issue 3, pp. 63–78.

[30] Gillard, J. 2008, Leading transformational change in schools, Address by the Deputy Prime Minister to the Leading Transformational Change in Schools Forum, Melbourne, 24 November.

[31] Regulation Taskforce 2006, *Rethinking Regulation: Report of the Taskforce on Reducing Regulatory Burdens on Business*, Report to the Prime Minister and the Treasurer, Canberra, January.

[32] Head, B. W. 2008, 'Three lenses of evidence-based policy', *The Australian Journal of Public Administration*, vol. 67, no. 1, pp. 1–11.

[33] CRA International 2007, *Implications of a 20 Per Cent Renewable Energy Target for Electricity Generation*, Report for Australian Petroleum Production and Exploration Association Limited, Canberra; McLennan Magasanik Associates 2007, *Increasing Australia's Low Emission Electricity Generation—An analysis of emissions trading and a complementary measure*, Report to Renewable Energy Generators of Australia, Melbourne.

[34] Productivity Commission 2008, *What Role for Policies to Supplement an Emissions Trading Scheme?*, Productivity Commission Submission to the Garnaut Climate Change Review, May.

[35] Banks, G. 2005, Regulation-making in Australia: is it broke? How do we fix it?', Public Lecture Series, the Australian Centre of Regulatory Economics (ACORE) and the Faculty of Economics and Commerce, The Australian National University, Canberra, 7 July; Banks, G. 2006, Tackling the underlying causes of overregulation: an update, Presentation to the conference Australian Regulatory Reform Evolution, Canberra, 24–25 October.

[36] Moggridge, D. and Johnson, E. (eds) 1982, 'The collected writings of John Maynard Keynes. Volume 21. Activities 1929–1939', *World Crisis and Policies in Britain and America*, Macmillan, London.

[37] Rudd, K. 2008, Address by the Prime Minister to Heads of Agencies and Members of Senior Executive Service, Great Hall, Parliament House, Canberra, 30 April.

[38] Moran, T. 2007, Leadership lecture, Leadership Victoria, Melbourne, 7 June.

[39] Office of Best Practice Regulation 2008, *Best Practice Regulation Report 2007–08*, Department of Finance and Deregulation, Canberra.

[40] Quoted in Franklin, M. 2008, 'Out, out damned waste', *The Australian*, 20 September.

[41] Edwards, M. 2001, *Social Policy, Public Policy: From problems to practice*, Allen & Unwin, Sydney.

[42] Cochrane Collaboration, <http://www.cochrane.org>

Part 3. Reflections on governance and leadership

11. The two cultures re-examined: a perspective on leadership and policy management in business and government[1]

Philip M Burgess

In this essay, I will reflect on my experience as a student of governance, working for many years in the academy and as a practitioner or clinician of the same, working in the United States, East Asia, Europe and, of course, Australia, in order to make some observations about the key differences between the political cultures of the United States and Australia as they relate to public policy making.

The two cultures of business and government

For a long time, I have been fascinated by the decision-making environments of public administration and business administration. I believe the differences are much more important than the similarities.

As shown in more detail in Appendix 11.A, these differences are many. For example:

- goal setting in the enterprise sector—to delight customers and reward shareholders—is relatively narrow compared with the comprehensive 'public interest' objectives pursued by government
- enterprise sector leaders almost always enjoy the support and encouragement of their policy board; by contrast, public sector leaders are nearly always opposed by a vocal segment of their policy board—the legislature—which tries to embarrass, trip up or otherwise undermine the authority and standing of the leader
- enterprise leaders have enormous control over the decision process—the who, what, when and how of decision making; the CEO can decide who will participate on what issues at what time in what arena; public sector leaders do not have this kind of control [2]
- enterprise leaders have substantial control over staffing and other 'factors of production'; public sector leaders are much more constrained in the hiring, sacking and assignment of people.

As a result of these differences, there is a lot of room for misunderstanding between the wealth-creating institutions of society and the institutions of government. It is often difficult for the CEO and his enterprise leadership to understand and take account of the fact that the public sector leader typically needs:

- a public interest rationale (that is, 'cover' or an inspired or 'creative' explanation) for doing something that involves or benefits the enterprise sector; because everything is public, the mission of the public sector is the public interest and the public is often sceptical (not without reason) of government–business relationships[3]
- time—because public leaders need to make sure key stakeholders are on board; this is a process that takes time, especially when some have a formal or informal 'veto' power
- occasions for decision (or decision situations) that bring distributed benefits (what the game theorist calls 'side payments') for relevant stakeholders—because the building and maintenance of coalitions require benefits (what the game theorist calls 'pay-offs') for everyone participating in the winning coalition.

These decision-making needs of the public manager—for a public interest rationale, time and distributed benefits to players beyond the buyer and the seller—are not typical considerations to the 'let's do it now' orientation of most enterprise leaders who value results and often devalue or don't understand the process requirements of coalition building.

Therefore, we should not be surprised that the two sectors sometimes find themselves on a collision course—and occasionally even collide, usually with a loud crash when it happens. And we should also not be surprised that the two cultures often find it hard to cooperate.

The two cultures of the enterprise sector and the government will never be totally comfortable with the other. Nor should they be. They have different missions and a different modus operandi. Instead, they should make things work in the context of a healthy tension.

The public order and the civic order

Let's look more deeply at the public policymaking equation in a democracy—one that involves a relationship between:

- the public order, which includes government and other public authorities (legislative, executive, judicial and quasi-judicial regulatory agencies) at every level
- the civic order, which includes the private or enterprise sector (for example, business enterprises) as well as voluntary and non-profit organisations such as neighbourhoods, sports clubs, peak industry associations, think tanks, service clubs, churches, mosques, synagogues, centres for the performing

arts, museums and other cultural resources—indeed, all the things voluntary associations do.

A strong civic order is a key element of a healthy and resilient democracy. The enterprise sector is a key element of the civic sector—not the least because it is the primary wealth-producing segment of society. Hence the domination of one over the other—in either direction—is not good for democratic governance, and we should all work to keep the relationships in balance.

In my view, that relationship is out of balance in Australia, where the public order dominates the civic order through agenda setting, money and expectations.

The political cultures of the United States and Australia

I arrived in Sydney on 4 July 2005 expecting to stay only a month or perhaps two at the outside. The first question people typically ask is, 'How do you like it here' or 'What do you like most about Australia?' That's easy:

- the people—the upbeat, curious, welcoming and down-to-earth character of the people
- the dominant values—such as 'mateship', 'a fair go' and a willingness to call 'rubbish' what it is
- the 'no worries' spirit that embodies a forgiving temperament and gives people a lot of latitude
- the 'good onya' that encourages, heartens, gives confidence and shows appreciation
- the whole concept of 'stuffing it' that shows an ability to impose standards without disparagement
- the breathtaking natural resources—the land, the flora and fauna, the coastal waters[4] and…the mines. I love mines, especially open-pit mines. [5]

Invariably, the second question people ask is, 'What has been your biggest surprise since arriving here?' Then they often give me 'hints', such as:

- 'You've taken some baths in the media, mate. Wasn't that a surprise?'
- 'Politics here is pretty "rough", don't you think? Were you prepared for that?'
- 'I'll bet you're surprised how well known your eighty-eight-year-old mum became in such a short time?'

I have to say the media hasn't been a surprise. I have spent most of my professional life in public positions so playing the role of the spear carrier—with the spears sometimes in my back—is something I'm used to.

Nor have I been surprised by the politics. For 15 years, during the academic part of my career, I taught comparative politics. We always covered the various forms of parliamentary government, including the Westminster system practised in the United Kingdom and throughout most of the Commonwealth.[6]

Put another way, I understand very well the differences between the presidential system of the United States and the parliamentary system of Australia—and I especially understand how the 'fusion of powers' in the parliamentary system concentrates enormous power in the hands of a minister. That is very different from the United States.[7]

In the presidential system, as most of you know, the cabinet secretary is one voice among many. He or she has enormous influence, to be sure, but is hemmed in on all sides by the realities of the 'separation of powers' invented by Montesquieu but first put into practice in the American *Constitution* of 1789.[8]

In the US system, if you don't like what the cabinet secretary is doing, you have many options—the most important of which include going to the White House or to Congress.

When you go to Congress, you have 12 choices to go after a minister's decision. You can go to the department's oversight committee in the Senate, or the House that might be chaired by the opposition, or the authorisation or appropriations committees that provide the department's money.[9]

These are each separate political systems, each with its own power structures and own rules—each of which is a constraint around the neck of the cabinet secretary. I must say, in passing, that my experience here has given me a new appreciation of Montesquieu's genius.

And, of course, in the United States, every major issue area is surrounded by a 'permanent' campaign that includes:

- research-based professional messaging
- tracking polls
- the segmentation and clustering of constituencies
- massive and ongoing constituency lobbying
- targeted advertising and messaging in the mass media
- wide use of new media such as the Internet (blogs, podcasting, social media such as YouTube) and talkback radio
- direct lobbying of the principals.[10]

Punchline: the enormous concentration of power in the hands of the minister limits the give and take that you normally ascribe to good policy making. When the minister is against you, your options are limited to what I call 'the four strategies': sit, fight, join or run:

- appeal to the Prime Minister (fight)
- grin and bear it (join)
- give in, retreat or go do something else (run)

- appeal to the people because in a democratic society the people, in the final analysis, call the shots (fight).

In the case of our National Broadband Plan proposed by Telstra in August and September 2005, when faced with ministerial opposition to broadbanding Australia with fibre and other fixed-line assets, we invoked three of the four options.

Option one: we appealed to the Prime Minister (John Howard). It didn't work.

Option three: when we hit a dead-end with appeals, we decided to move to the largely unregulated wireless space to build a nationwide high-speed broadband network. We call it Next G. It is now the world's largest, fastest and most-advanced wireless broadband network.

Option four: simultaneously, we decided to appeal to the commonsense of the Australian people. We informed and educated people through our Broadband Australia Campaign, called 'BACk'. We mobilised people through Telstra Active Supporters (TAS). We did all of this using our alternative web site (<nowwearetalking.com>)—the nation's first corporate alternative web site—and other channels, including:

- direct mail to shareholders, who have a big stake in what the government does that might devalue shareholder value
- personal visits by Telstra executives to more than 100 communities to get our story out (I personally visited 54 communities during the nine-month campaign)
- op-ed commentaries in mainstream national media as well as regional and local print and electronic media.

As a result of these initiatives, we were able to increase awareness and interest in broadband from the single digits (7 per cent in one early poll) to more than 60 per cent in about six months. Then the broadband issue was picked up as a campaign issue and public awareness and interest soared.

Now, let me turn to the 'roughness' of politics in Australia. I have not been surprised because we have a saying where I come from that 'politics ain't beanbag'. I've learned that this is also the case here. I think politics is rough everywhere—and, in a way, it should be. After all, a lot is at stake.[11]

So even though there are differences, the media and the politics have not been a surprise. However, there have been two other surprises.

First, I have been surprised by the lack of interest in real dialogue and debate by public authorities—regulators, elected officials and public servants—with the industry on matters that extend beyond laws and regulations. When we tried to have these discussions under the previous government:

- political operatives said their hands were tied by the regulators
- regulators pointed to the ministers
- ministers pointed to the departments
- the departments either went dark or gave a routine defence of established positions and that took us full circle to the four options, which were now down to two: grin and bear it and/or mobilise the public.

The lack of dialogue between government and business is not ever a healthy situation—but especially not in a sector characterised by intense global competition[12] and rapid technological change.[13]

My view is different: when people disagree, we should welcome argument and seek to resolve it, relying as much as possible on facts, data and reason—pushing emotion and prejudice as much as possible into the background. That way, more times than not, we will reach the right decision. And if we don't, we fix it.[14]

There was a second surprise. I was gobsmacked by the timidity of civic leadership and the lack of robust civic institutions.

Put another way, I am most surprised that think tanks, peak industry groups and other non-governmental organisations are not more assertive about the work they do addressing many of the critical issues of the day.

Many of these issue areas, where decisions will have an impact for generations to come, are too important to be left to governments. [15] They deserve broad public dialogue that is civil and informed.

I believe that democratic societies are stronger when the civic order can challenge the public order.[16]

The civic order must provide venues where serious people can come together to investigate and discuss issues of national importance around the rule of reason informed by facts and data.

In Australia, there are many, though not an abundance, of what I call 'civic leadership institutions' that do very good policy research and hold forums where serious people can come together to address issues of national importance.[17] For example:

- there are international think tanks such as the Lowy Institute for International Policy (Sydney) and the Australian Institute for International Affairs (Canberra)
- there are domestic policy think tanks, such as the Institute for Public Affairs (Melbourne), the Tasman Institute (Melbourne) and the Australia Institute (Canberra), and new ones are on the drawing board[18]
- there are peak industry groups that do policy research and hold forums, such as the Business Council of Australia (BCA, Melbourne) and the Committee for Economic Development of Australia (CEDA, Melbourne and Sydney)[19]

- there are consultancies such as Concept Economics (Canberra) and Tasman Asia Pacific (Melbourne) that do outstanding analytical work and hold forums from time to time [20]
- there are independent institutions that hold forums, but don't do research, such as the Sydney Institute, the National Press Club in Canberra, the Foreign Correspondents Press Club in Sydney, the Trans-Tasman Business Circle and Davos Australia.

Why are these other venues needed, one might ask? These kinds of groups assemble influential opinion leaders from all walks of life—the very people who should be exposed to balanced discussions or even formal, Oxford-style debates of the cardinal issues of our day, of which investment in telecommunications is certainly one.

When issues are taken up in the media, they are almost always discussed either in personal or political terms or in 'horse-race' who's winning terms.

When issues are taken up in forums dominated by lawyers or regulators, they are typically discussed in strictly legal terms that often drive out commonsense and shrink the opportunity for the creative, no-fault or win-win solutions.

Once issues get to the courts, a whole new dynamic, including new rules of evidence, takes over. This happens when politics fails and democratic policy making gives way to the judicial process—though Clausewitz might say, 'A law suit is an extension of politics by other means'.

When the issues are taken up in forums dominated by economists, well, everyone knows what happens then. They make a lot of money because no-one knows what they are talking about.

So, what surprises me is this: Australia has a wide range of accessible and capable civic leadership groups that do not seem to have as much impact as they should in sparking public debate, shaping the public dialogue and influencing public policy. Instead, they try to influence Canberra and leave the public to shift for themselves.

Maybe my 34 months in Australia are a bad sample of time. That could be. But I have also been told by elected leaders from different political persuasions and by public servants who have been around for a long time that the influence of civic leadership groups has waned in recent years, that they used to play a larger role in agenda setting, the clarification of alternatives and the assessment of results.

Speaking to the telecom issues I care most about professionally, I am surprised by the relative lack of interest in the long-term benefits of the digital revolution and its importance for the future of the people, enterprises and communities of Australia. Instead, people talk about the *politics* of telecommunications (not its societal benefits), about the details of regulation (for example, the role of the ACCC, structural separation and other diversions) and whether or not Telstra is a monopoly or a community property, when it is neither. But, they seldom talk about what the digital revolution means for jobs, growth, productivity and the economic development of Australia.

That, I think, is unfortunate, because, once again, these issues are too important to be left to government or the 'experts'. Indeed, the business and public service professionals along with the economists and the regulators have carved out a special language—such as 'unbundled local loop' and 'operational separation' and on and on with impenetrable jargon—that makes it impossible for the ordinary citizen to participate in the debate even if he or she wants to.

I will leave it to people such as Hugh Mackay, Bernard Salt and others much smarter than I to lay bare the reasons for an anaemic civic sector and timid civic leadership, but I think it is an issue that we need to address because a strong civic order goes to the heart of building a strong and resilient society that can withstand social, political, economic, demographic or natural resource tremors now unforeseen.

Some might suggest that the 2020 Summit was a breakthrough for civic leadership in Australia. I would argue it was almost the exact opposite: a gathering of delegates selected by government, elevated by government and media managed (brilliantly) by government. That is not an example of a robust civic society in action.

Leadership profiles in the United States and Australia

The other side of the coin of Australia's tepid civic leadership in public policy is a highly state-centric approach. It is the job of elected leaders to address any and all issues of concern to the public, but in Australia that also means senior members of the Public Service—bureaucrats, administrators and regulators—speak out regularly on matters of public concern. The views of public servants convey high legitimacy and authority in the political culture—not just in a formal legal and political sense but in a wider civic sense.

Hand in hand with this, there is great interest (especially in the elite media) in the lives and leadership perspectives of leading public service figures. Again, I'm not talking about elected leaders. One thinks, for example, of the high profiles of individuals such as:

- Treasury Secretary, Ken Henry
- ACCC Chairman, Graeme Samuel
- Productivity Commission Chairman, Gary Banks
- former head of the Department of Prime Minister and Cabinet, Peter Shergold
- Reserve Bank Governor, Glenn Stevens, and his predecessor, Ian Macfarlane.

The same could be said of Professor Allan Fels during his distinguished tenure as the Chairman of the ACCC.[21]

Punchline: the visibility, salience, 'presence' and authority of public service leaders are very high when compared with the voices of civil society in Australia.

That includes the voice of business. The difference, I would argue, is not just one of degree, but of kind. Like most social observers, I think of business as a key element of the civic order. But it's my experience that business leadership in Australia tends to be viewed more in a private domain—not unlike one's family or personal life.

As a result, business leadership is a fairly low-profile calling, at least compared with countries such as the United States, Germany, Sweden or Japan. When you think of a great Australian business leader such as Frank Lowy, for example, his civic role is viewed almost exclusively through the prism of his chairmanship of Football Federation Australia or as the founder and chief benefactor of the Lowy Institute for International Policy, rather than, principally, as a business leader. [22]

I have found that Australians are encouraged by the media to feel angry, or at least slightly embarrassed, about business leaders who are financially rewarded for their success. When an Australian actor or sportsperson commands millions to make a movie or play a match, they are treated as national heroes. Nicole Kidman demands $10 million per movie, the Wiggles earn $45 million annually and Hi-5 receives around $15 million a year. Yet, when a leader of business earns in the neighbourhood of six to eight figures, they are most often condemned as greedy and undeserving.

In the United States, by contrast, the views of leading business figures (and not just the salaries they earn) are the subject of intense interest—not just in the media, but in the wider public. Stroll around any book store in the United States and you find books by business giants such as:

- GE's Jack Welch
- Microsoft founder, Bill Gates
- Chrysler CEO, Lee Iacocca
- IBM CEO, Lou Gerstner
- Berkshire Hathaway CEO, Warren Buffett. [23]

They write on a variety of issues, including:

- leadership
- lessons learned in life and business
- the changing workplace
- the emerging global marketplace
- the future of technology

- challenges facing society.

Moreover, these books regularly find their way onto non-fiction bestseller lists.[24] In fact, there is pretty good evidence that a well-known and respected CEO can give a couple of points of lift to share values. [25]

In Australia, by contrast, the business book genre invariably is of the 'rise and fall', 'ups and downs' and 'trials and tribulations' variety. The market is defined much more by the shortcomings of business leaders than by the inspiration and insight their experience can offer to making organisations work or to making the world a better place. One thinks, for example, of works by Trevor Sykes, Paul Barry and Mark Westfield, shining a torch on the hubris and folly of the commercial world.[26]

Result: the civic authority and legitimacy of business leaders are diminished when they speak about the public interest in the public square.

If I'm right, what explains this contrast? To my way of thinking, there are two sources.

First, the diminished role of civil society means a diminished role for civic institutions and the men and women who lead them. This includes foundation executives, universities and think tanks as much as the big end of town. In fact, to the extent these civic leaders are 'players' they play in arenas organised by the public order—as evidenced by the 2020 Summit.

Second, there might be historical reasons for the diminished role of civic leaders—and of business leaders especially. I am new to Australia's history, but my reading over the past 34 months tells me that Australia did not experience the giant accumulations of private wealth associated with the heroic era of industrial growth in the United States in the nineteenth century. In the United States, heroic individual capitalist titans built:

- railroad, telephone and electricity networks
- oil and gas pipelines
- massive irrigation systems
- great financial, mining and manufacturing conglomerates.

This first wave of industrialisation was a time of rapid growth—and change—and was shaped by business leaders such as Andrew Carnegie, J. P. Morgan, John D. Rockefeller, Thomas Edison, Harvey Firestone and Henry Ford—household names to every American today.

Those capitalists and entrepreneurs acquired a profile, together with public and private power, that was a striking feature of America's political and social landscape. These men—and they were all men during this era—also articulated a public ideology of stewardship that expressed itself in philanthropy, reflecting a wide range of beliefs from the 'social gospel' to 'social Darwinism'.[27]

After the turn of the century, when the capitalist titans were replaced by business administrators, the new, bureaucratised 'managerial elite' were well-known, admired and influential individuals—the likes of Theodore Vail at AT&T, Gerald Swope at GE or Alfred Sloan at General Motors. In fact, AT&T executive Chester Barnard wrote *The Functions of the Executive*, which is a classic on executive leadership in business administration as well as public administration. [28]

In Australia, by contrast, the State took the lead in the building of national infrastructure, drawing mainly on capital borrowed from Britain. As a result, the leaders who helped forge that infrastructure—men such as Sir John Monash—were largely *administrators* of the business of the State, rather than forces separate from and external to it. As for manufacturing and mining, with a few exceptions, major Australian operations were foreign owned and those who ran them were subordinate to a head office located in London or elsewhere overseas.

Public policy also played a role, especially in the embrace of protectionism—'protection all round'—and centralised industrial relations in the early twentieth century.

Protectionism and industrial relations enmeshed business in the political system in a way that weakened its capacity to act as a counterbalance to the State in terms of civic legitimacy and authority.

These pillars of what Paul Kelly has called the 'Australian settlement' not only deadened the entrepreneurial impulse of Australian business; I would argue they weakened the civic culture of a new nation. [29] The result was a sort of corporatist, state-centred, 'mother-may-I' mentality that W. K. Hancock described so brilliantly in his classic study of Australia in 1930.[30]

Even when Australian business found a more outward-looking, reformist and competitive voice in the 1980s, there was a powerful view that it should try to come together around a national 'consensus', rather than simply accept that a degree of civic head-butting was a healthy, normal part of a mature democracy.[31]

Business leaders did engage in great policy debates at times; I think of episodes such as the bank nationalisation battle of the late 1940s, which appears to have played an important role in the defeat of Ben Chifley and the election of Robert Menzies. Yet, the individual presence of business leaders was less marked, their role was more in the backroom of politics and their civic standing was more contested.

There were, to be sure, business voices advocating the floating of the dollar, the liberalisation of tariffs and the deregulation of the labour market—but it also has to be said they were few and most often muted.

It reminds me of my own experience working at Telstra. When we were faced with difficult issues with the government and the regulator, we were advised that 'a public stoush with the government won't work', that 'it will offend the minister' and 'that is not the way we do it in Australia'. That might be true, but I think the record will show that what some people call a 'stoush' others call 'public education'—and when the public is educated, they can move issues a lot more effectively than all the lobbyists and backroom politics put together.

Conversely, biting your tongue and playing the backroom game serves only to reduce the voice and authority of civil society—including business.

I'm reminded in this context of a wonderful essay by the late Donald Horne, entitled simply 'Businessmen', which captures the diminished place of business in Australian civic life by the second half of the twentieth century.[32] Horne writes:

> Business and businessmen are almost completely unwritten about in Australia…Many intellectuals—especially those who are in the universities or the cultural world or the professions, or the more remote kinds of government departments—confidently express as fact about the nature of Australian businessmen what is really the repetition of fashionable myth. These people never meet businessmen; they never read about them (except to read a repetition of fashionable myth); they are not really interested in them and would not bother to cross the street to find out a fact about them; but they have them neatly taped and ticketed for all that—in the most unscientifically generalised terms that seem to include everybody who does business, from the local estate agent to the chairman of directors of BHP.

Horne goes on to list what he calls the 'hive-full of preconceptions' that swarm around the idea that Australian businessmen are 'uneducated, provincially ignorant, suburban-minded, vulgar, anti-intellectual, reactionary, materialistic bores, more Babbitt than Babbitt'.

This piece of socio-cultural commentary is grating to the ear of this American. It's like fingernails on the chalk board. I grew up on a diet of Horatio Alger stories that celebrate hard work, entrepreneurial drive and the American dream.[33] When I was in the seventh grade, we began each day with the pledge of allegiance to the flag and a 10-minute Horatio Alger story played over the school intercom.[34]

Let me pose as an open question to you: except for the need to replace 'businessmen' with a more gender-neutral term, how much has changed in the four and a half decades since Donald Horne penned that essay?

I'm not suggesting there is anything sinister here or that business perspectives on public policy deserve legitimacy independent of their merits. Nor is this a prelude to some latter-day version of 'what's good for Telstra (or Holden or BHP) is good for the country'.

Like many of you, I've read my Adam Smith. Good public policy assuredly demands alertness to rent seeking, brazenly self-interested behaviour and 'conspiracies against the public' on the part of business.

My real point concerns the degree to which good policy and a healthy democracy require multiple and, in some sense, counterbalancing voices of legitimacy and authority in public policy debates. Without this, we tend to be left with the comfortable status quo, and that can impose very large costs and extract very severe penalties.

Put another way, I believe that:

- the public interest is too important to be left to the public sector, however wise our public officials might be
- politics is too important to be left to the politicians.

Ordinary people and civic institutions have much to contribute in a literate and developed society. The late William Buckley, a giant among public intellectuals in the United States, once said, 'If I had a choice between being governed by the Harvard faculty or the first 100 names in the Boston phone book, I would take the phone book.' There is a lot to ponder in those words, especially in view of the mess that technocrats made of the twentieth century.

Telecommunications regulation in the political culture of Australia

Let me conclude with a few words about the business I'm in—telecommunications—and my job, to make the case for reform of telecommunications regulation in this country. The telecommunications debate in Australia highlights in stark relief the issues I have been discussing—in particular, a presumption that public policy debate should be a matter for government and its intimates, and not an open debate in which civic leaders, including business leaders, and civic institutions play a vigorous, transparent role.

Closely associated with that is a persistent confidence in the public sector in what regulation can achieve—despite overwhelming evidence to the contrary.

Indeed, the call for proposals to build high-speed broadband fibre out into the neighbourhoods of the nation—called FTTN or fibre-to-the-node—contains a 'gag order' that asks those making proposals not to speak publicly on the substance or the process of their proposals at the risk of being eliminated from the bidding process.[35]

The reality I deal with every day is that Australia's telecommunications regime is failing under a burden of regulatory overreach. I am not talking here about mere faults of implementation, but rather deep-seated, underlying problems with the design of the regime—its systems, style, structures and processes—and the reality that technology has changed, consumer preferences have changed and the competitive environment has changed, but regulations have not. That's why there is an urgent need to:

- reduce the scope of regulation
- place stronger limits on regulatory discretion
- separate the functions of cop, judge, jury and hangman
- increase overall accountability in the regulatory regime.

Good regulation serves three primary functions:

- it protects the consumer, including health and safety as well as providing more choices for consumers
- it encourages investment, in part to spark innovation to give consumers more choices and cheaper prices
- it fosters a healthy and competitive industry.

Using these established standards for assessment, the ACCC's performance in the telecommunications space is not just a failure, it is a dismal failure:

- consumers have been denied choices in the marketplace
- investment growth in telecommunications is *negative* over the past three years if you take Telstra out of the mix
- Australia's telecommunications industry is anything but healthy.

The ACCC has fumbled, badly, in the case of telecommunications and things need to be fixed.

More specifically, we need a regulatory regime that:

- affords regulated parties due process and procedural fairness
- makes decisions on the basis of facts and data—not conjecture
- applies consistent and predictable standards in both the application of the law and in the decisions made
- uses special powers judiciously and sparingly—particularly powers that impinge on fundamental rights
- builds and maintains trust.

Unfortunately, my experience suggests that these principles are honoured more in their breach by the ACCC in decision making about the telecommunications industry.

Effecting change involves a larger issue that goes to leadership and culture. It concerns Australia's willingness to embrace a dynamic, future-oriented approach to the regulation of telecommunications technology and to leave behind a static and defensive one.

Telecommunications seems to be one of those policy areas where this wonderfully successful New World country seems strangely ambivalent—and anxious—about the future. The ambivalence is found in the public sector and the civic sector. That's why it is time to engage. That's why the future requires a different approach. And that's why business leaders and others who speak for civil society and our civic institutions must stand up and be counted. Public policy is not just about government.

Appendix 11.A: Decision making in the public and private sector is different

Decision-making Function	Enterprise Sector	Public Sector
Goal setting of the Chief Executive Officer (CEO) and the Elected Executive Officer (EEO)	Relatively narrow: to turn consumers into customers, delight customers, increase shareholder value — though the corporate social responsibility (CSR) movement is advancing broader environmental, diversity and others stewardship objectives for corporationes.	Broad: to maintain a minimum winning coalition among competing interests and competing stakeholders in pursuit of multiple economic, social, cultural, environmental, and political objectives.
Orientation	Substantial resources pursuing limited goals.	Substantial resources pursuing unlimited goals.
Major constraints	Financial, regulatory	Coalition maintenance, talent
Validation	Year-end results, total shareholder return (TSR)	Election results.
Support of the policy making board	Boards of directors generally give high support to the CEO — or they get rid of him/her.	Legislatures typically have a large minority that continuously squabbles with the majority, consistently opposes the initiatives of leadership, and regularly tries to embarrass or otherwise trip up the EEO.

Control over the decision process	High control over decision process and the who, what, when, and how of decision -making. CEO can decide who will participate on what issues at what time in what arena.	Low control over the decision process and the who, what, when, how of decision -making. The legislature, public interest groups and other stakeholders, media, awareness of FOI vulnerabilities — all constrain the ability of the EEO to more than shape the process.
Decision rules	High control — though the CEO can and does set standard operating procedures (SOPs) for the rest of the enterprise, s/he can easily and quickly make exceptions or change them. Often requires board approval but 'common cause' facilitates flexibility. Somewhat less freedom to set rules in a regulated industry.	Low control because the EEO is formally constrained by procedures established externally by law (the 'bureaucratic process' ') and informally constrained by the decision criteria imported by stakeholders.
Flexibility	High, though for public companies the imperatives of disclosure and, for all enterprises, capital planning impose significant constraints.	Low, because in the process of forging a winning coalition entails commitments — promises and rewards;, threats and punishments — thant cannot be easily revisited.
Control over staffing	High in the hiring and assignment of people; some constraints on sacking imposed by laws and regulations.	Low in the hiring and sacking of people and very limited in the assignment of people.

ENDNOTES

[1] This essay was originally presented as an ANZSOG Public Lecture on 30 April 2008. These remarks are my personal views and are not necessarily the views of Telstra Corporation Ltd or of the Public Policy and Communications group that I lead.

[2] The legislature, public interest groups and other stakeholders, media, awareness of freedom of information vulnerabilities—all constrain the ability of the public sector executive to do more than shape the process.

[3] That means the value of initiatives must satisfy national needs and multiple stakeholders, and that expanded or 'spill-over' value is not always self-evident to stakeholders, opinion leaders or the public.

[4] I am a sailor. I love to 'mess about in boats', as Kenneth Grahame, the venerable English writer, put it in *The Wind in the Willows*, his 1908 classic that reflected a new way to look at the world. So, living on a large island between the Pacific and Indian Oceans suits me fine.

[5] I used to teach at the Colorado School of Mines and worked a lot on coal exports. I have to say, I love to visit large mines, as I have done in Australia—from the coalmines in Queensland and New South Wales to the awesome gold mine in Kalgoorlie. See Burgess, Phil (ed.) 1981, *Western Coal Exports and Pacific Rim Markets*, (Six volumes), McGraw Hill, New York, December 1981.

[6] The Westminster system, a series of procedures for operating a legislature, is used in most Commonwealth and ex-Commonwealth nations, originating in England and then transported first to the Canadian provinces and other colonies in the mid nineteenth century. It is also used in Australia, India, the Republic of Ireland, Jamaica, Malaysia, New Zealand, Singapore and Malta. The Parliaments of Italy, Germany and Japan take a different approach to parliamentary rule.

[7] In fact, I was amused to read a commentary this past weekend (April 2008) in *The Australian* where the writer talked about the 'strong' executive in the United States versus the strong Parliament in Australia. In fact, it is just the opposite. The United States has a relatively weak executive compared with almost any parliamentary system, where the Executive controls the Parliament through the party system, as it does in Australia. Senator Barnaby Joyce gave an insightful talk on this issue a couple of years ago, lamenting how the role of the Senate in Australian policy making had been fundamentally altered and weakened by Australia's strong party system—a diagnosis that seemed spot on to me. Joyce, Barnaby 2006, Crossing the floor: political hero or renegade?, Address to the Law Institute of Victoria, 26 July 2006, <http://www.barnabyjoyce.com.au/news/default.asp?action=article&ID=170>

[8] That America's founding fathers were deeply fearful of lodging too much unchecked power in the hands of one person or one institution was expressed most forcefully and persuasively in *The Federalist Papers* by James Madison, Alexander Hamilton and John Jay—and especially in *Federalist* no. 51.

[9] You can also go to an oversight, authorisation and appropriations committee on both the Senate and House sides and then choose between the Republican side or the Democrat side. So, in Congress alone, you have 12 options if you are having a problem with a minister or his or her department. Plus you can always go to the White House staff and to the party apparatus. So, there are at least 14 appeals to a minister's decisions.

[10] The opportunity provided by the issues campaign for broad public education and broad public participation in the resolution of political issues seems to be missing here, though I understand it has surfaced in the past around important issues—one of which I will discuss later.

[11] Let's not forget that governments are the only institution in society that can legally take away our freedom and our wealth and, in countries with the death penalty, our life. That's what sovereignty means. So politics should be rough.

[12] Though it doesn't get much traction with ministers, public servants or the media, the major threats to Telstra's future are not Optus and AAPT. The major threats are Google, Yahoo, Microsoft and other offshore enterprises. Achieving a common understanding about what the future holds is one of many important reasons why there should be a steady and continuing dialogue between industry and government.

[13] Just think of what you can do in the digital space today compared with five years ago. Yet, in 2005, we were told there would be no changes to regulations for five years. Five years is a lifetime in a sector driven by changing technology, changing consumer preferences and a changing competitive structure. For example, who would have thought five years ago that by 2009, 99 per cent of consumers and businesses in Australia would have access to 21 Mbps over the mobile Internet called Next G?

[14] In short, we find truth in a free society by mixing it up in the marketplace of ideas—and if we don't find the truth, then we can at least find an approach or a policy that will provide the greatest good for the greatest number. As Winston Churchill famously said, 'Democracy is the worst form of government except for all those others that have been tried.' Actually Churchill was sometimes ambivalent about democracy. He also said, 'The best argument against democracy is a five-minute conversation with the average voter.'

[15] For the role of think tanks in Australia, see Marsh, I. 1994, 'The development and impact of Australia's think tanks', *Australian Journal of Management*, December; Murray, Georgina and Pacheco, Douglas 2000, 'Think tanks in the 1990s' and 'The economic liberal ideas industry: Australasian pro-market think tanks in the 1990s', *Journal of Social Issues*, May; and Beder, Sharon 1999, 'The intellectual sorcery of think tanks', *Arena Magazine*, June–July. For an outstanding study of the role of think tanks in the United States, see Smith, James A. 1993, *The Idea Brokers: Think tanks and the rise of the new policy elite*, The Free Press, New York.

[16] On the distinction between the civic order and the public order, see the writings of Harold D. Lasswell—for example, Lasswell, Harold D. and Kaplan, Abraham 1950, *Power and Society: A framework for political inquiry*, Yale University Press, New Haven; Lerner, Daniel and Lasswell, Harold D. 1951, *The Policy Sciences: Recent developments in scope and method*, Stanford University Press, Stanford; McDougal, Myres, Lasswell, Harold D. and Vlasic, Ivan A. 1963, *Law and Public Order in Space*, Yale University Press, New Haven; Lasswell, Harold D. 1971, *A Preview of Policy Sciences*, Elsevier, New York; Rubinstein, Robert and Lasswell, Harold D. 1966, *The Sharing of Power in a Psychiatric Hospital*, Yale University Press, New Haven.

[17] Georgina Murray and Douglas Pacheco, cited earlier, cite research by B. Herd estimating a total of 80–90 think tanks in Australia (and six in New Zealand). They employ 1600 people, publish 900 reports and discussion papers and hold almost 600 conferences and symposia a year—but with a collective budget of around $130 million, they are not well funded.

[18] I've noticed that the media and other opinion leaders sometimes tend to dismiss their findings and conclusions as 'predictable'. That is unfair and unfortunate, based on what I have seen of their work. These critical issues of government regulation and the impact of advanced communications technologies need to be addressed from every vantage point—and not just from the point of view of the regulator or the government administrator or the competitors. At the end of the day, there is the national interest.

[19] These groups are membership organisations and their members include perspectives, skills and information from all points on the compass. They are already playing an important role on issues such as taxes, regulation, workplace relations, infrastructure development and economic and regional development—and they should, because they are uniquely positioned to inform and educate the public about the consequences of policy decisions and regulatory practices and how they affect the ability of the nation's wealth and job-creating institutions to survive, compete and prosper.

[20] Even though the work they do is properly guided by an agenda that grows out of their business and not out of the public policy agenda, groups such as this have a rich base of talent that needs to be enlisted to help educate the public as well as the policy makers and elevate the public dialogue about these critical issues.

[21] See Brenchley, Fred 2003, *Allan Fels: A portrait in power*, John Wiley, Sydney.

[22] For background on Frank Lowy's business career, see Margo, Jill 2001, *Frank Lowy: Pushing the limits*, Harper Collins, Sydney.

[23] See Welch, Jack with Byrne, John A. 2001, *Jack: Straight from the gut*, Business Plus; Welch, Jack with Welch, Suzy 2005, *Winning*, Collins; Gates, Bill 1995, *The Road Ahead*; Gates, Bill 1999, *Business @ the Speed of Thought*; Iacocca, Lee and Novak, William 1984, *Iacocca: An autobiography*; Iacocca, Lee with Kleinfeld, Sonny 1988, *Talking Straight*, Bantam Books; Iacocca, Lee 2007, *Where Have All the Leaders Gone?*, Scribner; Gerstner, Louis V. jr 2002, *Who Says Elephants Can't Dance?*, Harper Collins; Buffet, Warren, *The Essays of Warren Buffett: Lessons for corporate America*.

[24] In fact, in the United States we have 'business bestseller' lists and many listings are books not by academics or journalists but by business leaders.

[25] See Watson Wyatt Worldwide's *Effective Communication: A leading indicator of financial performance*.

[26] Examples include: *Two Centuries of Panic* (1988) and *The Bold Riders* (1994) by Trevor Sykes; *The Rise & Fall of Alan Bond* (1991) and *Rich Kids* (2003) by Paul Barry; and *HIH: The inside story of Australia's biggest corporate collapse* (2003) by Mark Westfield.

[27] See the essays collected by Kennedy, Gail (ed.) 1949, *Democracy and the Gospel of Wealth*, D. C. Heath, New York.

[28] Barnard was president of Pennsylvania Bell and then New Jersey Bell in the Bell system operated by AT&T. Barnard wrote *The Functions of the Executive* (1938, Harvard University Press, Cambridge). In 1948, he wrote *Organization and Management*, another widely reviewed and highly regarded book that is still cited today.

[29] See Kelly, Paul 1992, *The End of Certainty: The story of the 1980s*, Allen & Unwin, Sydney.

[30] Hancock, W. K. 1930, *Australia*, Ernest Benn, London.

[31] The use of controversy as a strategy to clarify ideas and the character of people is well established. It's not just the well-known idea that you have to break eggs to make an omelette. I like to think about it this way: Thomas Aquinas wrote that '[c]ivilization is constituted by conversation—that is, by argument'. However, G. K. Chesterton reminded us that arguing was not the same as quarrelling. According to Chesterton, 'The principal objection to a quarrel is that it interrupts an argument.' Theologian Michael Novak says 'civilized people…argue with one another. Barbarians club each other, as if values are mere "preferences"—and reason is nowhere to be found. So when people disagree, we

should welcome argument, and if the other side doesn't want to engage, well, that tells us something too.'

[32] Horne, Donald 1962, 'Businessmen', in Peter Coleman (ed.), *Australian Civilization*, F. W. Cheshire, Melbourne.

[33] Alger was a nineteenth-century author of more than 100 'dime novels' recounting rags-to-riches stories celebrating how the down and out might be able to achieve the American dream of wealth, success and social standing through hard work, courage, determination and concern for others.

[34] I attended the first school in Lafayette, Indiana, to have an electronic intercom. It was a big deal—not unlike today, where we have technology looking for content.

[35] See the FTTN tender RFP, Sections 11.1 and 11.2.

12. Leading the Australian Defence Force[1]

Air Chief Marshall Angus Houston AO AFC

The basis of successful leadership in the Australian Defence Force

There are five basic principles that are imperative to the successful leadership of the Australian Defence Force (ADF). The first principle is to provide clear direction. It is necessary to provide a vision, intent and goals that are successfully communicated to other people. If this clear direction is met effectively, people tend to follow you. The second principle is to establish and maintain the right culture, a value-based culture. Values should define the way the leadership in the organisation behaves. If you can establish the right culture in your organisation, goals are much easier to achieve.

The third principle is effective leadership. People demand and require leadership that is focused on people. Therefore, effective leadership is essential when dealing with people. Leadership is also about empowering your people and avoiding micro-management. The fourth principle is communication. Face-to-face communication is the most effective form of leadership and I find that if you engage in this type of communication you get much better results than if you try to lead via the written word.

Finally, the fifth principle is to develop cooperative and harmonious relationships. Having relationships with people in the leadership frame promotes good results and thus relationships are vitally important. Without being able to develop relationships, I would have got absolutely nowhere and, of course, the most important relationship of all for me, in the present context, is the relationship I have with the Secretary of Defence, Nick Warner. This relationship is known as a diarchy and forms a partnership and a very effective form of leadership.

Strategic direction

The Australian Defence Force needs to be a balanced, networked and deployable force staffed by dedicated and professional people who operate within a culture of adaptability and who excel at joint interagency and coalition operations. At present, every operation the Australian Defence Force conducts is a joint operation and it is imperative that these operations are run in this fashion. Single-service operations are no longer a viable option. The Australian Defence Force needs to be a balanced force with high-end capabilities as this is the ultimate insurance policy in terms of defending the integrity and sovereignty of the nation. There are no measured threats to the integrity of Australia as a nation at present, yet maintaining these capabilities is vital to this integrity and sovereignty.

Australia's defence force needs to be able to respond to all challenges in the strategic environment and this requires the ADF to have the ability to perform across the spectrum of operations, across the operational continuum and thus necessitates the need for a balanced force. Australia's experience in recent times demonstrates the need for high-end capabilities, as an ultimate insurance policy, to defend the integrity and sovereignty of the nation. In terms of a deployable force, most of Australia's combat power lives in the south. The north of Australia highlights a substantial deployment challenge. Indeed, operations in Australia's neighbourhood require a substantial deployment and in geographical terms Australia is a long way from the rest of the world. Thus, Australia needs to have a defence force that is able to deploy effectively.

An emphasis on joint interagency and coalition operations needs to be considered. Indeed, Australia has now moved into an era of a focus on interagency collaboration. We need to see all agencies within government working together. If we have a look at some of the stabilisation operations Australia is involved in at the moment, we need to work very closely with our colleagues in the Department of Foreign Affairs and Trade, with AusAID, the Australian Federal Police and, of course, with all the services within the defence force.

And, of course, there are other agencies as well who we have to work with, particularly when we go overseas. Inevitably, we are in some form of coalition and, in my view, this coalition requires a whole-of-agency approach or a whole-of-government approach. I think one of the deficiencies in Afghanistan at the moment is that we do not have a comprehensive whole-of-country approach to the resolution of the problems there. And we need to have the entirety of agencies—military, civilian, government, non-government—all working together cohesively to one common strategy with common goals and objectives.

Let me now move on to our strategic environment because I think it is important to focus on that for the moment. As you would all be aware, we have recently had a change of government, but one thing that is enduring is our strategic environment. It is important to highlight in the first instance that the most fundamental factors that shape our strategic environment concern the relationships between the big powers in our wider region. It is very important for us that the United States, China, Japan and India are able to coexist together in our wider region. I think we can manage the rise of China. Indeed, we are a very lucky nation to be leveraging off the rise of China at the moment. Australia has had 16 years of straight growth and very high levels of growth in our economy and that is due to our relationship with China.

So China is an important partner to us at the moment. Whilst it grows, it obviously becomes a much bigger and more substantial strategic entity. And as it does that, we do not necessarily have to have strategic competition in the old mould. What we need to do, and what other nations need to do, is manage our relationship with the Chinese so that we can avoid miscalculation and move into the future in a way that is a win-win for all those concerned. If we continue to effectively manage our relationship with China, it will have a positive impact on our prosperity as a nation. Thus, big-power relationships across our region are vitally important.

I might contrast that with some of the issues out there in the Pacific at the moment. If we have a look at what has been happening in the past 12 to 18 months, our region has been challenged by fragility in the smaller nations of the Pacific. Indeed, the crisis in May 2007 in Timor-Leste was testament to this. This fragility is something that we need to respond to and I think the challenges there are substantial. We do not have an easy way of dealing with the challenge of fragile nations out in the Pacific.

One of the challenges is to find a more effective way of dealing with the fragility in the region. Again, I would say, straight away, whilst a military response is quite handy in the first instance, at the end of the day, we need all agencies of the government working together to meet that challenge. The other really big challenge that we face in our neighbourhood and across the world at the moment is the threat of terrorism. We see a very lethal terrorist threat, not only in the Middle East and beyond, but in our own region. Interestingly, we have been very successful against the terrorist threat in our immediate region—particularly the threat that was resident in Indonesia. But it is almost impossible to exterminate it completely. Terrorism will be something we have to deal with into the future. Therefore, we have to find good strategies to deal with what will be an enduring threat in the years ahead. The problem between Israel and her neighbours is something that has to be resolved. Furthermore, we are in Afghanistan at the moment because the country was a haven for terrorists before the coalition became involved.

I might now move on to the operational tempo in the Australian Defence Force. Right now, we have the highest level of operational tempo we have had, certainly, for a generation. And it is probably the most challenging form of operational tempo, in that it extends not just in one area, but in a number of different areas.

If you have a look at what we have done in the past two and a half years, we have had about 20 000 individual deployments since July 2004. Compare that with the 20 years from 1980 to 1999. During that time, we were involved in the Gulf War, in the peacekeeping operation in Cambodia as well as in Somalia. Furthermore, at the end of the 1990s, we were involved in the intervention operation in East Timor. In all of those years, with all of those operations, we deployed only 17 000 individuals. So you can see already in the past two and a half years that we have exceeded the tempo that typified the environment in the 1980s and 1990s. This is highly significant, as the media tends to focus on those people deployed to areas such as Afghanistan, Timor-Leste, Solomon Islands and Iraq. Yet the level of deployment also puts a very heavy load on the defence organisation here in Australia. It does not matter where you go in the defence organisation at the moment, what you will find are very busy people, who are working incredibly hard, in a very dedicated way, so as to ensure that all the enabling support that is required is completed to ensure the success of those operations overseas.

Let me just give you a couple of examples. Our intelligence agencies are probably more stretched than they have ever been. Not only are they providing operational support to areas in which troops have been deployed, they still carry out the workload they would be undertaking in a more normal peacetime environment. Furthermore, if you go to the three services, although the service chiefs are not involved in operations, they and their people provide a vital 'raise, train and sustain' function. Furthermore, the Chief of Army prepares a force to go off to any of the operational deployments and spends six months preparing that force, and that preparation culminates in a full-blown mission rehearsal exercise, which involves not only all the traditional ways of doing business, it includes exploitation of modern technology, mainly simulation, where you are able to actually rehearse and practice everything that you are likely to face when you go on operations.

One of the big threats we face at the moment is improvised explosive devices. We can actually replicate all of that using simulation, so that our troops are very well prepared for the challenge they will face when they go onto operations. I think one of the reasons that we have been very successful on operations is because of that incredible investment that we make in the preparation and training of our people. One of the great things about our troops is their ability to work very closely with whoever we ask them to work with. They get on as well with the Afghans as they do with the Timorese. You can rely on them in very demanding circumstances wherever we deploy them.

Leading the Australian Defence Force

Seven broad themes define the way I lead the Australian Defence Force. First, I lead with a heavy emphasis on people. People are my highest priority. We have wonderful equipment in the Australian Defence Force, but it's the people who deliver the results. I've just spoken extensively about our people in operations, and if you invest in the right way in training your people, maintaining very high military standards, they deliver incredibly good results. So people are my highest priority, and I will work tirelessly for the welfare of the people of the

Australian Defence Force, and I expect all of my subordinate commanders to do likewise.

The second broad theme is leadership and values. I will not tolerate any form of poor leadership. This includes any form of bullying, intimidation or coercion. Leadership is about leading by example and treating people in the right way. In terms of the way that we treat people, we should empower people to the maximum extent possible. If you empower people, as I said earlier, you get very good results. Moving on to values, we have a set of values that we emphasise. We expect people to adhere to those values and, of course, the values also define the way we do business in the defence organisation.

The biggest strategic challenge we face in the Australian Defence Force at the moment is recruiting and retaining sufficient people to maintain our capability now and into the future. Our third theme, then, is operations and operational preparedness. If you talk to any chief executive officer around Australia at the moment you will find that this is not a problem that is unique to the Australian Defence Force. Our big problem is in the skilled areas. We are having absolutely no difficulty at the moment recruiting infantry men, but when we come to trying to recruit avionics technicians, electronics technicians, information systems specialists and health specialists, we have a huge problem. And the problem is probably greatest in the navy at the moment. We have 24 critical categories in the navy, three of which are perilous. The problem is a little bit better in the army, with 12 critical categories. The air force at present has no critical categories, although in the past three months, with the shortage of pilots worldwide, we have been starting to see very high separation rates with our pilots. And, indeed, right now, we have a separation rate of just fewer than 40 per cent for pilots who are not held by a return of service obligation. And, of course, they are our most experienced pilots—the people who instruct and lead in the flying game. Thus, we are taking steps to address that particular problem, which has come almost out of nowhere. We knew it was going to come at some stage. It is amazing what traction we have seen in recent times. And this reflects a shortage of pilots right across Australia at the moment and, indeed, right across the world. Fortunately, we have a 10-year return of service obligation on pilot courses, so we are not in a critical state, but we certainly have to address the problem and we are addressing that problem right now.

In the long term, I think we are going to be and will continue to be challenged by getting sufficient people into the defence force in all three services. If you have a look at the demographics, they are against us. And with a booming economy, with unemployment running at or about 4 per cent, it is a huge challenge to recruit sufficient people for the defence force. I am pleased to say that our performance in 2006 improved quite dramatically. We obtained just over 90 per cent enlistment, which was a marked improvement on the year before and the best result we have had for quite a few years. But we had to work incredibly hard to achieve that result. An area that I think we have to improve is in the retention area. In order to improve in this area we need to get our separation rates down to where the air force is at the moment, which is down below 10 per cent. Both navy and army have separation rates that are a little higher than I'm comfortable with.

A couple of areas I would just like to highlight on the way through are the military justice reforms. We are well advanced in the implementation of those reforms and indeed we would almost have the program finished now but for the fact that the election was called and some of the final pieces of the legislation were caught up due to the fact that the Parliament ceased and we did not get the final bit of legislation through. This will be readdressed with the new government.

In terms of operations, just to give you some facts about what is happening right now with our relief operation in Papua New Guinea, we have just fewer than 200 people in Papua New Guinea. Furthermore, at the moment, we have 4500 people deployed on operations. I think this reflects just what a high level of operational tempo we have. Of course, that also includes the 450–500 or so people who are involved in boarder security operations in northern Australia and of course the people who are involved in the Northern Territory emergency task force.

In terms of the fourth theme, strategic direction, I know many of you would be interested in that. We look forward to being involved in the writing of a new white paper. The last white paper process was conducted in 1999–2000 with the white paper published in 2000. The new government has made it very clear that in 2008 we will be embarking on another white paper process and it is very important that we seize the opportunity to review all parts of our organisation and of course conduct a thorough review of our strategic environment. That is probably the most important part of the work—to review our strategic environment and then, after we have reviewed this, look at the capabilities that are required within the full structure of the defence force. We need to have a look at all parts of the defence organisation, including the infrastructure, the information systems—indeed, everything that gives us the capability to do what government requires of us. And I relish the opportunity to be involved in that really important process.

One of the things that I wanted to do when I first came to the job of Chief of the Defence Force was to establish a good strategic framework so that we had clear direction as to where we were going. This has produced a very highly classified and very good document called the *Defence Planning Guidance*. Clearly, it will have to be updated as part of the white paper process, but it really provides the basis for a number of other strategic documents that guide the way we do business in the defence force. I am very pleased with where we are at with that documentation at the moment.

The fifth theme is capability. We have been very heavily involved in the investment in new capability in the past few years. I anticipate that out of the white paper process we will do another capability review and out of that will come another Defence Capability Plan. Again, I think that is going to be very important because it is absolutely imperative that we continue to invest in new capability to take us into the future. Whilst we are well placed at the moment, there is still much work to be done and, of course, the capability that we acquire needs to be the right capability for the strategic circumstances that are defined in the white paper. Because we are a nation of just over 21 million people, it is very important that we make the right decisions in that particular area. Over the years, governments of both sides have been very effective in coming up with the right force structure to give us the balance we need to face the strategic challenges that Australia has seen.

The sixth theme is based on collaborative relationships. Relationships across government are vitally important. I remember years ago we probably used to work in our stove pipes. I think the stove, the departmental stove pipes, are gone for good. It is absolutely imperative that we work across government in a very effective way and I think some of the forums that have been established, some of the committees that have been established, have seen us do much better work. Probably the best of those in my view is the National Security Committee in cabinet. I think that is a very effective way of running the national security business of government. That particular committee brings together not only the responsible minister, but the responsible officials in a very effective way of dealing with complex national security issues from the crisis that has just broken to the very important capability decisions that I have mentioned above.

Finally, the seventh theme is management, governance and accountability. Right now we are occupied with the business of implementing the *Proust Report*.[2] This is well under way. We have hit most of the high points, we are implementing all of the recommendations other than the one to do away with the diarchy.[3] Secretary Warner and I think the organisation works fine under our partnership, under our joint leadership and the areas that we are focused on are obviously improving advice to government, which is a high priority, improving our information technology systems and also rationalising some of the structures within the defence organisation. What we are doing is separating the policy part of human resources in the defence personnel executives from service delivery. We are moving service delivery functions out into the defence support group and we think that will give us a much more effective way of developing human resource policy.

One of the areas that I think has worked well as part of the reforms is separating the vice chief and the chief of joint operations functions. The vice chief will work in a number of areas that are important to improving governance and also improving the way we look after joint capability. We will have a three-star officer, General David Hurley, who will be initially at Fairbairn, but later out in our new headquarters in Bungendore and he will have total responsibility to run our operations. We have found with this very high level of operational tempo that it is imperative to have an officer who concentrates wholly and solely on operations. And already we are seeing the benefit of the split that was implemented about two or three months ago.

The final part of the *Proust Report* is improving our accountabilities. Because we are a very large organisation, sometimes the accountabilities have become a bit blurred. We will be looking at accountabilities and coming up with a much better way of doing business to ensure that everybody knows exactly what their accountabilities are, that they are not lost in this rather large and complex organisation that we call the defence organisation.

Conclusion

In conclusion, you can be very, very proud of your defence organisation and you can be particularly proud of those young people that we send off into harm's way to do the business the government has asked them to do. They always excel in the operational environment, they have great generosity of spirit, they are very courageous but they are also very compassionate and they represent Australia in a very fine way.

ENDNOTES

[1] This essay was originally presented as an ANZSOG Public Lecture on 28 November 2007.

[2] Proust, Elizabeth (2007), *Report of the Defence Management Review 2007*. Australian Government, Department of Defence, Canberra. The Defence Management Review was established by the Minister for Defence on 18 August 2006 to review and make recommendations in relation to 'Defence decision making, business processes, human resources, finance and information management processes and systems'.

[3] The *Proust Report* observed that 'The most unusual part of the Defence model is the diarchy, under which the Secretary and the CDF share responsibility and accountability for most of the functions in Defence' (p. 8:2.3). The report states that the Diarchy 'describes the joint leadership of Defence by the Secretary and CDF, both under the Minister for Defence. Within the diarchy, the Secretary and CDF are responsible for "joint administration" of the ADF. The CDF commands the ADF and is the principal military adviser to the Minister' (p. 30:5.6). The review 'formed the view that the diarchy, and the reality of a two-headed organisation, leads to a diffusion of commitment to and compliance with leadership visions and goals throughout the organisation. Moreover, achieving consistency in articulating a vision and strategy will always be more difficult in a diarchy than in an organisation with one leader' (p. 19:4.16). Although the review stated that 'we believe that the diarchy is still an appropriate way to run what is the most complex portfolio in Government' (p. 41:5.10) it nevertheless made two recommendations (Recommendations 17 and 18) aimed at giving 'greater definition to the individual and shared roles of the CDF and Secretary in the diarchy' (R17, p. 49). Neither recommendation was accepted in the Department of Defence response to the recommendations arising from the *Defence Management Review* (http://www.defence.gov.au/dmr/defence_response.pdf

http:/true/truewww.defence.gov.au/truedmr/truedefence_response.pdf), and it is these recommendations Angus Houston is referring to here. (Editor's note).

13. Essential linkages — situating political governance, transparency and accountability in the broader reform agenda[1]

Andrew Murray

I shall take the broader reform agenda as a given. It would be a strangely uninformed Australian who wasn't aware of the intense focus on infrastructure, climate change, education, the extensive COAG agenda, and so on, all set in the current maelstrom of financial, fiscal and economic troubles.

The economic, social and environmental reforms contemplated are very large. The reform is intended to make Australia more productive, more efficient, more competitive and a better society, and to better safeguard the future. These are noble plans that embrace nearly every sector in Australia, but leave the political sector largely untouched, as if only the political class at the apex does not need to be more able, have a higher calibre, be more productive, more competitive and professionally more suited for the future.

In times of trouble, it is important to stay true to the integrity and principles that will make reform lasting and sustainable. Money is scarcer than in good times. My thesis is that better political governance, more transparency and greater accountability will materially assist in troubled times and will add to the effectiveness of reform. They will assist the realistic measurement of reform achievements.

This point should not be lost in an atmosphere of crisis. A succinct, slightly crude business saying is apt: 'Even when you are up to your arse in crocodiles it is important to remember that your objective is to drain the swamp.'

These are times of reform opportunity. In times of trouble, the populace gives governments and parliaments greater latitude to act. These are good times to bed in major long-term reforms that would otherwise attract greater resistance, especially from vested interests.

My brief was to promote debate about how public sector performance and efficiency improvement could help meet the higher expectations of Australians. Debate is good, but persuasion is my aim; if you are persuaded of the merits of my arguments, I hope you have the determination to make change happen.

Australians are demanding much more of their governments. They want peace, prosperity and a good life. They want respect internationally and growth domestically. They want jobs and opportunities. They want their governments to be proactive, responsive, professional, far-seeing, productive and performance driven. They want their needs met. The push for higher standards and better performance is strong. The cry for economic, social and environmental reform is loud. Governments have said they will respond with a broad reform agenda. Expectations have been created. Success in meeting those expectations needs achievable plans, an accepted time line, constant credible reporting and measurable results—through key performance indicators, targets, benchmarks, review and analysis.

The gap between expectation and performance has to be addressed.

The major theme of this essay is the essential linkage between the need to reform political governance, the need to improve accountability regimes—financial and informational—and the democratic and managerial case for transparency and accountability resulting in more efficient, effective, responsive and sustainable business, government and not-for-profit[2] organisations delivering public services.

It is almost 20 years since the Fitzgerald Inquiry reported. The 'moonlight' state took a leap into the sunlight and there have been quantum improvements in politics and public administration in Queensland since. In terms of my broad argument, Queensland is living proof that there is a clear link between transparency and openness, better governance and improved outcomes in terms of economic performance, status, competitiveness and national influence. So the system works and major accountability reform really does help; it's scary and at times painful, but the long-term benefits can be quickly realised.

The problem is it took a horrible period and a remarkable judicial inquiry[3] to get such real change. We don't want that repeated to get more change. The benefits can be forecast and foreseen; more transparency and accountability will materially help Queensland and other Australian governments. The Australian people want more transparency and accountability—that is why each election campaign sees renewed promises, too often followed by later backsliding.

Essential linkages

I was educated in the doctrine of the political economy, a holistic approach to the functioning of the State and society that respects specialisation ('silos' in modern parlance), but believes the virtue of specialisation is to provide depth and understanding to overarching integrated objectives and programs. Such an approach requires linkage analysis; not just what will make the parts work better as a whole, but what linkages are essential to make it work well.

There are intangible links such as ethics and culture, but usually the links dictating consistent performance are tangible, bedrocked in statute, regulation, codes, guidelines, procedures and the like. The continuity and maintenance of standards require such tangibles, but without the intangibles, standards will decline. So the personal calibre, quality and character of political and public service leaders in government matter greatly in holding ethics and culture together, as well as in delivering performance.

In that context, a recent federal whole-of-government survey that said 45 per cent of employees agreed their agency was well managed and 46 per cent agreed that their agency's leadership was of a high quality implied that more than 50 per cent did not[4] —a worrying way to go therefore, on that front.

And the poor opinion the community has of politicians in general, with exceptions for some individuals, creates a large gap between expectation and performance.

Which leads me on to political governance; I have been anxious about the state of political governance for years.[5]

Governance through law regulation and process makes power subject to performance and accountability and leads to better outcomes and conduct, which is why so much effort has been put into better governance in the bureaucratic[6] union and corporate sectors, with great improvements resulting.

Political governance matters because political parties are fundamental to the Australian democracy, society and economy. They wield enormous influence over the lives of all Australians. They decide the policies that determine our future, the programs our taxes fund, the ministers that government agencies respond to and the representatives in parliaments they are accountable to.

Political parties must be accountable in the public interest because of the public funding and resources they enjoy and because of their powerful public role.

Conflict of interest and self-interest have meant minimal statutory regulation of political parties. It is limited and relatively perfunctory, in marked contrast with the much better and stronger regulation for corporations or unions.

We have law and governance in the public interest for corporations and unions because they make a real difference to their integrity and functioning. When I last looked, there were 2262 pages of laws to regulate the conduct of companies, 1440 pages to regulate unions, but few rules regulating political parties.[7]

The successful functioning and integrity of an organisation rest on solid and honest constitutional foundations. Corporations and workplace relations laws provide models for organisational regulation. Political parties do not operate on the same foundational constructs.

Political governance includes how a political party operates, how it is managed, its corporate and other structures, the provisions of its constitution, how it resolves disputes and conflicts of interest, its ethical culture and its level of transparency and accountability.

Increased regulation of political parties is not inconsistent with protecting the essential freedoms of expression and protection from unjustified state interference, influence or control.

Greater regulation offers political parties protection from internal malpractice and corruption and the public better protection from its consequences. It will reduce the opportunity for public and private funds being used for improper purposes. The federal electoral committee has previously agreed with many of these points, but nothing has been done.[8]

I haven't time to go into other areas of political governance that could help materially, such as constitutional and electoral law change and better remuneration and career opportunities.

Improved political governance will over time lift the overall calibre of the political class by requiring greater professionalism, better preselection, recruitment and training, a sustainable career path for professional parliamentarians as well as those who aspire to an executive ministerial career, and by reducing the opportunity for patronage, sinecures and dynastic factionalism. Australia is fortunate in having many very able politicians, but the overall quality and ability of politicians and ministers—local, state, territory and federal—need to be lifted.

A trained professional, experienced political class that is subject to the rigours of regulation, due process and organisational integrity will always perform better than one that is not.

If you are still resistant to the idea of political governance ask why the best talent is attracted to business, the professions or the public sector—all of which have strong governance—but not (with exceptions) to politics, which has little. Ask yourself if you are satisfied with the overall quality of political candidates, representatives and ministers—or with the branch stacking in political parties, their murky processes, the donations system and their standards.

Transparency

Transparency is usually bracketed with accountability, but it is not the same thing. Transparency means easily discerned, seen, open. Accountability connotes formal reporting and being 'responsible for' and 'to'.

The democratic case for transparency is that the public's 'right to know' is an essential principle and protection in a democracy. It is a right, like voting, or a fair trial. It aids efficiency.

Why is transparency often resisted? In essence, transparency means giving up power and freedom of action in the political market. In another context, Joseph Stiglitz recently alluded to this: 'Those working in markets see information as power and money, so they depend on a lack of transparency for success.'[9]

The managerial case is that transparency means activities and processes are easily seen, automatically providing an efficiency incentive and less opportunity for corruption, waste, mismanagement, incompetence or any other potential sins of public administration. Inefficiency, mismanagement and corruption can thrive in the absence of transparency.

As the saying goes, sunlight is the best disinfectant.

Right at the heart of my thinking is this: more transparency, clearer accounting and continuous disclosure will actually mean less need for scrutiny, because close and detailed scrutiny will not be necessary—and therefore there will be more focus on what is relevant.

Sunlight does not need torchlight.[10]

There are many good examples of improved transparency: legislation and forms that are in plain English; web sites that are user friendly, informative, easy to navigate and have analytical aids; public access to information that is provided helpfully and promptly.

Then there are the impediments: freedom-of-information systems that are nothing of the sort, whistleblower laws that are instruments of suppression, budget papers that are deliberately obtuse and appropriations whose design permits licence and impropriety.

Fundamental to transparency is the minimal use of secrecy by government. Secrecy is necessary for genuine reasons of security and privacy, but too much secrecy is unacceptable if Parliament is to fulfil its oversight function and if government is to remain open and accountable to the people.[11]

When information is blocked, it must genuinely be in the public interest, not in the political interest or in the private interest of those who would otherwise be exposed for mismanagement, waste or impropriety.

Freedom of information is vital

Alan Rose, former president of the Australian Law Reform Commission, made the point succinctly: 'In a society in which citizens have little or very limited access to governmental information, the balance of power is heavily weighted in favour of the government. It is doubtful that an effective representative democracy can exist in such circumstances.'

The New Zealand Court of Appeal once described New Zealand's freedom of information (FOI) legislation as of 'such permeating importance' that 'it is entitled to be ranked as a constitutional measure'. The 1996 *Constitution of the Republic of South Africa* provides for a constitutional right of access to information held by the State. British Columbia's FOI regime requires the government to disclose, among other things, 'information which is clearly in the public interest'. This is a mandatory duty to disclose, which arises even where no particular individual has specifically requested the information.

In contrast, Australia's commitment to freedom of information has been disappointing.

The provision of information is a public duty. The *Freedom of Information Act* should be the final resort for obtaining information, not the only means of doing so. Many agencies refuse to provide information without sound reason, forcing recourse to the act.

I have had a bit to do with FOI issues over the years, including producing my own bill in 2003.[12] At that time, our FOI laws were in serious need of reform and the Howard Government had no intention of delivering that reform.

Recently, Queensland led the way on FOI with the impressive Dr David Solomon having 116 of his 141 recommendations supported by the Queensland Government in full (and either partially or in principle supporting another 23 recommendations).[13]

Solomon[14] attacks the costly, legalistic and adversarial FOI culture and attends to such vital issues as having an independent FOI commissioner to oversee and monitor the act; broadening the scope of information that can be accessed under the act; creating a fairer, more reasonable fee structure; reducing the time limits for the processing of FOI requests to 25 days; limiting the right of refusal to essential public interest grounds; and so on.

The Queensland Government has issued two draft bills for simultaneous public consultation—the Right to Information Bill 2009 and the Information Privacy Bill 2009—for the very good reason that privacy is the flip side to public disclosure, and one should not be considered in isolation of the principles and practices of the other.

I won't deal with it here, but elsewhere I have had much to say about the misuse of privacy rules to prevent adults institutionalised as children from finding out their past or their identity.[15] FOI laws exist to help achieve open and accountable government, to allow access to certain personal information held by government departments and to provide a general right of access to government information.

Former Prime Minister Malcolm Fraser said that 'too much secrecy inhibits people's capacity to judge the government's performance', neatly encapsulating the very reason later governments and bureaucracies were to conspire to limit FOI, aided in some cases by executive-minded court decisions.[16]

In 1983, former Prime Minister Bob Hawke put the case bluntly: 'Information about Government operations is not, after all, some kind of "favour" to be bestowed by a benevolent government or to be extorted from a reluctant bureaucracy. It is, quite simply, a public right.' It is a public right, it is in the public interest and the principle of popular sovereignty demands that people have access to relevant information.

The power to access and independently scrutinise government information makes for a genuinely deliberative and participatory democracy. FOI opens government up to the people. It allows people to participate in policy, accountability and decision-making processes. It opens government activities to scrutiny, discussion, comment and review from the individual and from the media on behalf of society.

In our massive government sector, it is hard for watchdogs such as auditors-general or even management to keep abreast of everything. The military will tell you that troops and equipment are insufficient without good ground intelligence. That is what whistleblowers can provide.

Whistleblowers are people who by reason of their employment come across information that reveals waste, mismanagement, corruption, dishonesty or improper conduct in government or in private organisations. They play a vital role in ensuring the accountability of government.

The expert Dr A. J. Brown of Griffith University Law School has said:

> The willingness of public officials to voice concerns on matters of public interest is increasingly recognised as fundamental to democratic accountability and public integrity. At the same time, 'whistle blowing' is one of the most complex, conflict-ridden areas of public policy and legislative practice.

When whistleblowers reveal waste, corruption, dishonesty or improper conduct in an organisation, they deserve protection. If a person is bullied, defamed, demoted or sacked because they made a genuine and warranted disclosure, there must be processes that allow for investigation and restitution or damages.

Public administration and public accountability can only ever be as good as the frameworks that support them. Openness, rigour and the need for constant revision are required within public bodies to ensure they live up to the vision for which they were created: serving the Australian people.

Remaining accountable for the wide array of services provided by government and ensuring the Public Service remains productive and efficient needs good people, supported by competitive entry standards and competitive wages and conditions. Requiring employees to keep official secrets in the public interest or requiring security clearances for certain tasks to ensure that people are trustworthy are necessary.

You also need safeguards to ensure that proper procedures are followed and that maladministration is uncovered. This underdevelopment of effective whistleblowing procedures is bad for public administration, bad for the

Australian people and bad for public officials who are twice betrayed—first by the failures these officials see within the Public Service and second when they are punished for reporting the problems they see.

While all the states and territories have reasonably comprehensive, if inadequate, legislation for public officials making disclosures, Commonwealth public sector whistleblowers are afforded little protection. There is no specific legislation and the *Public Service Act* (s.16) provisions are very limited and problematic.

In federal law, secrecy prevails over the public interest. So a leak to the media resulting in a review and major upgrade of Australia's airport security resulted in a conviction for the official accused of the leak.[17] Such outcomes are perverse and mean that the active disclosure of corruption and wrongdoing is inhibited.

The Rudd Government has accepted the view that genuine whistleblowers perform a valuable and essential public service. They have asked a federal parliamentary committee to come up with a better approach. This is another accountability area in which I have my own bill.[18] This bill was used as a submission to the parliamentary inquiry.[19]

Whistleblower legislation must be carefully crafted to ensure that unworthy causes cannot be pursued in the name of good public administration and that there are sufficient safeguards to weed out the inappropriate use of complaints procedures.

Any public interest disclosures regime should incorporate three principles: create a framework to facilitate the disclosure of information in the public interest; create a framework that ensures such disclosures are properly dealt with; and provide practical protection—including relief from legal liability and workplace victimisation—for people who disclose information in the public interest.

Whistleblower legislation must create an effective and transparent framework through which genuine public interest disclosures are managed, from initial reporting to appropriate people through the life of the investigation and ultimately to the appropriate resolution of the issue.

It is important that the focus should be on the disclosure itself. This shift is designed to place primacy on addressing the issue raised rather than the person who raised it. This does not imply a lack of protection for those who raise the issue—quite the reverse.

A unique element of my bill is that it supports the role of parliamentarians and journalists in the whistleblowing process. After other options have been exhausted, a disclosure may be made to a senator or member if under all the circumstances it is reasonable for the official to do so and the disclosure has already been made to a proper authority but to the knowledge of the official has not been acted upon within six months; or the disclosure has been acted upon by the proper authority but it was not adequate or appropriate; or the disclosure concerns especially serious conduct and exceptional circumstances exist to justify the making of the disclosure.

After the disclosure to a parliamentarian, a public official may make a public interest disclosure to a journalist if they do not make the disclosure for the purposes of personal gain, whether economic or otherwise; and under all the circumstances it is reasonable for the public official to make the disclosure; or the disclosure has already been made to the senator or member but to the knowledge of the public official the response was not adequate or appropriate; or the disclosure concerns especially serious conduct and exceptional circumstances exist to justify the public official making the disclosure.

A culture of secrecy is damaging to the integrity of public administration and expenditure.[20]

Here are two examples of how apparently small transparency measures can bring about big changes. The Senate was constantly frustrated by the lack of a systematic filing and record-keeping system, abetting secrecy and hindering accountability and FOI requests.

The Senate continuing order (the Harradine motion) of May 1996 required that an indexed list of all files from each agency be tabled in the Senate annually.

The result was the entire government had to get its filing and record-keeping system into a rational, accessible order, and those file titles were now on the record. If my memory serves me correctly, defence reviewed its entire secret classification and halved the number of matters formerly designated secret.

Hundreds of billions of dollars of contracts are let annually by Australian governments. Strong, independently audited procurement and tender processes are essential.

Because 'commercial confidentiality' clauses in government contracts were often not genuine and were designed to avoid scrutiny, the June 2001 Senate Continuing Order (known as the Murray motion) required ministers to table letters annually confirming that their departments and agencies had posted on their web sites a list of contracts entered into in the preceding 12 months (or before, if not yet completed) worth $100 000 or more. They have to show, among other things, the name of the contractor, the value and duration of the contract, the subject matter, the commencement date, whether it contains confidentiality provisions and, if so, why.

This key accountability measure ensures all Commonwealth contracts are public, prevents the overuse of confidentiality claims and promotes more efficient, competitive and open contract practices.

The Senate Finance and Public Administration Committee noted in 2007:

Two notable achievements are the general decline in the use of confidentiality provisions and the now commonplace inclusion of standard disclosure provisions in government contracts [but] concerns remain about the continued misuse of confidentiality provisions in contracts and the reliability of the reported data in departmental and agency lists.

Sunlight has helped, through the devices of reporting, transparency and regular auditing.

All government agencies should conduct a thorough audit as to just how transparent their processes and public interactions are. In my experience, this is almost never done in any holistic way and never in a whole-of-government sense.

Generally speaking, accountability is a matter of formal process or of legislation: Senate Estimates being of the first kind and legislation requiring annual reports by agencies being of the second kind.

Accountability systems need review like anything else. The Productivity Commission and COAG red-tape reviews focus on the regulatory burden on the private sector. I have proposed[21] a similar approach to review the burden of overlapping accountability reports and governance systems in the public sector. Ministers and parliaments often address issues in one portfolio that are isolated from effects across government. It is wise to periodically do some thorough housekeeping to establish whether reports, systems or processes are outdated, irrelevant or ineffective.

Governments and bureaucracies might relish the opportunity to rid themselves of requirements whose primary purpose is to satisfy Parliament, and which they regard as costly, time consuming or onerous, or as limiting their freedom of action. Therefore it is unwise to let the government do this housekeeping, although obviously they must and should make proposals for periodic reform. It is the task of Parliament itself to periodically conduct a comprehensive review of cross-government accountability devices and measures, to ensure they remain necessary and relevant to the Parliament.

Accountability is very often dictated by statute, but its force derives from higher law. This is what I had to say in the Murray report on budget transparency: 'In important ways budget transparency and financial accountability are part of the rule of law, mechanisms which deliver integrity and a real underpinning to our political economy, and which enable law to operate effectively and affordably.'

The Commonwealth's power to tax and spend is arguably its most important power of all. It is fundamental to the Commonwealth's ability to achieve its policy priorities and objectives.

A simple proposition informs my approach to budget transparency and financial accountability. That proposition is that budget transparency and financial accountability are not only ethically, morally and managerially sound concepts with positive and beneficial consequences; they are not only the natural accompaniment of parliamentary democracy; they are legal requirements that flow from the higher law of the Australian *Constitution*, as supplemented by statute.

Budgetary transparency is fundamental to Australia's parliamentary democracy. Without it, governments are able to deny the Parliament effective oversight of government expenditure and effective and efficient administration can be subverted. In any true liberal democracy, where the electors are sovereign, transparency is an essential feature.[22]

As we come towards the end of this essay, are you asking why it is hard to get change, when the benefits are evident? Apart from the obvious—that it is always difficult to get change—what is it that causes resistance to reform, disclosure and openness; what is it that people and institutions fear? I have no academic studies to fall back on, but my personal and political experience tells me that many people in positions of power in politics and the bureaucracy like power and don't like giving it up.

Second, being asked questions by parliamentarians or the media or the public is an uncomfortable business, especially when such questions have a nasty edge to them and assail your motives or integrity.

Third, many people in politics and the bureaucracy know that if something has been concealed that will be widely criticised if known, it will make life difficult. Just see the resistance to publishing health system misadventures.

It is worth acknowledging the human, cultural and other barriers to be overcome, because they are formidable. But the consequence of openness is less discomfort, less squirming. Openness requires a rethinking of processes and reporting; as a result, a better product is created and integrity goes up a notch.

I am sympathetic to the dilemmas public servants face, given the personal and public stakes involved when something embarrassing happens; and for ministers also, especially in service delivery-intensive areas (health, education, transport, emergency management—the bread and butter of state governments). And I'm particularly cognisant of the difficulties an officer faces when dealing with ministers and advisers who have no or little professional management training or who are less than enthusiastic about openness.

Having police interviews video-recorded protects the policeman as much as the accused, and leads to more faith in the process. Having hospitals report misadventure and mistakes lessens the extent of those over time. Publishing kids' numeracy and literacy scores results in better schools and teaching. Federal politicians' travel used to provide endless copy for journalists; now that it is regularly published and open, it is much less so.

When matters are professionally dealt with and managed, media sensationalism and public distrust become harder to sustain.

My opinion is that the only way to overcome the human and cultural barriers to openness is through widespread advocacy, such as through an audience such as this, strong campaigns such as the media campaign on FOI and political and bureaucratic leadership founded on principle and integrity.

There is much more to be said, but can I end provocatively with respect to Queensland.

Although I think it matters enormously, in this essay, I have not dealt with aspects of political governance that mean reassessing the constitution, the separation of powers, a republic, whether the federation should stay and, if it should, in what form, and the powers states and the Commonwealth and the House and Senate should each have. That means reassessing how power is acquired and restrained, who has power over what, how money is raised and spent, and by whom. It means examining the question of imbalances between the people and their rulers, the issues of rights, liberties, obligations, protections, representation and accountability.

You do need to think about what is missing in your battery of protections. If you do not have an independent appointment-on-merit system, such as in the United Kingdom under the 'Nolan principles',[23] you are always at risk from partisan interference in what would otherwise be independent agencies or institutions. External, independent oversight bodies, staffed by people of skill, ability and integrity, are essential to good government.

Nevertheless, if you do have an auditor-general, solicitor-general, ombudsman, equal opportunity, human rights, privacy, FOI and public disclosure commissioners, an independent judiciary, an independent police force and a Crime and Misconduct Commission—and effective laws and adequate resources to empower them and to ensure their integrity—then you are on your way to the protections needed in a civil society against abuse of power, waste, inefficiency, corruption and mismanagement.

Your Parliament matters because it represents the sovereign people. If Parliament has less talent, integrity or judgment than it should, everyone loses. Law that is the result of a parliamentary tyranny where a political party with half the popular vote gets all the say is not as sustainable or durable as one where there is plural cross-party input and support.

Do not tell me the ballot box cures all, if all it results in is changing one parliamentary take-all majority for another. Your constitution, electoral system and representative system matter in sorting this out.

In Queensland, your unicameral system design is bad, because it raises the Executive above all else and diminishes the checks and balances explicit in the separation of powers. If Queensland wants to remain unicameral, it should go either to proportional representation or to having your premier and deputy premier directly elected and letting them appoint ministers outside of Parliament, so making your unicameral house a non-executive one.

The alternative is a bicameral system. An upper house is necessary for the nobler cause of the public good and public interest, by adding real value: ideally—heightened accountability, a restraint on executive and legislative excess, a repository of Parliamentary good governance and standards and fearless, open and extensive consultation inquiry and review.

Appendix 13

Expanding on political governance

In the green paper, the Special Minister of State says:

> [W]e rightly value core democratic values: fairness, transparency, political integrity. Australians also want a healthy political system, with impartial umpires and processes underpinning our electoral system, keeping our campaigning fair and transparent and ensuring our systems are free from corruption and improper influences.[24]

This is an argument for better political governance. Greater fairness, transparency and political integrity require improved political governance.

Political governance includes how a political party operates, how it is managed, its corporate and other structures, the provisions of its constitution, how it resolves disputes and conflicts of interest, its ethical culture and its level of transparency and accountability. As the green paper implicitly acknowledges, electoral reform also requires attention to aspects of political governance such as transparency and accountability.

All registered political parties should be obliged to meet minimum standards of accountability and internal democracy. Given the public funding of elections, the immense power of political parties (at least of some parties) and their vital role in our government and our democracy, it is proper to insist that such standards be met.

At present, there are two governance areas in politics that are regulated by statute to a degree: the registration of political parties, and funding and disclosure. The statutory registration of political parties is well managed by the Australian Electoral Commission (AEC), as a necessary part of election mechanics, but the regulation of funding and disclosure is weak.

Although they are private organisations in terms of their legal form, political parties by their role, function, importance and access to public funding are of great public concern. The courts are catching up to that understanding.[25] Nevertheless, the common law has been of little assistance in providing necessary safeguards. To date, the courts have been largely reluctant to apply common law principles (such as on membership or preselections) to political party constitutions, although they have determined that disputes within political parties are justiciable.

The AEC dealt with a number of these issues in Recommendations 13–16 in the *AEC Funding and Disclosure Report Election 98*. Recommendation 16 asks that the *Commonwealth Electoral Act 1918* (CEA) provide the AEC with the power to set standard, minimum rules, which would apply to registered political parties where the parties' own constitution is silent or unclear. This is a significant accountability recommendation.

The Joint Standing Committee on Electoral Matters' (JSCEM) 1998 report recommended (no. 52) that political parties be required to lodge a constitution with the AEC that must contain certain minimal elements. This recommendation was a significant one, but it did not go far enough. In their report into the 2004 election, in Recommendation 19, to its credit, the JSCEM again recommended that political parties be required to lodge a constitution with the AEC that must contain certain minimal elements.

Political parties exercise public power and the terms on which they do so must be open to public scrutiny. The fact that most party constitutions are secret prevents proper public scrutiny of political parties. Party constitutions should be publicly available documents updated at least once every electoral cycle. (The JSCEM was once told by the AEC that a particular party constitution had not been updated in its records for 16 years.)

To bring political parties under the type of accountability regime that befits their role in our system of government, the following reforms are needed:

- The *Commonwealth Electoral Act* should be amended to require standard items be set out in a political party's constitution to gain registration, similar to the requirements under corporations law for the constitution of companies.
- Party constitutions should specify the conditions and rules of party membership; how office bearers are preselected and selected; how preselection of candidates is conducted; the processes for the resolution of disputes and conflicts of interest; the processes for changing the constitution; and processes for administration and management.
- Party constitutions should also provide for the rights of members in specified classes of membership to: take part in the conduct of party affairs, either directly or through freely chosen representatives; to freely express choices

about party matters, including the choice of candidates for elections; and to exercise a vote of equal value with the vote of any other members in the same class of membership.

- Party constitutions should be open to public scrutiny and updated on the public register at least once every electoral cycle.
- The AEC should be empowered to oversee all important ballots within political parties. At the very least, the law should permit them to do so at the request of a registered political party.
- The AEC should also be empowered to investigate any allegations of a serious breach of a party constitution and be able to apply an administrative penalty.

Changes to political governance such as these do not need COAG approval, although its support would be welcome. Such reforms to Commonwealth law would inevitably flow onto the conduct of state political participants, since nearly all registered state participants are also registered federal parties.

ENDNOTES

[1] This essay was originally presented as an ANZSOG Public Lecture on 17 February 2009.

[2] For analytical purposes, the scholarly literature often divides society into four sectors: business (first sector); government (second sector); not-for-profit, non-government, voluntary, intermediary (third sector); family (fourth sector) (Senate Economics Standing Committee 2008, *Disclosure Regimes for Charities and Not-for-Profit Organisations Report*, Canberra, December, p. 11).

[3] A judicial inquiry into Queensland police corruption, political corruption and the abuse of power was presided over by Tony Fitzgerald QC (1987–89, Commission of Inquiry into Possible Illegal Activities and Associated Police Misconduct).

[4] Australian Public Service Commission 2008, *State of the Service Report*, State of the Service series 2007–08, Canberra, November 2008.

[5] Recent work on political governance includes two public submissions: by Andrew Murray (February 2009) in response to the Australian Government's December 2008 Electoral Reform Green Paper, *Donations funding and expenditure*; and by Senator Andrew Murray to JSCEM's inquiry into the conduct of the 2007 federal election (April 2008).

[6] For instance, see definition on page 13 of ANAO and PM&C 2006, *Implementation of Programme and Policy Initiatives: Making implementation matter, better practice guide*, Commonwealth of Australia, Canberra.

[7] As entities, political parties sit within the third sector (see Senate Economics Standing Committee, *Disclosure Regimes for Charities and Not-for-Profit Organisations Report*; Murray, Andrew 2006, *One Regulator One System One Law: The case for introducing a new regulatory system for the not for profit sector*, Canberra, July 2006, available from the Parliamentary Library, Canberra; Murray, Andrew 2009, Public submission by Andrew Murray February 2009 in response to the Australian Government's December 2008 Electoral Reform Green Paper, *Donations, funding and expenditure*).

[8] See Joint Standing Committee on Electoral Matters (JSCEM) report into the 2004 federal election (September 2005: Chapter 4).

[9] Joseph Stiglitz, Columbia University economist and Nobel Prize winner, quoted in the *Australian Financial Review*, Thursday, 29 January 2009, p. 14.

[10] Murray, Andrew 2008, *Review of Operation Sunlight: Overhauling budgetary transparency*, Report to the Australian Government, Canberra, June 2008, Chapter 3, p. 1.

[11] There are useful chapters on government and cabinet secrecy that remain relevant today in *Commission on Government Western Australia*, Report No. 1, August 1995, Perth.

[12] Murray, Andrew 2003, Freedom of Information Amendment (Open Government) Bill 2003, Private Senator's Bill.

[13] Government of Queensland 2008, *Right to Information: Explanatory guide. Right to Information Bill 2009* [and] *Information Privacy Bill 2009*, Queensland Government, Brisbane, December 2008, p. 4.

[14] See the report by the FOI Independent Review Panel (*The Right to Information: Reviewing Queensland's Freedom of Information Act*, Brisbane, June 2008).

[15] See, for instance, Murray, Andrew 2008, The forgotten Australians: identity, records and their search for the past, Public lecture for the Fourth International Conference on the History of Records and Archives (ICHORA 4), a conference organised in conjunction with the Institute of Advanced Studies, University of Western Australia, Perth, August 2008.

[16] The minority of judges in *McKinnon vs Secretary, Department of Treasury* said, 'The declared object of the *FOI Act* is to extend as far as possible the right of the Australian community to access information in the possession of the Commonwealth Government.' The majority of judges did not see it that way and that decision further limited access to information for the community.

[17] Allan Robert Kessing was convicted under the *Commonwealth Crimes Act* of leaking customs reports on drug offences and security breaches at Sydney Airport. Before the leak, the reports had not been acted upon; one had been buried for two years and was never even seen by ministers or senior bureaucrats. Following the leak, the Australian Government appointed Sir John Wheeler to conduct a review of airport security operations, which resulted in an exposure of serious problems and an extra $200 million expenditure to improve aviation security. Despite exposing a real and immediate danger to Australians at large, Kessing was made a criminal.

[18] Murray, Public Interest Disclosures Bill 2007.

[19] This House of Representatives Committee's report was due to be tabled in late February 2009 (http://www.aph.gov.au/house/committee/laca/whistleblowing/index.htm).

[20] The Australian Law Reform Commission (ALRC) has been requested by the Commonwealth Attorney-General, Robert McClelland, to review secrecy provisions in federal legislation. The ALRC will provide its final report and recommendations to the Attorney-General by 31 October 2009.

[21] Murray, *Review of Operation Sunlight*, Chapter 4, pp. 60–3.

[22] Ibid., Executive Summary, pp. i and ii.

[23] The Nolan Committee was appointed by the UK Parliament in 1995 to examine appointments on merit. It set out principles to guide and inform the making of such appointments. The UK Government fully accepted the committee's recommendations. The Office of Commissioner for Public Appointments was subsequently created (with a similar level of independence from the government as the auditor-general) to provide an effective avenue of external scrutiny. UK Prime Minister Brown later announced that even better scrutiny would be introduced for appointments in particular areas, including involving Parliament's select committees in the appointment of key officials.

[24] *Donations, Funding and Expenditure*, p. 1.

[25] *Baldwin vs Everingham*, (1993) 1 QLDR 10; *Thornley & Heffernan*, CLS 1995 NSWSC EQ 150 and CLS 1995 NSWSC EQ 206; *Sullivan vs Della Bosca*, (1999) NSWSC 136; *Clarke vs Australian Labor Party*, (1999) 74 SASR 109 and *Clarke vs Australian Labor Party* (SA Branch); *Hurley and Ors and Brown*, (1999) SASC 365 and 415; *Tucker vs Herron and others*, (2001), Supreme Court QLD 6735 of 2001.

Part 4. Reflections on adaptive change

14. Higher education: it's time…(to change the policy framework)[1]

Ian Chubb AC

Let me begin with a comment about self-interest. Experience tells me that self-interest is a vice often observed when somebody else says something with which you disagree. If ever you have a flash of insight and detect self-interest in your own comments, you know at least that it is pure because, as you know with certainty, that's how you are. I hope what I am about to say will be heard to be beyond pure self-interest. Although I am paid by The Australian National University to work in its interests, there are some issues that go to the state of the higher education sector and not just the state of a single university and I will address some of those.

But, when you get down to it, we are an odd sector. And up there on the scale of oddness is our perverse attitude to performance. As one of my former colleagues asked several years ago: are we the only country that penalises success? He was commenting on the fact that research council grants cover nothing like the full costs of the projects they support—so the more you have the more you have to top up. Naturally, this diverts resources from other, say, prospective activity and is quite antithetical to a strategic approach to research and research development. It means that the best are penalised to enable more to be funded.

More recently, the same sort of thinking intruded into evaluating teaching performance. The Australian National University, for example, lost roughly $1 million a couple of years ago because scores were adjusted as the students the year before the allocation (not those actually surveyed as graduates) entered the university with high average cut-off scores. It was assumed, I presume, that we added less value to those graduates than did a university whose entry scores were low. I will come back to this later.

But even if we are not the only nation to penalise success, we seem to be expert at perverse incentives. It is time to get past this implicit 'equalisation' strategy and to put in place sensibly enlightened policies that will reinvigorate and advance the sector in a way that is coherent. They need to acknowledge that we perform differently and that we should not hold back (some would say continue to hold back) the best-performing universities in the hope that some of the others will join them at some high level if we deflect resources, or spread them thinly, for long enough. As I will discuss later, the gap does not appear to be closing.

Holding back is a recipe for levelling down. And that, I would argue, is in nobody's interest. Even so, it is an issue about which we cannot expect consensus in the sector; it will need real political courage if we are to maintain at least some of our universities in the upper reaches of the world league.

While it is a vexed issue, it is raised, not in self-interest, but rather as part of an urging that we come to terms with what we want to be and our place in the world as a nation, as a community, as a sector.

This is as important now as it was when The Australian National University was established as part of postwar reconstruction. The minister declared then that the activity of the university should lead to it taking its rightful place among the great universities of the world and that by it doing so Australia would have taken one more step to align itself with the great and enlightened nations of the world. This might be even more important now.

Clearly, the circumstances facing the world are different from 1946 but still massively complex: the issues of climate change, the environment, terrorism, pandemics and the migration of people are a few examples of problems that don't respect national boundaries. And solutions will be found only if the best minds in the world work on them, are given the skills to work on them and are able to work on them across cultures and boundaries. This is no time for reducing the capacity of our best. This is no time simply to say that what used to be is still good enough. It is not the time to assume that a country with a small population can have its universities presume that they are essentially scale models of some ideal teaching and research university. Nor is it the time to reduce the opportunities for Australians to get access to university, if it is their wish and they have the talent to succeed.

I take heart from comments made by the Deputy Prime Minister, Julia Gillard,[2] when she said 'we can't compete with the worldwide higher education revolution unless we improve the quality of our universities and keep some [more] of the best minds here'. She went on to announce a doubling of undergraduate scholarships and new mid-career fellowships and she linked education, training and social inclusion. Good news.

But importantly, she acknowledges up front that there is a worldwide revolution; that starting point is crucial to our future. I argue that it is, indeed, time—time for a policy framework that is fresh, strategic and supportive. That would certainly be revolutionary for us.

We have an opportunity. We have an opportunity to rethink, fundamentally, public policy, because of a change of federal government following the lengthy incumbency of its predecessor. While it is an opportunity we can't afford to miss, there are some preconditions necessary for turning the chance into a revolution. Let me suggest five prerequisites.

First, the incoming government needs to be interested in substantive policy reform. There are early indications of renewed interest in ideas and debate, which is refreshing. The COAG initiatives, the commitment to Indigenous communities, the review of the National Innovation System and the 2020 Summit, for example, indicate a new energy and a commitment to consultative policy development. The real tests will come in choosing between competing ideas and taking the hard decisions to put into effect necessary policies.

Second, the government needs to have adequate capacity for policy development. It needs access to evidence, analysis and creative thinking to guide longer-term policy formulation and evaluation. The policy capacity of the Australian Public Service is stretched in responding to the demands of the new government, as a result of its recent focus on 'can-do' program delivery and generational change. In the circumstances, there is a role for people in the university community to assist in offering policy analysis and advice.

Third, the government needs to invest the resources required for reform. There seems likely to be fiscal capacity for targeted investment in future years, but now, with inflationary pressures throughout the economy, and large election spending commitments, we are asked to be patient. While giving the new government room to set the house in order, we also need some signals of intent to address pressing concerns. We would be wise to ensure that the case we make for future investment is sound.

Given the current environment and condition of the sector, it is unrealistic to expect government to increase public investment in higher education across the board without regard to cost effectiveness and adding value. In other words, if we want extra investment, we offer reform in return. It will take two to tango to bring about microeconomic reform in higher education.

Fourth, the community needs to be ready for change. The signals of this are ambiguous. On the one hand, the community is calling for more effective and efficient service delivery, such as in health and education. On the other hand, resistance can be expected to further structural reform that disconnects people from their anchors in society. It is particularly essential that the institutions involved are encouraged to embrace change constructively by the policies, regulatory frameworks and financial incentives that are put in place, and by the way they are put in place.

Fifth and, I think, foremost, reform needs to be guided by clear vision and values. Blurred policy signals and incentives lead to dysfunctional systems. Yet a prescriptive approach is inappropriate for a pluralistic society. Policy needs to be alive to differences in community circumstances and institutional missions while also having coherence of purpose. It becomes important for government to be clear about its objectives and also for universities to articulate how well they do what they do, and what they stand for. I believe we have not only an opportunity but a responsibility to help build a balanced and sustainable policy framework for the future. The government is asking us to contribute ideas, so

I will outline what I see as the key features of well-designed policy architecture and the building blocks necessary to support it.

But before considering where we might go in the future, we need to understand where we have come from. Australia's policies for education and research have been built around national and sub-national orientations, politics and ambitions. But at the sharp end, national ambitions will not be realised if Australia fails to sustain a cluster of globally networked research universities. At the same time, we will fail as a nation to achieve the goal of an inclusive, well-functioning society if we do not provide equitable access to quality education and training.

The course of educational policy development in Australia, particularly in the past decade, has been segmented across the schooling, vocational education and training and higher education sub-sectors, with fissures between public and private provision. Once we enjoyed a capacity to consider policies and developments across sectors. We were able to consider things such as trends in demand and supply, the interactions of incentives for educational participation and employment, the effect of changes in education costs on access and study choices of students, the destinations of graduates and changes in employer requirements and expectations. There were also structured arrangements for intergovernmental consultation and cooperation, and provision for input from business and the unions.

It is time to join the dots again, to take an arm's-length view of needs across sectors, a helicopter view of international developments and a contemporary view of regulation for the increasingly competitive operating environment. And now that there is recognition of those long-neglected bookends—early childhood education and adult and continuing education—it is all the more necessary to adopt a joined-up approach. But how to join the dots?

Although he was focusing particularly on the universities, Peter Karmel's view expressed back in 2000 is still apt today. He wrote then: 'The government needs objective advice unaffected by political/ideological and political/electoral considerations and by the pressures of lobby groups. It cannot receive such advice from a government department subject to ministerial direction and the lobbying of individual institutions.'[3]

In addition to requiring sound and objective advice, the government also needs to be putting in place policies that will stand above the fads and fashions of political expediency. The higher education sector suffers from the legacy of accumulated incremental policy shifts and drift. The result is a lack of policy coherence, an introspective and narrow view of possibilities and a limit to institutional futures. Both sides of politics have railed against 'one-size-fits-all' funding. Before the 2007 election, both sides conceded that the Dawkins' model of the unified national system had passed its use-by date. There is a consensus that greater flexibility is necessary.

But we know that flexibility is not easily achieved. Experience suggests that even when measures are introduced to dilute funding incentives that induce sameness, cultural norms remain powerful in a sector where institutional status is confused with institutional purpose and performance.

This problem is not unique to Australia, as the American commentator Martin Trow has noted:

> [A] central problem for higher education policy in every modern society is how to sustain the diversity of institutions, including many of which are primarily teaching institutions without a significant research capacity, against the pressure for institutional drift toward a common model of the research university...the effort alone shapes the character of an institution to be something other than what it is: a prescription for frustration and discontent.[4]

Amid the confusion, we cannot expect consensus within the sector about future directions for policy and financing, other than the kind of lowest common denominator position calling for a spread of funding increments that has resonated throughout the past quarter-century and has levelled the system downward.

Before the election, Labor offered mission-based funding compacts. This was intended as a way to manage the transition over several years from an outmoded model of central control to a more market-driven approach, while also safeguarding the essential public good of universities.

That approach might be regarded as a balance between the 'grand plan' and 'muddling through'. On the one hand, it envisages the government clarifying its objectives and policy principles and, on the other, universities identifying how they can best play to their strengths in fulfilling their missions and contributing to government objectives. It has appeal as a two-way process. We can't start again, as it were, with a clean slate and centrally prescribe some new model, just as we can't rely solely on the self-referenced aspirations of individual institutions to cater adequately to varying needs.

The compact model recognises that universities have multiple roles in contemporary society, and that different universities have different roles. The concept of compacts, as outlined in Labor's 2006 discussion paper, indicated the potential for new funding streams for community service and innovative activities, additional to funding for the traditional functions of teaching and research.

Labor in government has signalled its intention to use compacts as a means for effecting reform. The Innovation Minister, Senator Kim Carr, recently said:

> [C]ompacts will be instrumental in bringing about structural reform and cultural change, and in concentrating people's minds on our international competitiveness. They will enable us to manage the transition from the present centralised system to a more flexible environment in which each university can respond to the needs of its students, its community, the country and the global knowledge economy by exploiting its comparative advantages by leading with its strongest suit.[5]

It is not yet clear how far the government will adopt the details of the compacts approach outlined in 2006, what modifications will be made and where compacts will fit in the broader policy framework. It is timely, though, to emphasise that the notion of compacts is government policy; it is the detail that remains to be sorted. This fact is apparently a shock to some in our sector.

The government's decision to separate the portfolio of research from that of education allows a more open consideration of tertiary education possibilities, without the distractions involved in exaggerated claims of a 'teaching–research nexus'. Instead, we are being invited to explore the potential of strengthening the nexus between university functions and innovation, in ways that will enlarge the contributions that universities make to the community. Compact funding in that context can help to improve knowledge exchange between universities and enterprises, and government and community organisations.

The government has also linked compact funding to tightening the access of universities to funding for research and research training on the basis of verified research quality. Quoting from their white paper:

> A university will be expected to cease admitting research degree candidates to areas where adequate quality of research performance cannot be validated. The university may shift funds for research training to build its capability in those fields of research where it has rated well or it may transfer the funds to undergraduate or postgraduate coursework places, or to develop activities for community service or innovation.[6]

This approach has the potential to shore up Australia's research capacity, by focusing future investment in areas of best performance. The areas of strength may initially be identified through the work of the Australian Research Council (ARC) in developing a replacement for the flawed Research Quality Framework. One approach would be for each university to self-rate its research against the benchmarks it considers relevant for the type of research it undertakes. The ARC/NHMRC (National Health and Medical Research Council) could then validate that the benchmarks are appropriate and assess how well the research rates against the benchmark, using a combination of appropriate metrics and peer judgment.

A major outcome of this approach would be a greater concentration of investment in research and improved research training. Several universities will be able to sustain comprehensiveness in research and research training, others will be more selective and a few will be active in niche areas only.

The 'hub and spokes' element of compact funding, as outlined during the election campaign, and, like compacts, part of the policy that the government took to the last election (again a revelation to some in the sector), will complement this reform, by widening opportunities for individual academics to be active in their scholarly field irrespective of the research focus or capacity of their home institution.

Already there are rumblings in some universities about this direction, but the government must stand firm. All Australian universities should benefit through the profile and access that the best performers enable. Australia cannot afford any longer to dissipate resources and level down the performance peaks.

Australia's capacity and performance slippage against the international leaders reflect an underlying deficit of national investment in research, research training and research infrastructure. I hope that a number of ministers soon get to see the scale of investment in facilities and talent in the leading universities of China, Europe and elsewhere. Then they will understand just how far we have fallen behind and how precarious is our future. I would hope that they would see the benefits to be gained by adopting an approach that funds the full costs of research and by accepting that there needs to be some focus of funding notwithstanding some political consequences.

Australia's catch-up cannot be predicated on a thinly spread distribution of any additional investment because of the scale and pace of our competitors. The hard reality is that the rest of the world is not waiting for Australia, and if we play catch-up politics internally, waiting a few more decades in some vain hope that the Dawkins reforms will eventually give every university a place in the sun, we could be watching the world from the sidelines.

We cannot continue to be timid about this imperative. Despite government incentives encouraging research expansion in newer universities, the performance gap between the top research universities and the rest has widened, not narrowed, since 1992, on all available quantitative and, especially, qualitative indicators. For example, the leading eight increased their share of total research income from 66 per cent in 1992 to 68 per cent in 2004.

The bottom 12 increased their share from 5 per cent to 6 per cent, and the ATN universities from 7 per cent to 8 per cent over the same period. Among those in the middle, the performance trends have been variable. One fell from a 3.4 per cent to a 1.5 per cent share, one fell from 1.7 per cent to 1.1 per cent, while another rose from 0.3 per cent to 0.7 per cent.

It is no wonder that some are very vocal advocates of funding on the basis of potential rather than performance. Potential is a bottomless pit, whereas track record is finite. It is indeed ironic that a sector that bases so much on track record from the accomplishments of entering students to research grants and their allocation to what staff have done to earn promotion should suddenly discover that 'potential' is more important when it comes to funding. Sometimes, it might be thought, self-interest is not always pure.

Around the world research is funded, including in emerging areas, on the basis of track record. Research grants are not awarded and researchers are not employed on the basis of promise alone. Their promise is inferred from what they have done.

So for research, research training, research infrastructure and improved connections of universities to the innovation system, the compacts approach should drive much-needed reform. I would like to see this process moving in the direction of customised block grants to universities from the research councils reflecting true operating costs with accountability for quality of outcomes as the means by which we judge the quality of our work and adjust the block.

In the short term, compacts could provide opportunities for university repositioning, new incentives for mission differentiation and funding-envelope flexibility. Diversification is itself a means rather than an end. The key purpose is to modernise the structure of provision to accommodate more cost effectively an enlarged body of students with varying characteristics. The main point is, in the words of Peter Karmel, to achieve 'the twin objectives of widespread access to higher education and of nurturing the most intellectually able'.[7]

Access should be widened in ways that recognise differences in student readiness, ability and motivations. Particular effort is needed to enable those with poor readiness to progress—not to make it easy to succeed by lowering standards, but to ensure they acquire the skills necessary to achieve good employment outcomes. This means support: with study and the relevant skills and support mechanisms. It also means minimising distractions: if we are to improve access to post-school education, and completion of courses, we need to think creatively about how to ensure that all students are able to meet basic living costs while studying.

Unlike course fees, day-to-day living costs cannot be deferred through HECS. Living costs present as an upfront deterrent to access and recent studies have shown that ever more full-time university students are having to work longer hours in part-time and casual jobs just to make ends meet.

The student income support system has not been the subject of a proper government-driven review since 1992; there is an urgent need for reform. In higher education, we are more likely to see diversity flourish when we address policy across the whole spectrum of post-school education and training. Conceiving of a holistic system for tertiary learning has implications not only for institutional structures, but for student access, financing mechanisms and student income support.

In this wider context, we need to revisit the rationale for the education component of compacts as conceived in Labor's 2006 outline, and to move to a less bureaucratic discussion. There are many questions to be addressed and serious work needs to be commenced shortly to underpin future policy considerations. Matters requiring attention include: student-driven models and the allocation of funding; the balance between private and public costs; the continuity of scholarship in areas that are not sustained by student demand alone, as well as the balance between graduate output and labour market requirements; and the principles and operations of a more appropriate regulatory framework for a competitive services sector.

In recent years, the OECD has been undertaking a series of thematic reviews of tertiary education, with 13 countries participating in a program of visits by international assessors. Australia did not volunteer for a visiting panel and missed out on the benefits of international perspectives and comparative assessment. I am sure an international panel would have been struck by the disconnections within the tertiary education system and the disconnections between it and the labour market. It is time to take a wider view. There is a further matter that must be addressed, and that is the actual cost of teaching at acceptable standards. A better understanding of actual costs will be needed for a more deregulated system. Truer signals about quality will be needed to inform student choice and safeguard educational standards.

We have danced around the question of standards for far too long. There is a dizziness affecting our thinking and a reluctance to confront reality. We persist with a notion of parity of esteem of degrees even though we know there are sizeable differences in the entry scores of students, in the capabilities of academic staff, in campus environments and cultures and in amenities for learning and research. Through the Learning and Teaching Performance Fund, these differences are smoothed out in order to detect a notional institutional value add, on the assumption that the exit standards of graduates are equal.

We know that there are differences in graduate destinations that reflect differences in student preparation, such as in engineering and information technology (IT). For instance, employers look to one university for computer systems designers and to another for computer programmers and to another for computer operators. That is what happens in the real world, and it is a good thing, and we should reveal rather than disguise the fact. Yet we have not achieved acceptance, either in rhetoric or practice, of the concept of fitness for purpose.

In Australian higher education, we have a process of quality auditing that assesses processes but does not necessarily assure acceptable standards. It could even, by dint of the process, validate mediocrity, especially when the criteria are referenced only to national norms. I understand the Minister for Finance and his 'razor gang' are looking for savings options. I can nominate some for him.

Evaluating standards is inherently difficult, and that is probably why most of the higher education quality assurance industry treats quality of process as a proxy for quality of outcomes. Standards-referenced evaluation requires a focus on how well students learn and how institutions assess this, rather than a preoccupation with how well the paperwork is prepared and the records kept.

It is time to establish a minimum acceptable standard for a degree and to develop benchmarks for differences in performance standards achieved by graduates. There are various options available, such as comparisons of student work assessed at different grades across institutions in comparable areas of study, as well as examinations of the kind used in other countries, such as the Graduate Record Examination in the United States. We have responsibilities to our graduates to safeguard the reputation of Australian qualifications in the international market.

It is time to grasp the nettle and get around what, I remind you, Trow described as 'a central problem for higher education—the pressure for institutional drift toward a common model of the research university'.

Our Australian way of handling the 'central problem' has been largely to ignore it as we penalise success in order to spread the already thin largesse.

It is time to discuss the whole issue of standards and accept that there are differences, real differences, within the sector and that those differences lead to consequences. It is time to consider the relationships between our universities in order to provide better opportunities for staff and students.

It is time to focus on the purpose and performance of universities. It is time to seize this rare opportunity for rethinking, renewal and reinvigoration.

All in all, it is time.

ENDNOTES

[1] This essay was originally presented as an ANZSOG Public Lecture on 20 February 2008.

[2] Gillard, Julia 2007, Address by the Minister for Employment, Workplace Relations, Education and Social Inclusion to the Australian Industry Group, 3 December 2007.

[3] Karmel, P. 2000, *Reforming higher education*, Occasional Paper Series, 2/2000, Academy of the Social Sciences in Australia, Canberra.

[4] Trow, M. 2003, 'On mass higher education and institutional diversity', *University Education and Human Resources*, Technion-Israel Institute of Technology, Tel Aviv.

[5] Carr, Kim 2008, Address by the Minister for Innovation, Industry, Science and Research to The Australian National University, 7 February 2008.

[6] Macklin, J. 2006, *Australia's universities: building our future in the world*, White Paper on Higher Education, Research and Innovation, Australian Labor Party, Canberra.

[7] Karmel, *Reforming higher education*.

15. Achieving a 'conservation economy' in indigenous communities: a Canadian model for greening and growing local economies[1]

Ian Gill

Like Australia, Canada is a big place. It has the longest undefended border in the world, with the United States. While most Australians live in a thin band around the coast, most Canadians live along a thin line called the forty-ninth parallel that stretches along the US border from coast to coast—or, as Canada's motto has it, '*A mari usque ad mare*' ('From sea to sea').

In Canada, as here, there is a deep divide between urban and rural populations—a division that is about much more than just geography. John Ralston-Saul, one of our pre-eminent social commentators, believes that the growing gap between urban and rural populations is one of the most profound social issues in twenty-first-century Canada, and I agree.

Ours is a modern, pluralistic, democratic state. Ours is also a heavily resource-dependent economy; Canadians are 'hewers of wood and drawers of water' in the classic phrase, but we are also miners and smelters and car makers and farmers and drillers, and we don't always do all that as sustainably or sensitively as you might expect from a country such as Canada.

Like Australians, Canadians have stood alongside Britain and the United States through some of their most noble, and their most ignoble, adventures abroad. We didn't go to Iraq. You did. We are in Afghanistan, fighting, yet we are better known as peacekeepers. And let's face it, living alongside the United States, we have no illusions about being a regional military superpower.

By far our largest trading partner is the United States, and Canadians mostly like Americans—but these days don't much care for America. I suspect that if Canadians and Australians and, I guess, the citizens of Berlin were allowed to vote in the US election, it would be Obama in a walk.

Speaking of elections, we have a federal one of those under way right now, featuring Prime Minister, Stephen Harper, trying to convert his minority government into a majority one. Harper shares the distinction with George W. Bush of being possibly the only politician in the free world to have openly expressed admiration for your former Prime Minister, John Howard. And look where that got John Howard.

Harper is up against Stephane Dion, a highly cerebral man whose most popular contribution to public life has been to name his dog Kyoto. Canada signed the Kyoto Accord, by the way—by which I mean the real one, not an agreement with Stephane Dion's dog—but then we decided we wouldn't abide by it. I see that Australia has finally done the same thing: signed Kyoto. The jury is out on whether you'll have the courage to honour your commitments, or choose Canada as your role model.

Stephane Dion, by the way, is leader of the *Liberal* Party of Canada. In Australia, that would actually place him at the head of a very watered down Labor Party. Stephen Harper heads the *Conservative* Party, which truly is what it says it is. We have a more classically social democratic party, the New Democrats, who are a genuine force for good in Canada, possibly because they never come close to forming a government at the federal level. This election will also see a more prominent role for the Green Party, but it too is in no danger of making any significant electoral inroads.

Because the Queen is still our head of state, we have a governor-general—and, like yours, ours is a woman. Canada has also, briefly, had a woman prime minister. But our prime ministers, and our politics generally, go pretty much unnoticed in the world. Pierre Trudeau was really the only Canadian politician ever to make much of a splash abroad.

Still, some other Canadians have made it onto the world stage: think Joni Mitchell, Neil Young, Donald Sutherland, Margaret Atwood—but please *don't* blame ordinary Canadians for Celine Dion. Some Canadians, like Australians, have made it onto the world stage only to be asked to leave: you gave the world Alan Bond, we countered with Conrad Black.

Canada has a public health system that is said to be the envy of the world. Like Australia's, there is a good chance you will survive Canada's health system if you don't die waiting for a hospital bed.

Like Australia, ours is a sporting nation, although we spend more time on ice than in water. Judging by the results of the Beijing Olympics, bronze is the new gold when it comes to our athletes. When we do get a rare gold medal, they play an anthem that Canadians actually seem to like, *Oh Canada*. It's no *Waltzing Matilda*, but it's a big step up on *Advance Australia Fair*.

Our colonial, frontier history is poetically captured by Robert Service, the closest thing we have to a Banjo Patterson. You have 'movement at the station' and we have 'strange things done in the midnight sun'.

There are many more similarities and differences—some profound, some superficial—that I could list here. Suffice to say, ours is one lucky country. I seem to recall reading once that Australia is one lucky country, too.

The reality is, the majority of Canadians believe they live in one of the best places on Earth. I think a lot of Australians think they do, too. Ours are among the richest nations on Earth. We have money in our pockets and when we aren't grumbling about the weather or taxes—including that Canadian invention, the GST—well, we're a pretty happy bunch.

But let's talk for a minute about the money in our pockets. I have some right here: an Australian $50 note. The Australian $50 note has on it a drawing of David Unaipon, an Aboriginal inventor from Point McLeay Mission, down near the Murray mouth in South Australia.

Meanwhile, the Canadian $20 note has on it depictions of the artwork of Bill Reid, a Haida First Nations artist credited with producing some of the most complex three-dimensional objects the world has ever seen.

Think about it. Is there not some irony in the fact that in both our lucky countries, hundreds of thousands of times a day, our citizens unconsciously transact their business and their pleasure with currency bearing the images of people who have almost *no* currency in the modern economies of which we are all so proud? Or think of it another way. In Canada, we spend about $9 billion a year on First Nations at the federal level. That's 450 million $20 notes a year spent mostly on substandard social services that produce almost no positive outcomes for native people.

Canada, remember, is consistently ranked at or near the top of the UN index that ranks the livability of countries around the world. If the same indices by which Canada is deemed to be so successful are applied just to aboriginal Canada, the country would rank sixty-third in the world. That's a pretty big gap, by anyone's reckoning.

I won't burden you with the detailed numbers, but I can assure you that in Canada, as in Australia, aboriginal people live in substandard housing more befitting a Third World country; their rates of incarceration are higher than non-Native Canadians; their graduation rates lower. Lower average income, lower average life expectancy, higher suicide rates—the same terrible statistical rollcall.

If you look at the Canadian landscape—by which I mean the actual, physical condition of the country's lands and waters—in between all those postcards of the Rockies and the prairies and the Mounties are valleys and villages flooded for cheap power to run aluminium and lead smelters and to irrigate crops. There are areas of clear-felled forests so large that they are visible from outer space. There are rivers where two million fish used to return every year, now reduced to *2000* returning salmon. There are polluted lakes and streams and, lately, whole forests ravaged by beetles that used to die out in cold winters but no longer do.

Like Australia, Canada had a gold rush—literally for gold, but for other minerals too, and for forests and for fish and for furs—and in that resource rush the aboriginal people were pushed aside at best, and targeted for extinguishment at worst. Like Australia, we had residential schools and a *Stolen Generation*. Like Australia, our Prime Minister recently said sorry. Like Australia, there is much talk of reconciliation—but little consensus on what that actually means.

At the same time that we talk of reconciliation, we of course cannot bring ourselves to sign the UN *Declaration on the Rights of Indigenous Peoples*—for fear, we are told, that it might compromise our legal position. As for our legal position, you had *Mabo*, we had *Calder*. You had *Wik*, we had *Sparrow*. You had *Yorta Yorta*, we had *Delgamuukw*. And now, we have *Haida*—a case that so squarely argues for Haida title and rights that our federal government argues back that the Haida essentially don't exist. This, we are told, is necessary to safeguard our legal position. Some reconciliation.

But I'm glad to report it's not all bad news for indigenous Canadians.

In 2004, the Haida Nation won a landmark case in our Supreme Court that has put a burden on governments—and vicariously although not directly on industry—to consult and accommodate First Nations in the event of development on their lands, whether or not they have proven title. I repeat, to *consult* and *accommodate*. This does not give First Nations veto power, but it does put them at the negotiating table with senior governments in a way that actually gives meaning to the notion of negotiation. It is, in my view, one of the fundamental building blocks of a conservation economy.

Let me define the conservation economy, at least as we see it at Ecotrust Canada.

A conservation economy:

- provides meaningful work and good livelihoods
- supports vibrant communities and the recognition of aboriginal rights and title
- conserves and restores the environment.

The starting assumption of Ecotrust has always been that there is opportunity where conservation and the economy meet. The old paradigm is that you either have jobs or the environment—but you cannot have both. Our work instead takes place at the *intersection* of the two. I know this sounds all very nice in principle. What it means in *practice* is this.

As I mentioned, because of favourable court cases in Canada and because, in British Columbia, treaties were not signed and settled during the period of first contact, we now have a series of imperatives that demand that aboriginal people be dealt into decision making at every turn.

Spencer Beebe, the founder of Ecotrust, likes to say that 'societies do what societies think'. Well, part of our approach is to help communities think about their future, think about what to do or not do, based on a comprehensive understanding of their traditions and their current conditions.

We think of this as 'information democracy'. In the past, all the decisions about resource extraction and economic development were made in capital cities like this one, Canberra, or in cities with capital, such as London and New York…like Sydney, Melbourne, Perth…like Toronto, Calgary, Vancouver.

None of the decisions was made by the communities themselves, or even with their knowledge or consent. On the British Columbia coast, I can take you to First Nations villages where, literally, the first inkling that native people had that someone was logging their traditional lands was when they saw a massive barge laden with old-growth logs being towed past their communities—headed south to distant mills and markets.

At Ecotrust, our notion of information democracy is that decision making *has* to vest in affected communities. So we work with communities on use and occupancy mapping—on land-use and marine-use planning—in order that today, having been invited to the decision-making table 150 years after the fact, they can come equipped with culturally relevant and technically and scientifically defensible maps and plans of their own.

It is my contention that not a single new resource decision should be made—in Canada or in Australia—without affected communities first being able to articulate their traditional use and occupancy of their territory, or *country*, as you call it here. That knowledge should be the basis upon which communities can then articulate which economic opportunities they wish to pursue—or forgo. I think it is a fundamental human right to be informed, to be armed with knowledge that is your own.

So, as I said, information democracy is a core building block of a conservation economy.

But in a conservation economy, there also has to be an *economy*. I remember in a strategy session one of our board members taking us to task because, to him, it sounded like a conservation economy was just a set of principles—local this, sustainable that, value-added something or other else. He asked, not unkindly, 'Are there any *products* in a conservation economy?'

Well, yes there are.

Inevitably, when communities articulate a vision, it involves some kind of development. At Ecotrust, we have been fortunate to work for more than a decade now with Shorebank, one the world's leading development finance institutions. Shorebank introduced us to community development finance—and it is courtesy of Shorebank that we operate the only revolving loan fund for business development housed in an environmental non-profit in Canada.

We have done a modest amount of lending: about $10 million so far. We finance small and medium enterprise development. We finance mostly sustainable forestry, fisheries, tourism and renewable-energy projects. Our loans average about $125 000 at origination—not exactly micro-lending, but what we call 'whites-of-your-eyes' lending. Local, responsive and leveraged, our $3.8 million active portfolio in 2007 leveraged a further $13.7 million in capital to our clients. Of that, about 30 per cent went to aboriginal enterprises. We have slowly, patiently helped to create or sustain hundreds of jobs on our coast.

Somewhat emboldened by these results, we are currently looking to raise market capital for renewable energy and sustainable forestry funds because we want to work on bigger deals, at a larger scale, with our First Nations partners. But before I get to that, let me give you a concrete example of how Ecotrust has worked with a First Nations client.

Let me tell you about a company called Iisaak Forest Resources.

Some of you might have heard of Clayoquot Sound. It is an extraordinarily beautiful place on the west coast of Vancouver Island, a place that became notorious in the 1980s and 1990s when the industrial logging juggernaut that was consuming the forests of Vancouver Island at an insatiable rate was stopped in its tracks.

In the summer of 1993—after years of skirmishes in the woods and interminable negotiations leading nowhere—more than 16 000 Canadians rallied on the logging roads of Clayoquot Sound in what became the largest single act of civil disobedience in Canadian history. More than 850 people were arrested for stopping the logging in Clayoquot. Your current Environment Minister, Peter Garrett, led his band, Midnight Oil, in a protest concert at the Black Hole, a notorious clear-cut that became an emblem of the worst excesses of the Canadian logging industry.

The blockades came on the heels of a conservation plan that left two-thirds of the sound open to logging. The government of the day promised this would take place sustainably, but no-one believed the government had a clue what that meant. In the wake of such a furious backlash, the government appointed a 'blue-chip' science panel to report back on what sustainable forestry might actually look like. At this point, local First Nations stepped in and called a halt. In effect, they challenged the credentials of a band of white scientists—no matter how well qualified on paper—to properly understand what sustainable forestry could be, without fully understanding the position of First Nations people who had lived in the forest for thousands of years. In the end, the science panel was co-chaired by Hereditary Chief Umeek of the Ahousaht First Nation. In the end, the science panel produced a report that radically altered the regulatory and social landscape for logging on the coast of British Columbia.

When the science panel reported in 1995, the companies didn't like the significant new restrictions on logging practices, but the government went ahead and approved the panel's recommendations. Sure enough, there was a dramatic reduction in the annual cut and, soon after, the two big companies in the region were looking for a way out. One of them, MacMillan Bloedel—which later sold out to Weyerhaeuser—closed down operations in Clayoquot, but committed to a joint venture with the local First Nations in the form of a new company, Iisaak Forest Resources. The word *'iisaak'* is Nuu-chah-nulth for 'respect' and, in 2000, First Nations in Clayoquot were majority owners of a company that set out to produce just that: wood with respect.

Ecotrust Canada helped finance that first year of operations. In itself, that might be thought of as an unusual act for a conservation organisation: to finance a joint-venture logging company in Clayoquot Sound in which timber giant Weyerhaeuser was a partner. But, to our view, this is what everyone had been arguing for: a dramatic reduction in the cut, more local control, more *First Nations* control, more local benefits and preferably a product certified by an international body, the Forest Stewardship Council (FSC). So for us, financing this example of a triple-bottom-line company was a no brainer. We also helped it get FSC certification. And we aided the company in many other ways, including finding markets for its good wood and spreading the word.

In 2005, Iisaak bought out Weyerhaeuser's minority interest and the First Nations became sole owners of the company. In 2006, seeking new management after some poor years and substantial financial losses, Iisaak asked Ecotrust Canada to help find new managers. Instead, with a partner that had experience in ecosystem-based forest management, we decided to offer ourselves up as managers.

Why did we do this? Because environmentalists have a tendency to support things such as Iisaak in principle, but seldom offer much by way of tangible assistance where it counts: in the day-to-day operational reality of a business. And while environmentalists sing a good song about helping aboriginal people get access to resources as a way out of poverty, they get a bit weak-kneed when they actually do it.

So we stepped up with a plan, won a competitive bidding process to manage the company, and we did so for 18 months—a contract that ended a couple of months ago. At the end of our management turnaround contract, here's how things stood:

- 47 per cent of employment was First Nations
- 67 per cent of employment was local

- Forest Stewardship Certification (which had been lost) was reinstated
- we achieved a financial turnaround and left Iisaak with $1.5 million in the bank
- emerging markets were found for FSC-certified wood
- 18 months of advance engineering was in place (that is, plans for business going forward).

I have to say that assisting First Nations to cut old-growth forests in one of the iconic conservation areas in the world hasn't endeared us to everyone. As one of my staff put it in a report to our board, 'Our effort here inspired many, puzzled some, enraged a few, and left no-one indifferent.' So too, probably, will our upcoming work to raise venture capital to assist First Nations to invest in micro-hydro projects, and to acquire and manage private forest lands. But to me, conversation for far too long has been about access—and not about assets. Everyone wants access to indigenous lands—to exploit them, to 'save' them, whatever—but in very few cases do we see good-faith attempts to actually build an asset base in indigenous communities. At Ecotrust Canada, we think that is critical to the long-term success of the communities where we work.

This gets us to some of the challenges. I've read a bit about the deterioration in Australia of the so-called black–green alliance. Canadians are far too polite to ever colour code people. No-one up home would ever talk about a red–green alliance and anyway, in Canada, Red Green is the name of a TV comedy character, so they wouldn't know what you were talking about. But as in Australia, in Canada, there has long been an assumption that the indigenous agenda is at once and at least in part a *green* agenda. In truth, that *has* been the case for the past 30 years or so: about the same time that Greenpeace was founded in Vancouver, aboriginal communities were engaging in their own conservation efforts, linked to their emergent rights and title agenda. But today, as First Nations come into ownership and control—as they come to determine more and more of the *access* to lands and natural resources—those old allegiances will come under strain. In fact, they already have—as in the case of Iisaak Forest Resources, as I've already mentioned, but in many other instances as well.

In Canada, as in Australia, I predict a significant shift in the agenda towards new allegiances based less on conservation and more on *economic* imperatives—and a transfer of assets to communities that for the most part have none. That doesn't mean the end of conservation. But we should not assume that indigenous economic development choices will always be the good ones. Then again, they won't always be bad ones: well informed and well led, indigenous communities will make many good economic development decisions, and they could invoke their aboriginal right to say no to development. For all we know, they might say that more often than they say yes. The fact is, a new era is upon us, and I think the conservation community has a significant role to play in helping indigenous communities make good choices about conservation *and* development. Nature is resilient where it is bio-diverse. I would argue that communities are resilient where they are culturally strong and economically diverse.

One issue that does crop up in our work and which continues to limit confidence in First Nations—especially among investors—is that of governance. It's not as if non-native people have somehow perfected how to govern our political or economic affairs—the newspapers let us know that on a daily basis.

Nonetheless, just about everyone bemoans the problems of governance that afflict indigenous communities. We've seen our fair share of poor governance up our way. I understand that's a big issue here, too.

Some of you might have heard of the Harvard Project on American Indian Economic Development. It's a research project that has been running for more than 20 years now under the expert eye of Stephen Cornell, who argues that access to resources is not necessarily an essential ingredient for economic success in indigenous communities. He argues, and offers powerful evidence, that culturally relevant governance—regardless of access to resources—is absolutely essential to success in Indian country. He argues that there are significant parallels between the US experience and that of communities in Canada, Australia and New Zealand.

Cornell argues that self-determination in indigenous communities is key to their ability to progress. He says that for central governments, good governance means governance on their terms, so as to facilitate service delivery in a way that appeals to ministers and bureaucrats and, I would add, reporters. Central governments are terrified of self-determination, because where indigenous peoples control natural resources, there is a threat to the ability of the State to utilise those resources or get them to market, which undermines the State's ability to control what happens within its borders.

No wonder that Cornell says, 'Reluctant to address indigenous self-determination, states instead address indigenous poverty.'

Sound familiar?

Self-determination is critical. Good governance is critical. But I must say that on a visit last week to a remote community in Northern Australia, I saw something pretty discouraging. I saw a community that was getting a huge amount of money through a benefits agreement with an industrial concern, which had set up a corporation to manage that money. I saw nothing culturally relevant in any of this. In fact, I was told by their earnest non-Indigenous adviser that the corporation was run according to the rules of the *Corporations Act* in Australia. Minutes are taken, live on PowerPoint, before the Indigenous people's very eyes. However, this same adviser had just finished telling me that every adult person in the community was illiterate and innumerate. So whose agenda does this serve? Is this what the framers of the *Corporations Act* had in mind? I have in mind something less corporate. Perhaps something more *cooperative*—modelled along the lines of the cooperative economic experience of the Emilia Romagna region of Italy. Is there not a governance model based on principles of the gift exchange, on reciprocity, that is more relevant to Indigenous communities than trying to find a cultural way to build a corporation, or a corporate way to rebuild a culture? I don't know the answer to this, but I believe it is a question that deserves an answer.

In two trips—last week in the Kimberley and Kakadu, and three years ago to Kimberley and Cape York—I've seen some discouraging things in your Indigenous communities, and I've seen great potential. There are tremendous reserves of resilience based, I believe, on retained culture and on conserved country. While I haven't seen that much to inspire me in respect to new economic models, I think you have many of the conditions that I believe are essential to building a conservation economy.

Both of these trips to the north have been sponsored by the Australian Conservation Foundation and its partners (including Land and Water Australia), who see value in our approach in Canada. There is a proposal afoot to start an Ecotrust Australia, and it might just be up and running in six months or so. I hope it is, and I hope it is a remarkable success.

I don't for a minute imagine that Ecotrust's approach, adapted for Australian circumstances, will solve all the woes of your Indigenous communities or somehow magically convert an economy built on gross resource extraction and consumption into a conservation economy—at least not right away.

But surely what is happening to your climate (the drought)—and indeed to the Earth's climate—suggests that the need for alternative development models is urgent. And I think there is a way to pay for them, too. As you embark on emissions trading here, and as markets in carbon offsets and other ecosystem services continue their meteoric growth, I think we need a system not just of carbon capture, but 'capital capture'. Given that new capital markets are opening up precisely *because* of an awakening to the perils of climate change (among other environmental threats), surely we can find ways to spend that capital on solutions. To invest in new technologies, for sure—but also in new development models, and most urgently in indigenous communities.

My fellow Canadian Naomi Klein has written a remarkable book called *The Shock Doctrine: The rise of disaster capital*. Its focus is mainly on American global hegemony, both military and economic, over the past 50 years. But I think the post-contact, colonial experience has been one long, continuous spasm of 'disaster capital', and nowhere have its effects been more evident than in aboriginal country around the world.

We've seen a remarkable decline in cultural capital, and community capital, in the past 200 years. We have to start—*now*—building what Jane Jacobs has so wisely referred to as 'reliably prosperous' communities. These are the communities that we envision are the constituent parts of a conservation economy. I know that such a thing—a conservation economy—might seem somewhat wistful or quixotic. But it's the only one I want to live in—and it seems a much safer place to be than in an economy that is melting down around us as I speak.

Re-engineer the whole economy? Why not? The Berlin Wall came down. Who would have predicted that? Nelson Mandela got out of prison. The Soviet Union broke up. Suharto was swept from power. Or somewhat more tangibly to us mere mortals, consider that people no longer smoke in airplanes—or just about anywhere else for that matter. Thirty years ago, who would have predicted radical social change like any of the above? So why not a new economy? Why not reliable prosperity? Why not a triple bottom line? Why not economically, ecologically, culturally and socially successful indigenous communities?

My friend and an Ecotrust Canada board member, Eric Young, writes about how the world gets changed in a book called *Getting to Maybe*. 'If history shows us anything,' Young says, 'it is that the obdurate world *does* yield. Change—surprising and sometimes radical change—*does* happen. The world does turn on its head every once in a while. And what seemed almost impossible looking forward seems almost inevitable looking back.' So it is—or so I believe it will be—with the conservation economy.

ENDNOTES

[1] This essay was originally presented as an ANZSOG Public Lecture on 17 September 2008.

16. From crystal sets to the double helix in one journalist's lifetime[1]

Peter Thompson

When I was a child in the 1950s, my mother told me that she and other children at her school at Randwick rushed outdoors to see the fly-over of Charles Kingsford Smith on one of his epic voyages to Mascot aerodrome. My father was born in the same decade that the Wright brothers flew at Kitty Hawk. This bygone era of technology so dated my view of my parents that they might as well have lived in the time of fossils rather than in the world that I knew.

Now, I find myself caught in my own time warp. The change that communications technology has wrought has made my childhood experiences a remnant of a long-eclipsed era. I have spent my working life immersed in the technology of what used to be called 'mass media' but which somehow lost the 'mass' bit along the way. I realise now that I too am a fossil. Of the crystal set era!

I first marvelled at the gadgetry of *my* techno-age when I watched boys attach their crystal set radios to the wire fences of the school tennis courts. These ingenious little devices could tune into AM radio using only the power of the station's own transmitter.

The first inkling of my future as a journalist came when I accompanied my dashing Uncle Ray to his work as editor of the yellowish *Sunday Mirror* at the News Limited offices on the corner of Holt and Kippax Streets in Sydney. Could work be this exciting? Long screeds of copy were run back and forth by copy boys, each time bearing new coloured pencil notations and markings. They were handed to the typesetter, after which the apron-wearing compositor would lay out metal blocks of the text and images ready for the presses. I took home a block bearing my name and my destiny was half decided. At home, I laid out the first and last edition of *The International*, circulation: one copy. Later on, I was to find it easier to talk for a living rather than write.

In the school library, as a twelve year old, I read John F. Kennedy's *Profiles in Courage* to learn more about the hero president who had been killed the year before. These dramas of former statesmen stirred my own fantasies about pursuing a noble career as a politician. And it must be said I took down copies of parliamentary *Hansard*. How impossibly important to have your every spoken word recorded for posterity! Now, the two consistent pathways in my life began to merge: a passion for journalism (and communication) and an abiding interest in politics.

In the Sydney of my childhood in the 1950s and 1960s, *Cinesound Review* and its competitor, *Movietone News*, were entering their twilight years as the showcases of documentary newsreels that would accompany the 'shorts' before the feature film at the 'pictures'.

An all-newsreel cinema operated in the basement of the grandly ornate State Theatre, in Market Street, Sydney. I went there hand in hand with my parents. It was easy for me to imagine wartime crowds queuing up to get their fill of the latest sanitised documentary footage of conflicts raging in Europe and the near Pacific. Drama and atmosphere were added to the images by the exaggeratedly declaratory voice-overs and martial music. Much of the film work was masterfully shot by brave young cameramen such as Damien Parer, who trudged the Kokoda Track alongside the diggers. The introduction of television into Australia in 1956 slowly killed off the newsreel and ushered in a new communications age.

The television, the communications satellite (first launched in 1963) and the jumbo jet became symbols of a new era of 'speed' and 'access' that tore down the barriers that separated people by psychological and physical distance, mind and body. You could go anywhere in the world in a day; talk to anyone, any place, at any time; or sit numbed by a continuous stream of news, pseudo-news and entertainment on the box (and later on computers and mobile phones and a combination of the two). This transformation in 'connectivity' would help transform cultural norms and was a taproot of globalisation. Over just a few decades, one world had morphed into another. The world at war already seemed far back.

Imagine 1939–45 wartime Canberra and its physical isolation. The Prime Minister, John Curtin, sat in the bush capital, with telegrams still acting as a primary form of communication. A journey to his home town of Perth meant an arduous journey by transcontinental train or by coastal shipping for most travellers. A small coterie of print journalists tapped out the news from the press gallery to their head offices around the country.

Imagine wartime Washington. President Roosevelt had expanded his personal office in the White House to cope with the growing demands of the job. When he became president at the height of the Great Depression, one correspondence secretary was sufficient to handle the flow of mail into and out of his office. Roosevelt had mastered the new medium, radio, and in stentorian tones had delivered his renowned 'fireside chats', which sounded much more like lectures than chats. He made 30 of these broadcasts between 1933 and 1944.

Imagine wartime London. Winston Churchill made his great speeches in the House of Commons but an actor, Norman Shelley, then mimicked Churchill to repeat the same speeches for broadcast on the BBC. As the great American journalist Edward R. Murrow observed, Churchill mobilised the English language and sent it into battle. Television, with its demands for intimate speech rather than platform oratory, would soon bring down the curtain on the age of rhetoric of which Churchill and Martin Luther King Junior were the last exemplars.

Back in 1939, the ABC broadcast Neville Chamberlain's declaration of war live via BBC short wave and, soon after, Robert Menzies made a live announcement that 'Australia is also at war'. A 'Department of Information', of which Sir Keith Murdoch was briefly Director-General, censored all news reports.[2]

Voice was the breakthrough medium of the Second World War, presented with formality by posh-accented radio announcers (as broadcasters were then called). The head of the ABC, Charles Moses, for a long time held the view that announcers should remain nameless.[3]

Radio began in Australia in 1923 and the ABC came into existence on 1 July 1932 with a vision of helping to unite the continent's far-flung population. In those heady days of the 'wireless', families gathered around the radio console at night to listen to the mix of soap operas (so named because of their soap company advertisers on commercial stations), talks, music and news. Richard Boyer, appointed chairman of the ABC by the Chifley Government and after whom the Boyer Lectures were named, called radio more revolutionary than the internal combustion engine (an ambitious claim; at least it produced less greenhouse gas).[4]

During the war, the ABC still relied for news content on negotiated agreements with wire services and newspapers, although a number of ABC reporters, such as Chester Wilmot and John Hinde, became voices of the Australian war effort. An independent ABC news service was finally introduced on 1 July 1947, a year after the broadcast of Parliament began—an experiment that the politicians of the day were sure would raise the prestige of their debates.

The television era

It's now more than five decades since Bruce Gyngell stood in front of the camera at TCN 9 Sydney and uttered the words, 'Good evening ladies and gentlemen. Welcome to television.' When television was introduced into Australia in 1956 to coincide with the staging of the Melbourne Olympics, crowds gathered around shop windows to watch coverage of the games and marvel at the new medium. If a television set was beyond the pocket of the family budget then rental was a popular option. TV's socialising influence would soon far outreach radio's impact. Television spread with enormous speed throughout Australia. By 1960, 70 per cent of homes in Sydney and Melbourne had a TV set, rising to 90 per cent in established markets by mid-decade. The combination of 'live' variety shows, American movies, soapies, comedy, BBC dramas, sit-coms, sport and news proved irresistible to the growing consumer society.

The Menzies Government held in its hands the gift of granting licences to virtually print money. Those licences went to existing media owners after a royal commission and public hearings by the Australian Broadcasting Control Board. Fairfax got ATN 7 in Sydney; the *Herald and Weekly Times* got HSV 7 in Melbourne; a consortium of the soon to be defunct *Argus*, Syme, Hoyts and Greater Union got GTV 9 in Melbourne; and Frank Packer's Consolidated Press established TCN 9 in Sydney. By 1965, television advertising accounted for 24 per cent of total advertising spent. It climbed to more than 35 per cent after 1980.[5]

ABC—from promise to paucity

The ABC was granted a piece of the action with its own television network. The Australian model was starkly different to the United Kingdom's. The BBC commenced experimental TV broadcasts in 1932 and it took off its training wheels in 1946 when TV recommenced after being suspended during the war. The BBC had a monopoly on television for 20 years and then faced only limited commercial competition (Independent Television or ITV). BBC2 commenced broadcasting in 1964 with a brief to produce more specialist programs after the Pilkington Inquiry had roundly criticised the poor quality of ITV programs.

By contrast, the ABC never enjoyed a head start over its rivals although the postwar Chifley Government had proposed a public television service rather than a dual public/commercial system. In Australia, the weighting of licences in favour of commercial versus ABC was 2:1 then 3:1 after the launch of the third commercial network by 0/10 in 1964–65. In the United Kingdom, the playing field was tilted in the other direction. The BBC's monopoly on radio broadcasting extended far longer, lasting until the 1970s. The British population didn't appear to suffer long-term harm from its diet of BBC. Indeed, the Beeb's long lead time in establishing its culture of broadcasting goes a long way to explain why its cultural content is arguably Britain's most important export. The vision of the BBC's founder, Lord Reith, of building a platform of cultural excellence was more than half a world away from the ABC's founding purpose of helping unite a disparate and far-flung population spread over a continent.

Caution about innovation and looking after the interests of existing players has been the hallmark of governments' approach to new communication technology. Proprietors and politicians alike have a mutual love of exercising power and coexist in a relationship of considerable nervous tension towards each other. The politician doesn't want to alienate the interests of the media owner for fear of being turned on by the press. On the other hand, the media proprietor steps warily around the politician for fear of loss to their commercial interests in the carve-up and regulation of public assets, like access to the airwaves. This softly-softly approach delayed colour television in Australia, it permanently shelved the introduction of a fourth commercial network and it long postponed the introduction of pay TV.

My first appearances on television, mustering all the authority of a nineteen-year-old Walter Cronkite, were in black and white. Colour television was finally switched on in 1975, more than a decade after its introduction in the United States and eight years after Britain. The network owners wanted the competitive advantages of colour but sought time to gear up for the change.

Sadly, the legacy of 50 years of Australian television is a notable underachievement in creative output. This is not to say that our talent pool has been lacking. Far from it. There have been many flashes of outstanding drama and miniseries such as *Brides of Christ* and *Changi*. There has been genuinely brilliant natural history and wildlife documentary making, especially in the hands of David and Liz Parer. Cop shows turned out by Crawford Productions such as *Homicide* (500 episodes), *Matlock Police* and *Division 4* had their heyday. Closer to the bone were shows such as *Blue Murder*, *Phoenix* and *Wildside*. Soapies such as *Bellbird*, *The Sullivans*, *A Country Practice* (a 12-year run), *Neighbours* and *Home and Away* have done well for domestic audiences and in some cases as exports. Variety had *Mavis Bramston*, Graeme Kennedy and *Hey, Hey It's Saturday*. Children's television has enjoyed the consistently strong backbone of *Play School*. Comedies such as *Frontline* and *Kath and Kim* have tickled audiences. And the reality television era made its dubious debut with *Sylvania Waters* in 1992. And, who could deny the value of the invention of one-day cricket as a television product?

Yet, all in all, audiences have been fed a 50-year diet of mostly American junk TV. Local content rules brought about the production of cheap product such as game shows, sport and low-end variety and did not so much raise the bar of quality as produce a lowest common denominator response to meet the minimum required hours. Alas, the failure of Australia's television industry to achieve much of its cultural potential has been a missed opportunity in the nation's social development.

The creative arts are the mirror and conscience of a nation. It is through our stories that we come to know ourselves and what we stand for. Perhaps it was a manifestation of our notorious cultural cringe in the foundation years of television that such an opportunity to develop our cultural industries was stillborn.

The founding of the National Institute of Dramatic Art in 1959 and the Film and Television School ('Radio' has been added to its title) in 1973 were important steps in the direction of developing a talent base on which to build a robust performing arts/media industry. The renaissance of the Australian film industry in the 1970s and 1980s created brave hopes that it might nurture and sustain the excellent credentials of filmmakers, but it turned out to be more like a short-lived gold rush to pour money into the 10BA tax scheme. It was a policy tragedy: a combination of good intentions to support an industry and a tax rort that was bound to draw adverse attention to itself.

A serious blow to the ABC was the scrapping of the television and radio licensing fee by the Whitlam Government and substituting direct funding from the federal budget. It was a popular move at the time and supporters of the ABC were blindsided by the temporary largesse of the government. The licence fee was a nuisance for consumers to pay and for government to collect. But the licence had the virtue of making funds for the ABC quite an explicit commitment. Funding has been on a gradual downhill slide ever since and the blood flow wasn't staunched by David Hill's 'eight cents a day' campaign. Now, the BBC, still paid for by licence fees, enjoys nine times the income of the ABC.

A flickering bright moment in the history of television came with the introduction of SBS by the Fraser Government. Its TV service was launched in October 1980 to serve Australia's ethnically diverse communities. It has been one of the more visible examples of our multicultural society at work. More than half of its broadcasts are in languages other than English. Always under-resourced, SBS has in recent years been playing with the devil by introducing commercials in the hope that government will still feed it basic funding.

The decline in the output of Australian drama by the ABC has been alarming. In 2001, the ABC produced 102 hours a year but this had fallen away to 21 hours in 2004 and it continued its decline in 2005 when it produced barely a dozen hours a year of new TV drama. This decline has been echoed in the independent television sector, where in 2004–05 the number of productions was just 33, the second lowest in 15 years. [6]

This feeble contribution to the nation's culture was the legacy of a federal funding squeeze on the one hand and the extension of new services such as online, ABC 2, NewsRadio and digital radio networks on the other. The Howard Government continued to pare back ABC funding, following the lead of the Keating Government, which had conspicuously ignored the ABC in its boost to arts funding under the 'Creative Nation' program of 1994.

Radio

FM technology brought a high-fidelity breakthrough to radio. First patented in 1933, FM became widespread in the United States in the 1950s. FM radio was one technology where the ABC did get a break on the field. ABC FM, now Classic FM, began broadcasts in January 1976 to Adelaide, Melbourne, Canberra and Sydney. A year earlier, the ABC had launched its 24-hour-a-day youth station, 2JJ (later Triple J).

The launch of FM led to a migration of music formats to the new band and a consolidation of talk radio on AM. In the case of the ABC, the reorganisation led to the birth of Radio National, which replaced 'Radio 2' in 1985. Over the next decade, the service was extended to more than 300 transmitters throughout Australia. Radio National developed a fiercely loyal audience and fulfilled ABC obligations to provide specialist programs that were culturally diverse and educational. Australia is lucky to have such a culturally rich resource.

The commercial launch of FM came in 1980 with the inauguration of 3EON (now Triple M) in Melbourne. The existing AM proprietors were understandably frightened of the competitive threat posed by FM and poured lobbying efforts into protecting their interests. The new licences were auctioned for big sums.

The potential of pay television to wrest market share from the free-to-air networks rattled vested interests too. Cable television was introduced to the United States in the late 1940s. Yet again Australia lagged behind, holding up the introduction of pay TV until 1995. It's now in about 25 per cent (1.27 million) of Australian homes, a low penetration rate compared with countries such as Canada, where there is 70 per cent connection. Pay's early years were marked by the madness of a duplicate roll out of cable across suburban Australia by Telstra and Optus as the telcos competed to take big equity positions in the converging world of telecommunications and media. The slow take-up and big investments squeezed both players until ultimately the Telstra-backed Foxtel won the competitive game. Its digital service, introduced in 2004, now offers 100 channels. Fearing a backlash from viewers/voters who stood to lose free-to-air access to major sporting events, the government drew up a long list of events that would be protected from 'siphoning' to pay TV.

The long battle waged by the old media proprietors to protect themselves against the onslaught of new media has prompted a reordering of investment priorities. Rupert Murdoch's News Corporation has poured capital into upstart digital services such as MySpace while James Packer has turned his attention to gaming. Of the big players, Fairfax is the only one that still looks like a traditional media company, though it has made some costly investments in the digital world.

Decline of newspapers

In a speech to the American Society of Newspaper Editors in 2005, Murdoch reminded the audience that while four out of five Americans read a newspaper every day in the mid 1960s, only half that many did today. The figures for younger readers are far bleaker:

> One writer, Philip Meyer, has even suggested in his book *The Vanishing Newspaper* that looking at today's declining newspaper readership—and continuing that line, the last reader recycles the last printed paper in 2040—April, 2040, to be exact. There are a number of reasons for our inertia in the face of this advance. First, newspapers as a medium for centuries enjoyed a virtual information monopoly—roughly from the birth of the printing press to the rise of radio. We never had a reason to

second-guess what we were doing. Second, even after the advent of television, a slow but steady decline in readership was masked by population growth that kept circulations reasonably intact. Third, even after absolute circulations started to decline in the 1990s, profitability did not.[7]

In Australia, the first newspaper to go after the advent of television was the Melbourne *Argus*, founded in 1846. In the classic mogul style of smothering competition, the *Herald and Weekly Times* bought the *Argus* and the parcel of shares it owned in GTV 9 (the *Herald and Weekly Times* already controlled HSV 7) and soon onsold the shares and closed the paper in 1957.

The arrival of the bright new national titles, *The Australian* in 1964 and the *Australian Financial Review* (weekly 1951, twice weekly 1961, daily 1963), marked an important stage in the development of more specialised political, industrial relations and business reporting in Australia. Also, for the first time, newspapers were starting to reach over state borders and take a national perspective on public affairs.

Almost inevitably, television's octopus grip on leisure hours made life unsustainable for afternoon papers. They still limped on for quite some time. The Sydney *Sun* was closed in 1988. Even Canberra had an afternoon paper, *Canberra News*, a Fairfax publication from 1969 to 1974. Perth's *Daily News* ceased in 1990. Brisbane's *Sun* closed in December 1991 (it had been a morning paper from 1982 to 1988). The closure of the Adelaide *News* in 1992 brought down the curtain on the last afternoon paper in the country.

Valiant efforts were made to save the nation's most successful afternoon paper, the Melbourne *Herald*. It had been published in the evening since 1869 and, with Keith Murdoch as editor-in-chief after his return from being a war correspondent at Gallipoli, it became the largest circulation newspaper in the country. It reached a peak of 500 000 in 1964.[8] Energetic editor Eric Beecher pushed the *Herald* upmarket in its final years but the venerable masthead went down. A limp attempt was made to create multi-edition '24-hour' newspapers with the closure of the Melbourne *Herald* and Sydney's last afternoon paper, the *Daily Mirror*, but this was really a smokescreen for morphing the titles into their morning stablemates, the Melbourne *Sun* and the Sydney *Daily Telegraph*.

Internet

The sunset year for the Melbourne *Herald*, 1990, marked a key moment in the dawning of the Internet age. Tim Berners-Lee created a hypertext system for use among scientists. Two years later, the offspring of this technology, the World Wide Web, was born. The idea of networking had first been outlined in a series of memos written by J. C. R. Licklider at MIT in 1962. He imagined a 'galactic network' of linked computers that could instantly access data and programs from other computers.[9] With the Internet, like many advances in science and technology, effort was poured into developing the ideas as part of the US response to the Russian lead in the space race and as part of efforts to improve command-and-control systems of nuclear missiles. What's been called the first 'hot' application of the technology was sending emails in 1972. Another breakthrough idea that shaped the Internet we enjoy today was Bob Kahn's notion of an 'open architecture' Internet protocol, which meant there was no international controlling body that operated the system.

The giddying potential of the Internet for information exchange fuelled the dot-com bubble on Wall Street that burst in 2001. Amid the hysteria, many back office staff of internet companies became overnight paper millionaires after stock market floats. The absence of sustainable business models that could generate revenues to match the burning of cash was something of a problem.

Despite the excessive exuberance on the part of crazed investors who could see only dollar signs in their eyes, the Internet did go some way to rewriting the rules of commerce. From banking to ordering and distribution services, to knowledge industries and media, the Internet was revolutionary. Names such as eBay, Google, Amazon and YouTube grew from minnows to whales in the digital pond.

The Internet and digital revolutions posed two dilemmas for traditional media companies. How could they beat the anywhere, anytime accessibility of the Net and digital space? And, how could they staunch the flow of advertising dollars to the new media?

In Australia, companies such as Fairfax were especially vulnerable. They had built revenue models heavily dependent on classified advertising. Even though the *Sydney Morning Herald* and *The Age* were easily outsold in their markets by rival newspapers, they held sway over the classifieds. It would no longer be so easy. Competitors emerged with internet classifieds in the key areas of housing, cars and jobs. At Fairfax, incoming CEO Fred Hilmer was set the task of taking $40 million a year in costs out of the business to meet dwindling revenues. A wave of journalists or, as Fred called them, 'content providers', went. Then, as part of the company's positioning in the dot-com business, Fairfax paid $625 million in 2006 for New Zealand's net classified site, TradeMe.

Internet technology was decoupling the nexus between the news business and advertising. News was expensive to gather, with the bigger newspapers and the ABC each employing hundreds of journalists. Its high cost base demanded sizeable revenues to sustain. If advertisers had a dwindling need to use old media 'channels' then it followed that their business models were at risk.

Step into the ABC's compact online news operation in Brisbane and glimpse the future. A journalist writes a story and instantly edits the text, walks a few metres into a studio that's little more than a telephone booth in size, dabs on a little make-up if their vanity demands it, switches the camera on, records the story, steps outside to edit it, then presses 'send' and it's all but ready for viewing by a global audience. No waiting for the seven o'clock news anymore. In 2006, the ABC web site averaged 22 million page views a week.[10]

Newspapers are catching on. Their web sites are rapidly becoming interactive, boundary-less news operations, featuring written text, audio and video clips as well as blog sites and mini-polling stations that invite people to express attitudes about news of the day. Visits to these sites are growing rapidly. In the year to June 2006, smh.com.au grew 30 per cent, theage.com.au was up 32 per cent and news.com.au visits rose 31 per cent. The awkward issue for the accountant seeking to balance the books at traditional media organisations is that audiences see little need to pay for any of these basic services.

Some theorists of the new communication technology claim that the Internet has profoundly shifted power relationships in the media towards consumers. They equate 'connectivity' with 'control' and envisage an unstoppable democratisation of the Net. In this model, everyone becomes a journalist. There are famous examples of where previously anonymous individuals have gained worldwide attention through blogging. Remember the diary 'Where is Raed?' by the blogger using the name 'Salam Pax' that chronicled day-to-day existence in Iraq after the invasion of 2003? Of course, if you do know about his story, chances are you learned about it through traditional media.

China makes an interesting case study in government efforts to retain censorship controls. The Net is widespread in China. Next to Tsinghua University, Beijing's version of MIT, the multicoloured Google logo stands on top of a technology park building adjacent to the campus. As their price of admission to the lucrative Chinese market, Google and Yahoo have done deals with the central government restricting access to certain topic areas. You won't find reference to Falun Gong in a Chinese search engine. Access to sites on the Tiananmen Square uprising of 1989 is limited. The big net companies have been just as willing to bend to China's whims as Rupert Murdoch did when his publishing house dropped the book *East and West* by Hong Kong's last governor, Chris Patten. The risk to his Star TV satellite rights was too great.

New genres of journalism

Inevitably, the emerging technologies have brought with them new forms of journalism. The ABC introduced *4 Corners* in 1961 based on the BBC's *Panorama*. Early programs that questioned venerable institutions such as the RSL soon upset the establishment but the genie was out of the bottle. *4 Corners* programs would often take many weeks to research and this particular culture of long-form journalism made challenging demands on reporters and producers. Chris Masters, the doyen of the art, joined in 1983. Two of his programs had profound political repercussions. His very first report, 'The big league', led to a prosecution of the chief stipendiary magistrate in New South Wales and a commission of inquiry during which the Premier, Neville Wran, stood aside from office. 'The moonlight state' shone the torch on police and political corruption in Queensland, led to the Fitzgerald Commission of Inquiry and was a factor in a change of government after decades of National Party rule.

Pilots for a possible nightly program on the ABC began in the mid 1960s. The unfortunately named *Week* created nightmares for the promotion department when announcements were made to the effect, 'Next week on *Week*'. *This Day Tonight* began broadcasting in 1967 and rapidly had its impact on the nation's political culture. For the first time, politicians were subjecting themselves to tough cross-examination from a new breed of self-assured journalists. There were many celebrated incidents in the program's early days, such as federal police storming a studio in pursuit of a draft dodger conducting a live interview. He was spirited out the rear door.

The arrival of nightly current affairs programs put politicians into lounge rooms in a way that had not occurred before. Inevitably, it enhanced the fortunes of political actors who were quick on their feet, looked good on television and could sell a political message in quick grabs.

The coaxial cable, laid between Sydney and Melbourne in the mid 1960s, made possible simultaneous network broadcasts between the two major cities. Prior to the cable, television film was flown in the TAA and Ansett ANA fleet of Electra turbo-props and would need to leave one city early in the afternoon to make the evening news in the other.

Before the introduction of microwave technology, Tasmania remained dependent on air shipping of film. For example, Gough Whitlam's short-lived weekly news conferences were held in Canberra on Tuesdays and made the TV news in Tasmania on Wednesdays.

Commercial television was not far behind the ABC in introducing nightly current affairs. Mike Willesee, the talented presenter of *4 Corners*, created a start-up show for the Nine Network, *A Current Affair*, that brought a tabloid feel to its content in order to generate audiences. Politicians such as Whitlam, Fraser, Hawke and Keating would make appearances on *ACA* in days gone by, but *A Current Affair* and its imitator on Seven, *Today Tonight*, have exited the field of politics altogether in favour of a line-up of stories dominated by diets, celebrities and rip-offs.

60 Minutes brought a new style to journalism. Its founding philosophy, unchanged to this day, was to personalise stories so that an issue could be explored through the experience of one person. This produced a time-honoured maxim that journalists needed to 'forget the flood and find Noah'. A clever formula of creating celebrities out of its team of reporters and its populist story selection built and sustained an unrivalled Sunday night audience for the show. Where necessary, *60 Minutes* gets out the chequebook and buys access to sensational stories such as the sky-high dalliance of actor Ralph Fiennes and the airline stewardess.

An amendment to the law allowing broadcasting of telephone calls in the mid 1960s, so long as they were accompanied by a beep or pip, changed the direction of radio. Talk radio was born. Some of the top personalities of radio turned their talents to the new genre. Ormsby Wilkins, Claudia Wright and Norman Banks at 3AW in Melbourne built strong audiences by tackling topical issues, as did John Laws in Sydney. John Pearce discovered that calling an irritating caller a 'nitwit' or other insult created controversy that attracted rather than repelled most listeners.

In the later 1960s, a number of serious journalists entered the commercial radio world as presenters and set a high standard of discussion and debate. Brian White pioneered a news-talk formula at 2GB and Anne Deveson brought a then rare female voice to her *Newsmakers*. At 2UE, Steve Liebmann broke similar ground. Their work was an inspiration to me and I somehow convinced the management of provincial 7LA in Launceston to allow me to try a similar format by calling guests to discuss the day's events.

In 1967, the ABC introduced *AM*, followed by *PM* in 1969. Their arrival marked a coming of age for radio journalism in Australia and they soon set the standard for reporting and analysis on the medium. A listener to the programs today would be quite shocked to hear the scratchy sound quality of 'circuits' that carried reporters' voices in those early days. The content has changed too. In the 1970s and 1980s, *AM* would regularly carry stories of high drama in the House of Commons and BBC reporters were often heard from places where no ABC journalist had reached. *AM* was short and snappy with items not often exceeding two minutes. Reporters were given a razor blade and editing block on their first day on the job and learnt the art of fine cutting audio tape. Office floors were festooned with miles of discarded tape. Today, everything is edited digitally.

Skilful politicians such as John Howard have exploited the opportunity offered by talk radio to the full. In a keynote address to the centre-right parties' International Democratic Union in Washington in June 2002, Howard shared his thoughts about the power of the medium:

> The Australian experience with the media is instructive. Like all democratic nations I guess, Australia is no different in the sense that there is a greater preponderance of people in the media of a…how should I put it mildly and gently and diplomatically…of a gentle centre left

disposition. Talk back radio is tremendously important in Australia. Enormously important. It has played a greater role in shaping and determining the outcome of elections over the last few years than perhaps has been the case with other sections of the media. I was having a discussion with Ian Duncan Smith [then UK Conservative Party Leader] earlier and I said to him that radio in Australia I found to be the iron lung of Opposition. We would always get a run. There is so much of it. And you couldn't devour enough of it. And whether that is the same in all of your countries, you individually will know.

John Howard was certainly a welcome guest on *Radio National Breakfast* during my eight years at the helm. Covering politics was central to our program brief and our audience's expectations. In the final two years of my tenure, 2003–04, I worked with the talented producer Jacquie Harvey, who was a veteran of commercial current affairs programs (3AW and Mark Day in Melbourne) and of ABC programs such as *Lateline* during Kerry O'Brien's period as host. We wrestled with a dilemma to which there was no easy answer. While we remained fully committed to covering politics, we worried that audiences were bored by the utter predictability of politicians' spin where virtually everything was said for its effect rather than enlightenment.

So, instead of covering politics mostly by talking to politicians, we experimented with a different approach. First, we overturned a convention that all breakfast segments must be short in duration and introduced long debates on the salient issues of the day, often of 20 minutes or more. Though politicians were not disqualified as guests, we much preferred talking to people at least one step removed from the frontline. Following John Maynard Keynes' aphorism that 'even the most practical man of affairs is usually in the thrall of the ideas of some long dead economist', we searched out people at the source of ideas that were shaping political actions. Often we would seek policy wonks or leading global thinkers on issues.

Audience response was overwhelmingly positive. For the first time, *Radio National Breakfast* achieved its peak share of the market after 7.30am, just when we ran these debates. What explains its apparent success? It certainly convinced me that there is a substantial audience hungry for a high-calibre discussion of public affairs that goes beyond the banalities of much political discourse. Go to writers' or ideas festivals around the country and you get the same sense. People want to engage with ideas.

Sadly, at the other end of the spectrum, there's money in muck. From the early days of the 'top 40', Australian commercial radio was always derivative of trends set in the US market. Radio programmers would make the pilgrimage across the Pacific to air-check new formats and DJs. In time, the emergence of a nasty brand of 'shock jock' radio in the United States was imitated here. To be charitable, you might call the offerings populist. It's closer to the truth to say that they are often bullying, vindictive towards vulnerable groups and individuals and just plain ugly. Technical gizmos ensure that the shock jock can override the voice of any incoming dissident caller and, of course, they can choose to terminate the conversation at any time.

Talk radio has been lorded over by demigods with inflated egos and a tiresome sense of self-importance but it has also operated as something of a release valve for public pressure. It has become a sort of permanent 'vox pop', the modern-day equivalent of neighbours yakking over the back fence.

In 1999, the lucrative commercial arrangements that greased the incomes of radio millionaires such as Alan Jones and John Laws were exposed in the notorious 'cash for comment' affair. It worked like this. If a sponsor wanted favourable comment on their business, they paid up. In return, they received not advertisements but favourable editorial mentions. Banks, for instance, which had been under sustained consumer pressure for years for closing branches and offering terrible service, suddenly became the subject of friendly editorial comment. Telstra was another case in point. One moment it did no end of harm. In the next, Telstra was praised as a good corporate citizen after all. Too bad if these inconsistencies were confusing to listeners. There was big money at stake. Expensive lawyers for all the main players argued out the issue before the Broadcasting Authority and it was decided the arrangements could stay so long as the presenters made occasional mention of their friendly sponsors' names.

The talk phenomenon plays best when presenters work themselves into a lather of righteous indignation. Taking a populist 'moral' position on a highly charged emotional issue is a ratings winner. This 'opinion-led' journalism on radio soon began to infect newspapers. Pick up a smartly edited tabloid paper and you'll find no absence of moral guidance about how to interpret the leading story of the day and you won't have to go to the opinion page to find it.

A sample of weekday front-page headlines of the *Daily Telegraph* amply demonstrates the point. In the space of just over a week in January–February 2007, on Tuesday: 'Save our state. Cut property taxes now—or ruin the next generation of young homebuyers.' On Thursday: 'Drug barons: sick Aussies ripped off as pharmaceutical companies create sham medicine shortages.' On Friday: 'Two years of total chaos. Exclusive: what Labor didn't tell you about its water desalination plant.' And, on the following Tuesday, 'All torque. What has 904 wheels, 226 fuel tanks, 1356 cylinders and exposes our MPs as climate change hypocrites?' And, on Thursday: 'Road to ruin. Tunnel's final disgrace: $60m lost from public servants' superannuation fund.' Are you feeling happier about the world after reading that litany? The headlines all work to provoke a high emotional response in a low-trust environment about the perceived sins of big government and big business.

It is still early days for journalism on the Net. In the United States, the *Drudge Report*, originated by Matt Drudge about 1994, achieved notoriety by being first with the scandalous Monica Lewinsky story that by a long chain of events led to the impeachment of President Clinton. In Australia, Stephen Mayne, a former (unsuccessful) political minder to Jeff Kennett, began *Crikey.com*, a site that is a mix of gossip and titbits.

In the United States, there has been a migration of some serious journalists to the Net, including John Harris, national politics editor of *The Washington Post*, who has joined a subscription web site, *The Politico*, which is building a reporting staff of 30 journalists.[11] Sites such as Salon.com offer serious commentary and analysis and are a bright alternative to the mainstream press.

Efficiency is the great advantage of accessing news on the Net. It is available anywhere, anytime. There's no need to wait tiresomely for the next radio or television news bulletin and then find that it doesn't cover the item you are interested in. And good sites make for quick and easy navigation to the stories of interest. Radio and television, which had the great advantage of immediacy over newspapers, are now the slow coaches.

Double helix

What can we say about how 'the media age' shapes politics? In turn, how does politics shape the media world?

A metaphor from biology seems appropriate. In 1953, just as the nascent television industry in Australia was gearing up for its launch, two scientists, James D. Watson and Francis Crick, offered the world the image of the 'double helix' to describe how DNA was constructed. Watson was supposedly on an LSD trip when he saw the vision.

In many respects, the 'double helix' fits the media/government relationship, where both strands twist together to form its DNA. Like the image of the double helix, both spirals engage in a dance around each other, centred on the same axis. Neither strand manages to fully dominate the other.

One strand contains 'money' elements of the relationship, the other the 'black box' of content. The 'money' thread holds the 'legislative' codes that have unlocked the enormous market power of the technological revolution that is modern media. Government paced the introduction of key technologies (where it could) and bestowed favours on media proprietors through regulating the playing field. It is the politicians who enact the laws. So, appearances give the impression that the government is the dominant force in shaping the structural thread but the reality is somewhat different. No government idly transgresses on the commercial interests of the handful of owners. Indeed, a media proprietor expects his calls to the Prime Minister to be returned. As former NSW Premier

Bob Carr remarked, the only thing that separates Jamie Packer from the other dozen billionaires in Australia is that he has media interests.[12]

The 'black box' thread of the DNA contains the 'editorial' codes of data and information that make up the daily news agenda. It's the journalists who write the headlines, present the news, interview the politicians and pen much of the commentary. So, appearances give the impression that this role makes journalists the dominating force in the content thread. Again, the reality is somewhat different. Journalists and politicians live in a tightly woven relationship of co-dependence. Both sides are busy 'framing' the news to put their own interpretation on events. Neither side wants to yield to the other's version. A prime minister expects his or her calls to an editor to be returned. The editor will call, but if they are worth their salt, will not necessarily buckle.

The helix shape, of course, corresponds to a 'screw' and perhaps that is the more fitting image, as both sides of the relationship seek to screw down the other, fastening, keeping in check, protecting their source of power as they play the great game of politics and media.

ENDNOTES

[1] This essay was prepared for the ANZSOG Strategic Media Management Workshop held on 22 August 2006.

[2] Inglis, K. S. 1983, *This is the ABC*, Melbourne University Press, Melbourne, p. 78.

[3] Ibid., p. 216.

[4] Ibid., p. 128.

[5] See < www.freetvaust.com.au http:/true/truewww.freetvaust.com.au/true >

[6] ABC submission to Review of Australian Government Film Funding Support, August 2006.

[7] Murdoch, Rupert 2005, Speech to American Society of Newspaper Editors, 13 April 2005.

[8] See <Ketupa.net>

[9] See Internet Society's history at < www.isoc.org http:/true/truewww.isoc.org/true >

[10] ABC submission to Review of Australian Government Film Funding Support.

[11] Button, James 2007, *Sydney Morning Herald*, 13–14 January 2007.

[12] ANZSOG Media and Government Seminar, August 2006.

www.ingramcontent.com/pod-product-compliance
Lightning Source LLC
Chambersburg PA
CBHW061245270326
41928CB00041B/3416